W9-BPM-391

THE FEDERAL
MANAGEMENT
PLAYBOOK

PUBLIC MANAGEMENT AND CHANGE SERIES
Beryl A. Radin, Series Editor

SELECT TITLES IN THE SERIES

Collaborating to Manage: A Primer for the Public Sector
Robert Agranoff

Collaborative Governance Regimes
Kirk Emerson and Tina Nabatchi

Collaborative Innovation in the Public Sector
Jacob Torfing

The Collaborative Public Manager: New Ideas for the Twenty-first Century
Rosemary O'Leary and Lisa Blomgren Bingham, Editors

Crowdsourcing in the Public Sector
Daren C. Brabham

The Dynamics of Performance Management: Constructing Information and Reform
Donald P. Moynihan

Federal Management Reform in a World of Contradictions
Beryl A. Radin

Federal Service and the Constitution: The Development of the Public Employment Relationship, Second Edition
David H. Rosenbloom

How Information Matters: Networks and Public Policy Innovation
Kathleen Hale

Managing Disasters through Public–Private Partnerships
Ami J. Abou-bakr

Organizational Learning at NASA: The Challenger and Columbia Accidents
Julianne G. Mahler with Maureen Hogan Casamayou

Program Budgeting and the Performance Movement
William F. West

Public Value and Public Interest: Counterbalancing Economic Individualism
Barry Bozeman

Public Values and Public Administration
John M. Bryson, Barbara C. Crosby, and Laura Bloomberg, Editors

The Responsible Contract Manager: Protecting the Public Interest in an Outsourced World
Steven Cohen and William Eimicke

THE FEDERAL MANAGEMENT PLAYBOOK

Leading and Succeeding in the Public Sector

IRA GOLDSTEIN

Foreword by Tom Davis
former US Congressman

Georgetown University Press   *Washington, DC*

Library of Congress Cataloging-in-Publication Data

Names: Goldstein, Ira
Title: The federal management playbook : leading and succeeding in the public sector / Ira Goldstein ; foreword by Tom Davis.
Other titles: Public management and change.
Description: Washington, DC : Georgetown University Press, 2016. | Series: Public management and change series
Identifiers: LCCN 2016007097| ISBN 9781626163720 (pb : alk. paper) | ISBN 9781626163812 (ebook : alk. paper)
Subjects: LCSH: Public administration—United States. | Civil service—United States—Personnel management. | Administrative agencies—United States—Management.
Classification: LCC JK421 .G597 2016 | DDC 352.23/60973—dc23
LC record available at http://lccn.loc.gov/2016007097

♾ This book is printed on acid-free paper meeting the requirements of the American National Standard for Permanence in Paper for Printed Library Materials.

17 16   9 8 7 6 5 4 3 2 First printing

Printed in the United States of America

Cover design by Charles Brock, Faceout Studio.

This book is dedicated to the many devoted public servants, career and appointed, who work each day to deliver services and improve government.

Contents

Illustrations

Foreword

As chairman of the House Committee on Government Reform and Oversight, I oversaw investigations of literally dozens of failed federal programs, from the huge cost overruns at deepwater ports to soldiers being electrocuted in shoddily built showers in Iraq to bribery and incompetence in handing out government contracts. In nearly every case, the failures were driven by poor leadership or management decisions (or nondecisions) and were readily preventable. Often regulations were adhered to, but with such rigidity that foreseen poor outcomes actually were reinforced by managers who were afraid to take a risk or step outside their comfort zones or were just plain conflict averse.

These problems usually arose because the bureaucratic standards being followed and annual reviews of progress only measured inputs, not outputs. Decisions were not based on mission needs but on adhering to regulations and not making mistakes. Too often the mission itself became not making a mistake! Many times a congressional hearing on a failure became a finger-pointing exercise between the federal manager, the contractor, the agency head, and the Government Accountability Office. No one did anything technically "wrong," but the failure to focus on the outcome, the lack of specificity in the requirements, and the failure to communicate resulted in wasted dollars, cost overruns, and project failures.

I cannot tell you how many times I would say to myself, "I wish someone had written a book on this," so that the managers would not continue to repeat the same mistakes over and over and over again.

But now, someone has written a book. Ira Goldstein, drawing on decades of experience in key roles in the public and private sectors, both inside the federal government and as a consultant, has written a must-read for any federal leader or contractor who wants his or her program or agency to succeed or any student who wants to learn how to avoid making these same mistakes.

Although numerous books have been written about corporate management and effective leadership, Goldstein offers a unique perspective on management within the federal arena of arcane rules, unique metrics, and unprecedented transparency and oversight. Why do so many leaders fail in the government arena? It's a game like no other, where innovation is too often punished, mediocrity is rewarded, and thoughtful programs and policies fail under the burden of stifling rules and unreliable resourcing.

As chairman I presided over scores of hearings concerning government programs, IT procurements, modernization initiatives, and large, complex enterprise-wide systems that had been thoughtful during their inception but failed in implementation. Mark Antony said: "The evil that men do lives after them; the good is oft interred with their bones." So it is with government programs. The overruns, the delays, and the failures make headlines and result in congressional hearings. The projects that run smoothly, on time, and under budget get no quarter.

Goldstein's book is a thorough treatise on how to manage intelligently, how to avoid failure, how to identify problems while they are still correctable, and how to manage both the difficult and the unpopular. He livens it up with numerous case histories and anecdotes and draws on his vast experience in the public and private sectors, both as a federal executive and manager and as a contractor and consultant, to disseminate in readable prose how federal leaders and managers can succeed with the most difficult tasks. The book provides an extraordinary "What to do" and "What not to do" guide when facing difficult tasks and missions.

For example, Goldstein explains in some detail how today's managers can legitimately work the system within the massive and complex acquisition requirements to decide whether a project should be outsourced and, if it is, how to determine the correct requirements, the right vehicles, and the best communication techniques to align contractor performance to goals and expectations. By contrasting the success of the politically charged 2010 Decennial Census with the flawed launch of the Affordable Care Act website, the author delves into how these two "failure is not an option" projects differed in their implementation and management approaches. This chapter alone is worth the read.

Goldstein also focuses on practical problems faced by everyday contractors and federal managers in an era of continuing resolutions, sequestration, and government shutdowns. In the wake of unpredictable funding, changing administrations and policies, and the continual scrutiny of the press and elected officials on the hunt for headlines, too many managers tend to keep their heads down, follow the regulations to a tee, and take no risks. Unfortunately, this common approach too often results in missed opportunities—or worse, failed projects, cost overruns, and unnecessary delays—while keeping the managers and contractors pointing at each other and saying, "it's not my fault." The author takes these tendencies to task and notes that agility, innovation, and risk can be appropriately managed to ensure the best outputs and outcomes rather than just checking the boxes and measuring inputs.

One of the most difficult and seldom-reported conflicts in federal management is the relationship between politically appointed leaders and career civil servants. These interactions are often a clash of cultures and a difference in priorities. Drawing on his experience as a federal leader, Goldstein artfully and insightfully presents the perspectives of both sides and describes how the long-term experienced view of the career employee can mesh with the shorter-term agenda of the political appointee. The failure of these two camps to connect has led to project and policy failure and career destruction, but these institutional conflicts can be avoided if Goldstein's rules are followed.

The complexity of federal acquisition rules and civil service regulations has made even the simplest tasks difficult to achieve unless one knows how to artfully navigate the unique web of federal requirements. Goldstein's work is a literal and constructive playbook on what works best and what doesn't work at all. I can say emphatically that if this book had been read and the lessons learned, many of the project failures I investigated could have been avoided and taxpayer dollars saved.

In *The Federal Management Playbook* Ira Goldstein has offered all those who work in and around government, as well as students of public management, a tremendous benefit by giving us an essential and practical guide for success.

Tom Davis
former chairman
Oversight and Government Reform Committee
US House of Representatives

Preface and Acknowledgments

For decades I have seen and read many books analyzing what's wrong with government, especially the federal government. Many address broad structural deficiencies and propose management transformations or reforms needed to fix them. Federal politics, whether personal or partisan, often take center stage, not just because they are important to policymaking in the United States but also because they are entertaining (and frustrating) to a diverse audience.

These broad analyses have good purpose: they move the debate forward, toward needed government improvements. But usually they contain little real-time instruction that helps actual federal managers and leaders, or those who aspire to join or help them, to achieve great day-to-day results in a federal realm few can individually change. While others are working on much-needed structural improvements over longer timeframes, real people have to get the job done within today's government environment. This book is addressed to practitioners of public management and leadership—and to junior employees and college students aspiring to join their honorable ranks—and is intended to identify the nuts-and-bolts things they can do to be effective under conditions that dominate their world.

In writing the book I have focused the lens largely upon the federal level, because that has been the longest-term concentration of my own career. Most of the discussion, however, is transferrable to state and local levels, and to nonprofit management and leadership as well. After all, in the US system, services are most often delivered at the state or local level, so the multiple government and nonprofit sectors must be included to successfully meet program goals anyway. My hope is that the book identifies strategies and actions that will enhance the effectiveness of government practitioners at all levels.

At the same time, I believe that students in programs of government management and policy will benefit from a book with specific tools and techniques that can better prepare them for the unique challenges of government management and leadership. While there is extensive research literature on government effectiveness and policy reform, it is more limited in its application to the individual- and junior-practitioner levels. This book proposes individual actions students can learn to use at the intersection of politics and management that are based on interesting cases and my personal experiences, in language I hope will meet the expectations of new generations.

Government consultants are also an intended audience for the book. They play an important role in helping career staffs and leaders achieve program and organizational goals. I spent over half my career as a consultant. Indeed, some of the intellectual capital and insights for the book come from member firms of Deloitte, because Deloitte Services LLP was the "last stop" in the consulting part of my career. I am indebted to the leaders and principals of Deloitte Consulting LLP, to its CEO, Janet Foutty, and in particular to its federal leader, Dan Helfrich, for the support, access, insights, and intellectual free reign to use the organization's resources and luminaries, from both the federal and commercial markets, throughout the project.

During the development of this book I received valuable advice from many other colleagues and friends. In particular I am indebted to Beryl Radin, Tom Davis, and Bill Eggers. Additionally I thank Umair Alam, Catherine Cloud, Brian Diederich, Marielle Larson, Adriel Lyons, Andrew Mincheff, Dan Roseman, Megan Schulman, Holly Wilmot, Patrick Zubin, and my assistant, Heather Llewellyn.

I am especially grateful to Carmen Medina, Shrupti Shah, and Jonathan Walters for invaluable conversations and insights about innovation that informed my thinking in Chapter 8. Their experiences with government innovation challenges and successes were particularly helpful—for Medina, as director of the Central Intelligence Agency's Center for the Study of Intelligence; for Shah, based upon her work at the European Commission; and for Walters, built on decades covering "the innovations beat" as an author and senior editor at *Governing Magazine*. I am particularly thankful to Jonathan for the numerous good ideas and substantial case study information used in the innovations chapter, as well as for his skillful editing support throughout the entire book.

Special appreciation goes to my daughter and sons, Sara, Matthew, and David, who continuously challenge and update my thinking to help me stay relevant to today's world.

I am indebted to my wife and true life partner, Linda, whose insights and counseling (at the kitchen table and in the study) on innumerable aspects and passages of the book—and beyond—help me refine my thinking about what matters most in leadership, in management, and, most important, in life.

Abbreviations

ACA	Patient Protection and Affordable Care Act
ACSI	American Customer Satisfaction Index
AFDC	Aid to Families with Dependent Children
AFERM	Association for Federal Enterprise Risk Management
BIT	UK Cabinet Office's Behavioural Insights Team
BPA	blanket-purchase agreement
CTO	chief technology officer
CFPB	Consumer Financial Protection Bureau
CFTC	Commodity Futures Trading Commission
CNCS	Corporation for National and Community Service
COSO	Committee of Sponsoring Organizations
CR	continuing resolution
CRO	chief risk officer
DARPA	Defense Advanced Research Projects Agency
DISA	Defense Information Systems Agency
DOD	Department of Defense
DOE	Department of Energy
DOL	Department of Labor
EOP	Executive Office of the President
ERM	enterprise risk management
FABS	Financial and Business Solutions
FAFSA	Free Application for Federal Student Aid
GAO	Government Accountability Office (previously General Accounting Office)
GPRA	Government Performance and Results Act
GSA	General Services Administration
GWAC	Government-wide Acquisition Contract
HEW	Department of Health, Education, and Welfare (now HHS)
HHS	Department of Health and Human Services
HUD	Department of Housing and Urban Development

IG	inspectors general
IRS	Internal Revenue Service
IT	information technology
NIH	National Institutes of Health
OFPP	OMB's Office of Federal Procurement Policy
OMB	Office of Management and Budget
OPM	Office of Personnel Management
OSHA	Occupational Safety and Health Administration
PIO	public information officer
PMP	program management professional
PPP	public-private partnerships
PPS	Partnership for Public Service
RBD	risk-based decision making
RCT	randomized controlled trial
RFI	request for information
RFP	request for proposal
SOW	statement of work
SSA	Social Security Administration
SSTD	Surface Ship Torpedo Defense
VA	Department of Veterans Affairs

Introduction: Why This Book?

On October 28, 1962, the world breathed a sigh of relief as word spread that the Soviet Union had backed down from its deployment of intercontinental ballistic missiles in Cuba, just 90 miles from US soil and within easy striking range of all US major cities and centers of governance. In a real sense this was the closest our modern world had come to a nuclear war between superpowers. The clash involved a naval quarantine and ship-to-ship confrontations (including US Navy authorization to fire shots at Soviet ship rudders), along with the not inconsequential global stakes of pride and posturing. During the hottest moments it seemed as if neither superpower would flinch. Then, as popular history would have it, "the USSR blinked" and the world went on with its business.

The US policy that forbade offensive nuclear weapons stationed so close to its shores existed long before the confrontation arose. But figuring out how to actually enforce that ban—in this case, how to successfully meet the Soviet challenge—was the new and high-stakes wrinkle in what eventually was dubbed the Cuban Missile Crisis. Executing successfully on the commitment was no small challenge.

For almost two weeks in October the top-most levels of the US military, national security, diplomatic, and intelligence communities had to figure out how to successfully enforce the no-nukes policy in an unprecedented pressure cooker and under the glare of a worldwide spotlight. Below the leadership level, countless midlevel managers and executives provided unending scenario plans, strategic options, risk strategies, action choices, and defensive postures to support their leaders. In the USSR, comparable organizations, choices, and consequences were at play, and comparable players were involved.

Three Lenses

In his now-classic 1971 book *Essence of Decision: Explaining the Cuban Missile Crisis*, Graham T. Allison, professor at Harvard University's John F. Kennedy School of Government, analyzed the activities and decision-making processes of both governments in order to better understand how the successful outcome to the crisis occurred.[1]

In this landmark book Allison looks at three points of view from which the crisis can be analyzed: using a "rational actor model" that treats the decisions of each government as if made by a single, *rational person*; an "organizational process model" that is based on an analysis of agency *operating procedures*; and a "governmental (bureaucratic) politics model" that explores the personal behaviors and motivations of the key *individuals* involved, including the leaders of the various agencies and departments that fed both President John F. Kennedy and Secretary Nikita Khrushchev intelligence, advice, and action plans (both offensive and defensive).[2]

The first model—the rational actor—is often appealing for its romantic simplicity: a heroic young president faces down what a later and very popular President Ronald Reagan would label the "Evil Empire." That unidimensional analysis is, of course, just the variety that the media loves and that popular leaders court. But using the rational actor model gives limited insight into why certain actions were chosen and how the successful outcome was actually achieved.

This is why the second and third models of analysis employed by Allison are far more useful. In fact, these models provide the **first set of principles** of successful federal governance and management on which this book is based: that understanding what really drives successful organizational and personal outcomes in the real world of federal governance is key to learning how to achieve the results presidents and taxpayers alike require.

Through an analysis of the organizational and leadership prisms at work, Allison makes a convincing argument that the successful outcome in the crisis was really the product of a far more nuanced, even "softer" set of organizational and interpersonal behaviors and actions, rather than simply being the result of the bold actions of a charismatic president standing tall in the Oval Office.

The same is true for the Soviets. It's not that Khrushchev suddenly buckled under Kennedy's withering will. The Soviet first secretary, like Kennedy, made decisions based on a wide variety of organizational and individual inputs and advice provided to him by Soviet military and civilian authorities. This intelligence and advice, not incidentally, was itself being shaped by the organizational processes, personalities, and personal and political motives of the leaders and managers that ran the Soviet entities.

Indeed, both leaders ultimately made deliberate choices to achieve the goals of their respective governments. Both gave and got value in return. While the United States appeared to "win" more visibly, recently the history of the crisis has been updated to include the not-inconsequential fact that the United States, for its part, secretly agreed to pull missiles out of Turkey in return for the Soviet retreat. The complex and wrought interplay of organizations and personalities in the end steered the two countries—and the world—around the crisis; it wasn't just the simple interaction of two powerful international leaders squaring off.

Success in the Federal Realm

This connection—between organizational processes, personal behaviors, and successful outcomes—is not a unique dynamic. The only things unique to the Cuban Missile Crisis were the massive stakes involved, the global visibility of the event, and the sheer size and complexity of the two governments involved. US history is full of examples in which great and lasting federal policies have been expertly implemented by competent organizations run by smart, agile individuals. These individuals understood the complex organizational interplay and the wildly varying personalities involved in getting big jobs done in the federal realm. These include Franklin D. Roosevelt's program to pull the country out of the Great Depression and the successful bipartisan deployment of Social Security in 1939; the Marshall Plan to rebuild Europe and Japan in the wake of World War II's devastating destruction; and the bipartisan creation of Medicare in 1965. More recently, federal programs to meet twentieth-century challenges have provided new successes, such as the much-ballyhooed Year 2000 Y2K initiative to avoid what some predicted would bring the nation to its overly tech-reliant knees and the massive and rapid airport security deployments immediately following the attacks of September 11, 2001.[3]

There are, of course, many examples of the opposite. No matter one's opinion of the policy decision to create a national health insurance program—The Patient Protection and Affordable Care Act (ACA)—there is little debate that initial deployment of the federal website that was supposed to allow citizens to quickly and easily figure out if they were eligible for coverage, and to then sign up, was flawed. This may forever be a dominant memory when anyone mentions the Affordable Care Act, regardless of the law's ultimate impact on the health and well-being of Americans.[4]

What these successes and failures all have in common, though, is that there aren't simple reasons or explanations for what happened. Despite the famous admonition that "failure is an orphan," a massive number of employees and contractors were involved in the top-priority effort to design, build, and launch the ACA's website. All of them were operating—one would hope—under at least one immutable imperative: the executive branch's primary constitutional responsibility is to "faithfully administer the laws." And yet, in following a model close to Allison's "rational actor," we sometimes favor overly simplistic explanations of cause and ignore the complex organizational and personal dynamics that provide lessons from both successes and failures.

In the federal case, for example, attribution too often is attached to whether the federal workforce or leaders are skilled enough or competent enough. In reality there are specific and unique skills and capabilities among the individuals who operate successfully in our highly complex federal environment—and positive results follow from carefully defining, honing, and using those skills. These comprise the *second set of principles* on which this book is founded.

Unique Challenges of the Federal System

In that regard, the US federal system is, of course, unique. All democratic governments struggle with how to do programming and management well—how to "faithfully administer the laws"—at a level not encountered in other more authoritarian or limited democracies. The government of Singapore, for example, is a model of strong management success precisely because there is no lack of clarity as to management goals or authority to implement needed actions.[5]

By contrast, our own federal system is truly a daunting combination of shared authority and responsibility, diversity of goals and constituents, and massive size and breadth. Assistance to the poor, for example, is a crazy quilt of cash and services that are fractured among nonprofit organizations and federal, state, local, and tribal governments with wildly varying delivery approaches. Shelters are run locally; housing is as well, but it is heavily controlled (and subsidized) by the federal US Department of Housing and Urban Development (HUD). Income support levels and rules vary by state and tribal government, each under its own rules, but those rules are supplanted by a second federal department, Health and Human Services (HHS), when there are children in the family. Food stamps come direct from a third federal entity, the Department of Agriculture; and, if it's health care you need, it will come to you via state-administered federal Medicaid coverage—unless you are marginally employed, in which case you must register under the Affordable Care Act.

In fact, James Madison's Federalist Paper #51 makes it very clear that the Founding Fathers deliberately created this web of government "of the people," with its multiple branches, multiple power centers, and "checks and balances" everywhere you look. They did it to protect freedom. They didn't want a top-down carbon copy of a monarchy with an elected king. They wanted multiple factions led by states, with the national government secondary in many respects, and all of it sliced three ways by the executive, legislative, and judicial branches. Even the alignment between legislative and executive leadership inherent in the British system, where the majority party or coalition must form a government, was cast aside in favor of fully independent executive and legislative control.[6]

Baked into this marble cake of governance, authority, and control are a wide variety of structures and issues that make operating in the US federal sphere particularly challenging, including the frequently vast distance that often exists between the federal government and its "customers" or "clients." This distance makes it much more difficult to deliver quality customer service to a population that cannot as easily make its needs known directly. It has led to the creation of innumerable "surrogates"—ranging from contractors to states to city mayors to nonprofit educational, social service, and healthcare entities—for delivery and customer interaction. Each layer adds complexity to the management challenge of responding to the vast spectrum of "customers" and "clients" that the federal government ultimately serves or regulates, ranging from veterans to social security recipients to national park visitors to food stamp recipients, prisoners, and airline passengers.

Then there's the "big P" party politics, manifested recently by massive gridlock on Capitol Hill, and the "small p" stakeholder, interest group, and personal politics, which can range all over the organizational chart, from the front lines of service delivery to the highest-level national decisions—each of which can sometimes be excluded or underestimated in decision making.[7]

A powerful seat at the decision-making and implementation table is also accorded to stakeholders and interest groups, whose rights and desires must be accommodated in virtually every program implementation because of the economics of the US election process and the freedom to contribute politically (recently reaffirmed by the Supreme Court in its famous *Citizens United* decision[8]). And, of course, our representative government model assures that programs must consider geographical interests when determining where to locate (or close) offices, facilities, or activities.

At the same time, successful federal managers must negotiate arcane and com plicated budget, personnel, and procurement processes, as well as a steady accretion of rules, regulations, and standards, none of which is designed to accommodate action but rather to control the worst actors in and around government. With the current pace of change in technology and rising citizen expectations—largely driven by rapidly improving commercial service levels—federal managers face the added challenge of finding solutions that will not be obsolete immediately upon deployment.

Just simple spending decisions involve appropriations, authorizations, apportionments, obligations, expenditure limits, committee earmarks, and rescissions. These don't even address whether an overall budget is in place any given year. And all of this occurs, of course, in a fishbowl—with the "gotcha" media and other aggressive advocates all waiting to pounce—that creates a risk-reward balance massively trickier in the federal environment than elsewhere.

Add to this litany of complexity the important role our courts play in assuring the important rights and freedoms of the Constitution—including the Bill of Rights—and the resulting statutes that govern and protect us. Frequent differences in interpretation of statute, regulation, or implementation, or sometimes just the pursuit of self-interest, can lead to years of litigation and redefined requirements under a system deliberately configured by the Founders to protect important individual rights. As I write this manuscript, for example, yet another Supreme Court decision that could have struck down the ACA and left millions of enrollees in the lurch was resolved in favor of supporting the program.[9] The courts are critical to the protection of our freedom, but many court decisions can be hard to manage.

The sheer magnitude and reach of the federal government also presents a management challenge that is both historically unprecedented and unparalleled in today's world. Expenditure levels of $3.5 trillion in 2014 and the weight of interests that include not just domestic needs but broad global peacekeeping and democratic goals virtually assure complexity to any federal initiative.[10]

Finally, there is the challenge of short-time-line political cycles, which only serve to exacerbate one of the other great challenges of the federal service: managing the relationship of career managers and appointed executives (a dynamic that both groups struggle with constantly). With major changes at least every two years, with total change possible every four years and guaranteed at least every eight—try running a major corporation under those conditions!

It is this massively complex and fractured authority of the federal management environment and all the attendant complications that together create the special challenges for all those who are trying to effectively implement federal programs and policies. Simplistic or rote plans for successful management—like the singular decision-maker model of Graham Allison's theory—don't get very far in managing well within the federal ecosystem. "Think outside the box!" "Set lofty goals!" "Lead boldly!": all these aphorisms massively oversimplify the challenge, at least when taken in isolation.

Public awareness and debate over the relatively good or poor performance of the federal government is often fed by misperceptions and misunderstandings of what actually can work at the federal level. We've all heard the now-aging adage, "If they would just run government more like a business." It might seem intuitive that, for example, some technology-based program, policy, or product rollout would unfold seamlessly were federal officials simply to follow the lead of an Amazon or a Sony. Maybe some of them, yes. But there are profound differences in the private and public sector spheres that we need to acknowledge—and many that are "special" to the federal level and contained in the "litany" of challenges detailed above.

Keys to Successful Management

Yet there are many successes occurring every day. Social Security checks go out with high accuracy, air traffic safety levels are unprecedented, and trillions of dollars of federally administered economic stimulus payments recently helped keep large corporate employers from bankruptcy and the nation from a potential modern-day depression.[11] Some successes are born of crisis but many are not, like the cleanup of polluted water sites, reduction in smoking, or improvements in child health. How do successful federal managers move programs and policies in effective and innovative ways in such a complicated environment made that much more difficult because of the political polarization we're seeing in Washington these days?

Allison used his organizational and personal-political analyses to better understand what happened during the Cuban Missile Crisis. Others have also addressed the challenges of broader management reform.[12] In this book I turn the lens to the specific practitioner level to address the question: "What are the organizational approaches and personal skills that produce more successful outcomes in running complex federal government entities and programs?" I do so by supplementing my forty-five years of personal experience with insights gleaned from interviews of successful practitioners and consultants, review of the literature, and case examples to place the focus on specific personal and organizational practices that work best in the highly complex, diffused-power, stakeholder-driven, politically charged federal environment. Through case studies of both solid successes and unhappy failures, including some with which I was intimately involved, this book explores how careful attention to four key dimensions of success and three essential phases of action can help government managers and leaders achieve better outcomes.

Organizing Frameworks

Major cases start each chapter with observations from real-world challenges and real-world experience, the best teacher of all. Other shorter vignettes are dispersed throughout the text. The Cuban missile case, studied in graduate school soon after the actual events, framed my career-long belief that understanding the complex interactions of people and bureaucracies, rather than trusting simplistic top-down explanations, provides the best understanding of organizations' decision making and actions.

Many cases are based on my personal experiences as a young federal employee at the Department of Health, Education, and Welfare, or as a Senior Executive Service (SES) leader at the Government Accountability Office (then called the General Accounting Office). GAO's own transformation, in which I played an active role, provides the summary case at the end of chapter 1.

Other cases come from my experience in consulting or contracting to government entities such as the Department of Labor, the Federal Bureau of Investigation, the National Institutes of Health, or the White House. Still others result from personal interviews of current and former officials or consultants with live experience—such as the Veterans Affairs, the Census Bureau, and the Maine OSHA (Occupational Safety and Health Administration) cases—supplemented and validated using documents and published research. Often more contemporary, these can be more relevant for younger generations of practitioners and students.

I selected some cases because they provide lessons which, although well reported in the literature, seem ill-mastered in the actual government actions. Analyses of the accidents that destroyed the *Challenger* and *Columbia* space shuttles, for example, or of what went right and what went wrong when Medicare was expanded to cover prescription drugs, can provide sound footing for applying broad lessons for today.

Chapter 1 establishes a framework that is used throughout the book by defining **Four Dimensions of Success** that have worked well for me over almost twenty years in government service and subsequent decades as a consultant: **goal** *clarity and alignment;* **stakeholder** *communications and impact;* the *right* **resources and** *tools;* and *attending to critical* **timeframes.** Specific elements within each dimension are addressed, such as considering the personal goals of key stakeholders or attending to both politically important short-term timeframes and longer-term plans essential to achieving outcome goals. The discussion shows how these elements can be used to create strategies for successful planning and launching of initiatives and organizations, and, like the needs of any successful team, the importance of creating a "game-day" offense and the basic techniques that prove valuable as the "game" proceeds. The chapter concludes with some suggestions on defending against the criticisms and expectation shortfalls that inevitably surface in the hyperpolitical, oversight-laden, and often-poisonous federal environment.

Subsequent chapters present specific examples of success and failure—both large and small—that illustrate the competencies and building blocks necessary for success, along with the all-too-familiar barriers and booby traps that derail good government and good governance at the federal level. The chapters are organized around basic groupings of organizational achievement familiar to us all—motivating people, deploying technology, picking the right organizational structures, communicating and teambuilding, acquiring and contracting services, risk-smart decision making, and finding innovation—with the chapters near the end focused on helpful "Tips" for specific groups.

At the end of each chapter, **Key Takeaways** are structured within three essential phases of action that are roughly aligned with the way many federal initiatives and programs must be managed, from planning to implementing to defending: **Create Your Offense, Execute Effectively**, and **Play a Smart Defense**. These takeaways are short descriptions of strategies, tools, and action steps that can enhance the likelihood of successful results. They are intended as a sort of "agenda for action" that practitioners can select from when planning, executing, or defending programs and activities day by day.

Key Takeaways also recur thematically throughout the book and are summarized in an easily exported shorthand format in the appendix.

Chapter 2 focuses on the personal, hands-on aspects of motivating and managing any initiative's or organization's most valuable asset: your people. The chapter discusses ways to manage "up" with supervisors, "across" with peers, and "down" with subordinates. It provides strategies for overcoming the largely dysfunctional federal human resource system to attract, motivate, and retain top

talent and seize opportunities presented by millennials and other new generations of staff and consultants.

Chapter 3 turns to information technology (IT) adoption, management challenges, and opportunities. The chapter focuses on the observed difference between successes and failures in federal tech deployments (which are seldom at-
tributable to the technologies themselves), how to balance the "three big rocks"
of tech deployment (scope, cost, and schedule), and what should be considered
when selecting new technologies (as opposed to working with older more familiar ones).

Chapter 4 addresses organization and resource management, including practical lessons and strategies specific to the federal realm, such as managing resources under a never-ending string of continuous continuing resolutions; understanding the difference between the president's budget and the real budget;
and finding ways to do more with less and less and less. The chapter explores
which organizational structures work best under what conditions, including
when it pays to take on a restructuring and the value (and challenges) of using
shared service solutions.

Chapter 5 focuses on listening and communicating, using the tools and information all around us, including effective media techniques. Since a federal
leader's personal style disproportionately drives effectiveness compared to other
more clearly defined hierarchical environments, the chapter defines some arche-
types—from "listener" and "strategist" to "hammer," "cowboy" and "consensus
builder"—and looks at both which style seems to work best to achieve specific
goals and at what personal cost.

Chapter 6 is a discussion of acquisition and contracting—a federal-government
perennial. The focus is on when and how managers and leaders can successfully
achieve program goals within massively complex procurement requirements,
and how to get the requirements right when writing solicitations, picking the
right vehicles for implementing contracts, or finding ways to ensure that the contractor's goals are aligned with yours.

No twenty-first-century federal management book can provide value without
paying attention to both risk management and innovation, the topics of chapters
7 and 8. Some consider them opposite sides of the same coin: innovation is inherently risky. While the familiar elements of enterprise-wide risk management
are addressed in chapter 7, the focus is on risk-based decision making and the
importance of taking smart risks. The innovation chapter illustrates situations
where innovation was done well in the public sector and describes some keys to

successfully finding and supporting innovation and innovators and to importing successful approaches from commercial and worldwide venues. The chapter capitalizes on dialogues with two successful public sector innovators and a twenty-year observer and reporter of government innovation success, all of whom were invited to discuss with me how to support and sustain innovation in the everyday operations of federal organizations.

Chapters 9 through 12 provide "Tips" on how to meet the special challenges that are presented when working with four specific communities that exist in the federal realm in order to help us manage and lead successfully: oversight organizations, political appointees, career civil servants, and industry consultants. Each of these is embedded within our current federal ecosystem and can provide critical value if roles, interests, and operating procedures are well understood. But each presents special management challenges as well.

Drawing on my nine years at GAO, chapter 9 offers some strategies and techniques for getting the most value from organizations such as GAO, inspectors general (IG), the Office of Management and Budget (OMB), or Capitol Hill oversight committees and, where possible, co-opting them to your agenda. Chapter 10 addresses lessons learned for political appointees on how to use career civil service staffs to achieve goals (both yours and the president's). Chapter 11 provides help for career civil servants in "managing" the political appointees they have to live with for up to eight years at a time. Both chapters address the common desire to be "on the team," which is of critical importance in achieving common purpose and mutual respect as well as developing an understanding of each other's hot buttons and sensitivities.

Chapter 12 is geared to consultants seeking to provide value to federal leaders and managers as well as the leaders and managers who hire them. Having been on both sides of this table, it's clear to me that the relationship provides incredible value when it works well but represents a huge waste of time, resources, and goodwill when it doesn't. The chapter seeks to offer the perspective each has of the other's views and motivations as a way to help both get the most out of the relationship.

The conclusion highlights some themes that repeatedly arise throughout the chapters and explores the positive role certain success factors seem to play, such as negotiating goals with stakeholders, making the right political trades, or finding an imminent crisis, real or manufactured. Appendix A provides a consolidated summary of the **Key Takeaways** from the chapters—retaining the "strategy," "execution," and "defense" distinctions—in a format readers can use day by day.

Why Me?

The book is written from the multiple perspectives reflective of the diversity of my career experiences. Starting as a contractor to the Naval Air Systems Command during the Vietnam War, I entered federal service as a GS-7/9 "entry-level hire" at the Department of Health, Education, and Welfare (HEW, now HHS). After moving up through program management and leadership positions in the HEW Office of the Secretary under Caspar Weinberger (a Republican) and then Joseph Califano (a Democrat), I moved to the Social Security Administration (SSA) as policy director for family assistance. At SSA I became a charter member of the Senior Executive Service and eventually served as acting associate commissioner for family assistance (normally a political position) in charge of the $14 billion federal cash welfare program.

Departing the executive branch, I moved to GAO, which gave me firsthand experience in the world of legislative branch oversight and performance oversight. I concluded my federal service as assistant comptroller general, leaving government for tours of duty with one large technology contractor and two large consulting firms, where my focus has been federal performance.

Whatever value is provided in these pages combines insights acquired through hands-on experience in actual federal support, in program and organizational management and leadership roles, in GAO oversight responsibilities, and in independent consulting and contractor experiences over a combined forty-five years. My experiences are the source of many of the examples and cases used throughout the book, culled from observing or participating in inspiring successes and painful (but essential) "learning experiences." All of the individuals cited in these pages are real people, although I have altered a few names of those who didn't hold publicly visible positions.

Free but Hard to Manage

Our country's founders presented us with a government that is based primarily on protecting freedom, but it is not so easy to manage. Even the initial governance framework, expressed in the Articles of Confederation and Perpetual Union ratified in 1781, needed an astoundingly immediate "management" rewrite; it was replaced by our Constitution in 1788. As a result of their dedication and brilliance, more than two hundred years later we remain free—and still challenged when discussing how to best manage within that complex structure. The key is to identify and focus on skills and approaches that drive success in our uniquely free and diverse federal enterprise. This book is meant to provide a practical and useful road map for how to succeed in the increasingly complicated and scrutinized operating environment of the federal government at a time when the stakes are getting higher every day.

Notes

1. Graham Allison and Philip Zelikow, *Essence of Decision: Explaining the Cuban Missile Crisis,* 2nd ed. (New York: Addison-Wesley Educational, 1999).
2. Ibid., 2–7.
3. Donald F. Kettl, "Ten Secret Truths about Government Incompetence," *Washington Monthly,* January-February 2015, http://www.washingtonmonthly .com/magazine/januaryfebruary_2015/features/ten_secret_truths_about _govern053468.php?page=all.
4. Tom Cohen, "Rough Obamacare Rollout: Four Reasons Why," CNN.com, October 23, 2013, at http://www.cnn.com/2013/10/22/politics/obamacare-website -four-reasons/.
5. "Go East, Young Bureaucrat," *The Economist,* March 17, 2011, http://www .economist.com/node/18359852.
6. James Madison, "Federalist Paper No. 51" (1788), http://www.ourdocuments.gov /doc.php?doc=10&page=transcript#no-51.
7. See Tom Davis, Martin Frost, and Richard Cohen, *The Partisan Divide: Congress in Crisis* (Campbell, CA: Premiere, 2014).
8. *Citizens United v. FEC,* 558 US 310 (2010).
9. *King v. Burwell,* 135 S. Ct. 2480 (2015) (No. 14-114).
10. Office of the President of the United States, *Fiscal Year 2016 Historical Tables, Budget of the US Government* (Washington, DC: Government Printing Office, 2015), 28, https://www.whitehouse.gov/sites/default/files/omb/budget/fy2016/assets /hist.pdf.
11. Donald F. Kettl, *System under Stress: The Challenge to 21st Century Governance,* Third Edition (Los Angeles: CQ, 2014), 19–20.
12. See, for example, Beryl A. Radin, *Federal Management Reform in a World of Contradictions* (Washington, DC: Georgetown University Press, 2012).

CHAPTER 1

Key Dimensions of Success

It was in the 1990s when we first began to hear that computer time and date codes were bringing us toward a potentially apocalyptic situation in the year 2000. The root cause of the looming crash was simple enough: in their push to conserve space in computer codes, an earlier generation of programmers had recorded the year in two digits rather than four. At the time, "11/10/67" clearly meant November 10, 1967 (or October 11, 1967, if you lived in Europe). The efficiency of presuming that the first two digits in the date indicated the twentieth century seemed self-evident, and across the enormous number of computer programs efficiency trumped precision. After all, most computer programmers of the 1960s and 1970s never dreamed their original work would still be running on computers in 1999 and beyond.

However, by the nineties it began to dawn on the tech community that many of those original programs were still in use and that the first two digits of the year were going to change from 19 to 20. In other words, at 12:00 a.m. on January 1, 2000, an unknown but significant percentage of the world's computers wouldn't know whether "00" was the first day of the year 2000 or the first day of a century earlier.

What would happen then? Would elevators stop abruptly at midnight on New Year's Eve? Would air traffic control systems and power grids stutter with confusion over the date? Would defense guidance systems come down? We simply didn't know.[1] And thus began the great "Year Two Thousand" challenge (dubbed "Y2K" in digital jargon). With it came lots of thinking and planning (and spending!) aimed at protecting computer systems worldwide. Many predicted a total worldwide cost of between $300 and $600 billion.[2]

Given public concern, as well as an understandable desire to ensure continuity, the federal government launched its Y2K initiative in 1998 to coordinate and support the review of the nation's computer programs and adjust or replace code as needed—and to do so before 11:59 p.m. on December 31, 1999.[3] Most of the systems involved were commercially owned, making for a classic public-private partnership in which companies as well as state and local governments ultimately would play key roles.

Federal efforts began late in the decade, reflecting the limited but critical linchpin role Uncle Sam often plays in overcoming cross-sector national challenges. But, given the potential of the Y2K event as it was understood at the time, it was a prudent action and an exciting challenge. The effort involved was intensive, yet none of those involved could know whether their time, energy, and money had been worthwhile until the two-digit millennial turnover. The nation, or some parts of it, held its collective breath as the fateful evening approached. Otis Elevator executives weren't partying that night; they were on high alert. So were FAA executives, power grid operators, key members of the armed forces, and the global media.[4]

And then came a planetary sigh of relief when the new millennium began without frozen elevators, empty bank accounts, downed planes, or darkened skylines. Those who had met the challenge of ensuring the continuity of existing systems felt they'd succeeded.

There were skeptics, of course; many suggested that Y2K was mostly hype and overblown worry in relation to the actual risk.[5] After all, they argued, nothing much happened to any of the millions of taxpayers who had footed the hefty bill for Y2K "fixes." But Uncle Sam viewed the risk as too great, so the Y2K campaign was launched—and a massive technological project was completed. The do-nothing option was never tested.

The purpose in highlighting Y2K isn't to question the necessity of the effort. The advertised alternative—massive shutdowns of innumerable key systems—clearly was unacceptable, and in the end the lights did in fact stay on as midnight of December 31, 1999, clicked by.

In terms of the response to risk, the Y2K initiative provides a case study in effective operation and illustrates the often-essential collaborative role of the federal government. It's a good launch pad from which to introduce four characteristics, or dimensions, that are key to succeeding in the federal realm, and some frameworks that can be used to manage them.

Framework of This Book

This book provides some insights on when and how to consider and manage what I call the **Four Dimensions of Success**—the goals, the stakeholders, the resources, and the timeframes—and the strategies and activities a federal manager or leader can choose to maximize effective use of all four under very challenging conditions. As winning coaches (sports or otherwise) will tell you, these can be organized into **Three Essential Phases of Action**:

1. Create your offense
2. Execute effectively
3. Play a smart defense

Effective managers include consideration of the activities of the **Four Dimensions of Success** in all three phases, addressing needed changes as the program or initiative progresses through each phase of action. Throughout the book the analyses demonstrate this focus. The Dimensions are knowledge based, and define **what** to focus on, like a specific goal or a particular timeframe. The three strategic phases are activity based; they define **how** to organize and execute them. A change in one dimension, such as a change in stakeholders or resources, demands reconsideration of the others, such as goals or timeframes. The cases in each chapter illustrate the consequences of doing this integration well . . . or not.

This first chapter sets the two frameworks for analysis: the **Four Dimensions of Success** and **Three Essential Phases of Action**. It opens with Y2K because it illustrates attention to all four dimensions in a multisector environment and presents an interesting challenge common to preventive programs: the ability to demonstrate goal achievement when no outcome noticeably changes. The chapter explains and expands upon the second framework used throughout the book—the three essential strategic phases of activity—and identifies core strategies and activities that generally should be included in each. It illustrates the consideration of key dimensions phase by phase. A case study on the long-term transformation of GAO illustrates the use of the phases and dimensions.

In subsequent chapters, I use cases and insights from experts in each field, as well as my own experiences, to highlight strategies and activities that are specific to the function under scrutiny, be it motivating people, designing an organization, or managing risk.

Other management themes emerge throughout the book: the value of defining and communicating your own goals clearly and often, even though they can't always prevail in the political environment; the overriding importance of people as your primary resource and communications as your principal tool (even when objectives are technical, such as in technology or procurement programs); and the positive role that a threat or crisis can play in getting focus and priority handling. But it all starts with understanding the Four Dimensions of Success and the components of each.

Four Dimensions of Success

The Y2K response illustrates the first and most critically important dimension of success: **choosing and communicating the right goals**. Y2K is a clear example of how beginning with a clearly described outcome—even one as seemingly mundane as "continuity"—and effectively communicating that outcome to all stakeholders can be a key to success.

Of course, the Y2K challenge faced a special public relations hurdle in that the desired result was that absolutely nothing out of the ordinary would happen. This is also why some people viewed the whole episode as anticlimactic. Those leading the charge at the federal level, however, began by making it crystal clear that the status quo was the desired result.[6]

This focus on outcomes is a standard subject in modern performance literature and typically receives at least lip service throughout every level of government. But few truly understand the flexibility that the federal system provides to use the power of outcomes effectively. In essence, *negotiating goals you can achieve also defines the terms by which success will be judged.*

Explicitly defining the goals is only part of the job, however. Goals must be negotiated among competing interests and they must be communicated clearly. Too many failures in the federal realm are actually due to poor communications. To succeed you have to clearly communicate your ultimate goals—and the need for the associated spending—to the communities affected by your decisions, particularly since federal initiatives often involve a huge cast of disparate players. Y2K leadership, for example, channeled all major information and action requirements through existing networks of industry councils and associations rather than trying to dictate actions directly to businesses and states.[7] In the federal environment, with its highly diffused power and authority, those who **best communicate achievable goals** by defining expected program outputs and outcomes have the greatest chance to succeed.[8]

The second dimension of success is **understanding the key interest groups and stakeholders**, both internal and external, and communicating with them early and often.[9] Which groups will be most influential in deciding success, and what impact will the program or activity have on them? The federal system has many players, each with its own priorities and rivalries and each with a different perspective on success, so the question remains: Who *will* define success, after all? The congressional staffer who wrote the legislation? The committee chairman who appropriated the money or the implementing agency? Or will it be the broader national pool of interest groups and potential customers for the program or policy?

Despite the myriad players and their individual definitions of success—or perhaps *because* of these different points of view and their different levels of power—successful program managers and executives must explicitly define results in a way that balances, as best as possible, the often-diverse needs of key interest groups and focuses on their real-world wants and needs.

This is certainly not easy, especially because of what I call the "poison politics" dominating the federal environment. The constant drumbeat of criticism and discord from opposition or campaigning politicians in a polarized and divided government has created a public distrustful of almost anything governmental; this is reinforced by record levels of budget uncertainty and 24/7 media and oversight reporting that frequently takes issues out of their broader contexts. When government leaders find ways to swim against this current to build coalitions around goals they can achieve, successes like those chronicled in this book seem to result.

In the Y2K example, federal agencies and individual employees worked with other governments, nonprofits, commercial companies, and consumers, all of them with different goals and incentives. Success depended as much as on orchestrating these divergent interests as it did on technical solutions.[10] In fact, director John Koskinen deliberately kept his staff small, which helped frame the federal support and partnership role for his team rather than the more usual authority-based federal approach.[11]

Beyond goal setting and stakeholder communications lies the challenge of **defining the resources needed and deploying them effectively,** the third dimension of success. The resources any effort needs to succeed involve *people, processes,* and *technology.* Specific questions must be answered: Will the right talent be available and in place? What processes are needed to roll out and manage the program effectively? Will the right technologies be used to support the program and its services? Often it is necessary to revise goals and stakeholder expectations based on the realities of limited resource availability.

The fourth dimension of success is **setting timeframes,** with short-term, midrange, and long-term activities and goals throughout implementation. Clear and relatively easy short-term goals can build to more complex and comprehensive

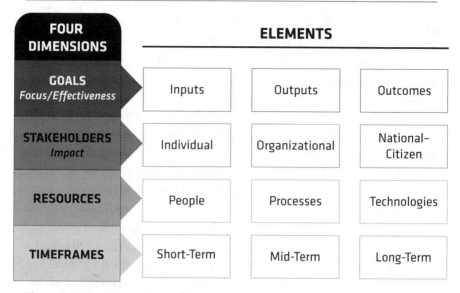

Figure 1.1 Four Dimensions of Success

changes over time. This stepwise approach can marry short-term political, organizational, or resourcing needs with ultimate outcomes.

For example, the Y2K program established different program timeframes based upon different industry and business group needs. "Y2K Action Weeks" focused the efforts of twenty-three million small businesses on systems needs in a concentrated way; "100 Days to Y2K," begun one hundred days before January 1, 2000, highlighted how some businesses got it done in fewer than one hundred days to help remaining last-minute outliers.[12]

Figure 1.1 summarizes the **Four Dimensions of Success: Goal Definition, Stakeholder Impact, Resources,** and **Timeframes**. It's a framework I've used for over twenty years to organize and focus goals, resources, and action in a complex, highly politicized, and rapidly changing work environment.

Each of these dimensions of success has three elements to its right that must be considered: Are the **goals** clear, and are the three elements necessary to achieve them—inputs, outputs, and outcomes—satisfactory to meet the goal? Have key **stakeholders** been identified, and their expectations understood at individual, organizational, and national levels? Are adequate **resources** available, particularly the necessary personnel, processes, and technology? Are **timeframes** realistic and comfortably separated into the three elements of near-term, midrange, and long-term activities and expectations?

Clay Johnson, deputy director for management at the Office of Management and Budget (OMB) under President George W. Bush, has described these challenges:

> Whether determining how to find a cure for cancer or attacking more easily quantified federal challenges like security clearance reform, it has to start with clarity of outcome goals [and] timeframes that make sense for the goals you set, addressing intelligently what the needed spend must be and who the vital stakeholders are.[13]

The **Four Dimensions** and their twelve second-level elements interact dynamically as a program rolls out or an agency meets different challenges. When some elements change, as they inevitably do over time, other elements will usually need to be "rebalanced." If I don't get planned resources, the outcomes and goals must be reexamined. When the timeframe shortens, organizational stakeholders may need to be alerted because outputs are likely to be more modest.

In the short term you can report inputs, such as the level of appropriated funding, to assure stakeholders that acceptable resources have been dedicated. But at the national level it will be more important to express longer-run planned outcomes, such as protecting endangered wildlife or reducing highway mortality. In any event, each of the elements should be considered when creating strategies and plans and when measuring and reporting progress.

Not every element in this framework will be equally important at any given time. Depending on the program, project, organization, or environment, different elements will be more or less pivotal to progress. But many program failures I've seen could inevitably be traced to undervaluing or ignoring one or another of these elements and the relationships among them.

Defining the Terms

At the beginning, it is important to understand and agree upon some key terms: inputs, outputs, and outcomes.

> **Inputs** are the resources expended toward the achievement of some output. They include items such as personnel costs, administrative overhead, and the cost of consultants and contractors.
>
> **Outputs** are the nuts-and-bolts "tangibles" created and delivered as a result of applying the inputs, such as additional veterans' hospital beds cre-

ated, highway or rail miles built or improved, acres of national parkland purchased, navy destroyers acquired, or tax returns processed.

Outcomes are the broader improvements in some condition or social situation that are the intended result of the outputs. In relation to the examples above, these could be, respectively, healthier veterans, safer and more efficient transportation systems, improved recreational opportunities, a country safer from foreign attack, and increased tax receipts or happier taxpayers.[14]

Consider real-world examples. The production and distribution of flu vaccine is the result of staff and facilities (inputs) working to create and administer doses of vaccine (outputs) intended to build to a healthier population (outcome). Added highway safety funding (inputs) is expected to produce highway improvements (outputs) that result in reduced morbidity or mortality among highway users (outcomes).

Three Essential Phases

But how can a manager or executive actually work with the elements that make up the **Four Dimensions of Success**? Good consultants and leaders have learned that you need a methodology or *systematic* way to tie the factors that matter into a logical sequence of planning, executing, and defending over many years and many projects. These **Three Essential Phases of Action** form this book's second framework. We will review each phase in turn, exploring core components for each.

PHASE 1: CREATE YOUR OFFENSE

A good offensive strategy involves three aspects:

- **Define the right goals**
- **Focus on stakeholders**
- **Set strategic timeframes**

Define the Right Goals
Your key goals will define your mission and align your stakeholders behind you, but only if there's adequate agreement about the goals and the way to get to the outcomes. If there isn't, you've got trouble, and often this is "easier said than

done." With the predictable diversity of goals that is so often present in modern-day programs—some themselves unclear and competing with others—settling on a manageable combination can require real negotiating skills.

The highly successful 2010 Decennial Census, for example, had to overcome major shortfalls in information sharing, organizational readiness, and technology. Various stakeholders had very different expectations for things as fundamental as staffing levels and basic IT needs. In fact, the whole exercise was on the brink of collapse when the Census Bureau asked Arnold Jackson to help the team regroup. Jackson, known in the agency as "A.J.," was the logical person to tap; he played a key role in the 1990 Decennial Census and won an Al Gore Hammer Award for leading the team that launched the bureau's website in the mid-1990s.[15]

"It became clear that we had to get everybody, from Hill appropriators to oversight organizations to key agency leadership, to agree that more funding and a 'working together' approach was needed to save the day," says Jackson. His strategy was to literally assemble the key players in a room and refocus the whole team on the ultimate goal of conducting a successful census.[16] Parochial interests were set aside, says Jackson, when it became clear that the group would either stand and work together or face the unthinkable: no census. Bringing the players together and helping them focus on the distinct possibility of failure led to critical decisions that significantly boosted budget and staffing to save the day. "When the crisis passed and it became clear that we would meet the constitutional requirement to conduct a census every ten years, the respective stakeholders returned to protecting their parochial positions," Jackson says. "But by then we were fine, in terms of getting the quiet cooperation we needed."

Jackson was fortunate that his key stakeholders could find common ground. When they have a strong-enough commonality of goals, as this group did in the 2010 Census, "getting them together" can work. If not, as with tobacco growers and anti-smoking programs, a mediator's technique can help by defining what matters most and what is minimally acceptable to each major stakeholder, paying attention to where power resides.

Focus on Stakeholders

It's important to assess the relative influence of various stakeholders. Their needs and goals frequently diverge and are often in competition with one another. But they are not all equal in power or importance, so it is possible (and wise) to offer different levels of performance and results for different categories of customers, clients, and beneficiaries—what one observer calls "negotiating treaties with multiple stakeholders that balance various goals."

Providing the highest value to those with the most clout obviously helps to secure and sustain resources. Politics and interest-group influence permeate the federal process. Legislators and other powerful players who support a particular program often find their state or district "blessed" with a new facility or a nice infusion of highway or mass transit funding. It's always wise to understand which legislators control which resources and assure that their constituents' needs are top priority in your plan, especially since they can help persuade others to be supportive.[17]

In its plan to establish the Defense Department Financial Training Institute, the Department of Defense (DOD) located the facility in Worcester, an economically depressed city in central Massachusetts, to gain support from then–committee chairman Ted Kennedy. The senator, in addition to ensuring funding and legislative authorizations, brought the support of other members in both houses as well as key business and nonprofits.

It is also good to be aware of constituencies important to high-level executive leadership (cabinet secretaries or other key administration officials), whose support can be crucial to ensuring that programs continue to receive attention in the president's budget.

One grassroots example of mustering stakeholder support was HEW Secretary Joseph Califano's 1978 launch of his war on smoking. Califano knew that the tobacco companies would be the most vocal and powerful opponents. Recognizing that Big Tobacco wasn't going to have a sudden change of heart, Califano created an "equal and opposing constituency" by enlisting the support of doctors and medical researchers as well as federal and state health regulators.

He addressed the stakeholder challenge by empowering and funding the surgeon general, the National Institutes of Health, the Center for Disease Control (since renamed Centers for Disease Control and Prevention), and the Food and Drug Administration, to focus on the consequences of smoking, as well as comparable state and private entities, all of which he knew would weigh in convincingly on the healthcare aspect of the debate. Virtually every congressional district had a constituency Califano supported in return for their help on the anti-smoking campaign.

The key is to define which people and which groups will matter most in terms of visible results, and then focus on the outputs and outcomes needed to satisfy and mobilize them. In Califano's case, he also found the right people to challenge potential opponents in their home districts and on the national stage of public opinion. Realistically, of course, it's seldom easy to balance stakeholder interests. (Later in the chapter I explore some balancing strategies that can help.)

Such calculations don't have to be made from personal knowledge or quantitative analysis. They can be based on a stakeholder survey or on feedback from focus groups—yes, sometimes you just have to ask. But, whatever the mechanism used, it's important to have a clear idea of what "success" should look like for each of your most influential affected groups.

Set Strategic Timeframes

The more ambitious the task, the smarter it is to establish short-term goals by which you can mark progress or, if needed, alter the strategy. The media, high-level executives, and politicians tend to focus on what's countable, that is, hard numbers they hope will tell a story. But hard numbers aren't always necessary.

For example, if the Internal Revenue Service (IRS) or the Social Security Administration (SSA) were to launch a long-term campaign to boost compliance by overhauling forms and instructions, an interim read on the impact of the new forms could offer insight into what works and what doesn't. You can interact directly with representative groups and collect their reactions early on, just to get their impressions of progress. Early interaction is important.

The smart use of timeframes also can help achieve goals in a federal environment that can shift dramatically over time. Plans that include short-term milestones that build to longer-term achievements allow for better risk management, including the unanticipated risks that are inevitable in a complex and ever-changing operational environment. These milestones can provide all-important "pivot points" between each segment, which allow leaders to adapt. Short sprints with "risk pivots" can keep progress aligned with changing expectations, whether from changes in leadership or simply the normal evolution of expectations over the lifetime of a program.

One simple way to get an early read on progress is to monitor the inputs that have been committed to the effort. If available resources simply aren't adequate (as in the case of the 2010 Census), it may be time for a pivot—either toward more modest goals or by capturing additional resources.[18]

Without milestones for early output progress, the results can be unhappy as well. In 2006, for example, the Department of Labor (DOL) began working on a "performance dashboard" that department leaders could use to gauge their performance in key program areas. The department defined some initial parameters, hired a consultant, and got to work.

Over time, as different DOL leaders engaged with the dashboard project, needs and expectations changed, at least informally. The project plan, however, didn't provide for progress evaluations and possible pivot points along the way. Predictably, the gap between DOL's expectations and what it was receiving grew noticeably over time. By the time leaders recognized the gap, though, the effort was too far down the road for easy adjustment, and so the "dialogue" devolved into finger-pointing and laying blame.

Setting and monitoring short-term milestones would have allowed the department and the consultant to manage and adjust expectations, resources, and activities as needed and produce a final product of great utility. Instead, a "rework" was required.

PHASE 2: EXECUTE EFFECTIVELY

Once a strategy is in place, effectively executing the plan essentially involves six components:

- **The right people with the right skills and motivation**
- **The right processes and procedures**
- **Risk-based decision making**
- **The right information technology, deployed correctly**
- **Constant communication with stakeholders**
- **Force multipliers**

These components should be considered in any significant federal endeavor, whether it's a new policy or program or an organizational review. Each will be more or less important depending on the task at hand, but all will come into play.

For example, in the wake of a series of high-profile citizen-interaction incidents involving the Federal Bureau of Investigation (FBI) in the 1990s, a consultant was hired to review a host of issues within the bureau, from training and staffing to policies, procedures, and technology. Big questions were in play: Was the FBI's workforce ready to meet multiple, ever-shifting challenges? Were its processes properly defining crisis events so agents could deploy with appropriate force and clear terms of engagement? In dangerous situations, what technologies could improve communications among its own agents and with other responders? Would the bureau need additional resources to meet its goals?

Working with staff in every role, the consultants helped the bureau develop a comprehensive set of recommendations for all areas, aligning mission, resources, and training with effective planning and deployment. They also conducted a complete review of the bureau's communications technology, including interoperability issues related to working with state and local partners.

The case study illustrates the need to consider and balance the six components of implementation. The people, process, and technology components are, in fact, the elements of the **resources** dimension of success that are visible in Figure 1.1. In the federal environment, players seldom have all the resources they really need. Coping with resource constraints requires clarity in understanding the risks, defining the essential tools, and usually finding some "force multipliers" (that can magnify impact when resources are constrained). Precisely defining the skills and resources needed, and the capabilities of the available technologies and contractors, can mean the difference between success and failure.

The Right People with the Right Skills and Motivation

These are the questions important to the people element:

Do your team members have the right knowledge and skills, and do they share a common view of success? Do they have the right technical skills, or will you need outside specialists like consultants or contractors?

Does the team include people who possess problem-solving skills and the social skills needed to build partnerships with stakeholders? Do they have experience in similar deployments, including in-depth knowledge of the playing field and the nonfederal sectors that may actually deliver the services?

As part of the American Recovery and Reinvestment Act, the Federal Railroad Administration (FRA) needed to distribute $10 billion in high-speed passenger rail grants among nearly five hundred proposed projects. The goal was to stimulate jobs and economic growth while supporting the most urgent regional passenger-rail needs. The FRA needed a team with the skills and experience capable of working well with the states, the District of Columbia, and Amtrak. The team would have to make its decisions rapidly to support economic stimulus goals, but prudently, to avoid public criticism for wasting taxpayer dollars.

To perform the job well and quickly, FRA supplemented its team, which was already strong in working constructively with state transportation agencies, with modest consulting support that could provide process and surge capabilities and technical specialists in fields such as grants management, passenger and commuter rail, and environmental considerations.

The FRA team's prior knowledge of the "players" and the terrain, supplemented by the added surge skills the consultant possessed, enabled them to evaluate over $75 billion in requests and launch 150 high-speed rail projects in 32 states, the District of Columbia, and Amtrak in record time (between August 2009 and April 2011). One indicator shows they got it right: the American Association of State Highway and Transportation Officials passed a resolution lauding FRA's outreach efforts and guidance throughout one of the largest discretionary infrastructure investment programs in US history.[19] (Chapter 2 addresses in more depth the definition and deployment of motivated personnel with the right skills.)

The Right Processes and Procedures

Defining the right processes and procedures is the second element in the **resources** dimension. In any complex deployment—a national website, for example—having "short-sprint" timeframes with technical and program milestones at identified intersection points should be standard operating procedure. These sprints are only effective, though, if team members are encouraged to be honest about their progress. A team must ask itself: Are additional resources needed? Do output time lines need to be adjusted, or, if you can't be flexible about deadlines, are the expectations of key stakeholders being managed properly? Setting overly long sprint intervals risks losing the chance to monitor progress and maintain control, and a team may miss the chance to pivot—which can leave it to defending poor progress or begging for more time or resources.

Risk-Based Decision Making

An important implementation tool to include in any set of procedures is risk-based decision making, or RBD. RBD is a key component of enterprise-wide risk management, a process for assuring that organizational threats are understood and managed from the start.

RBD can be used at every decision point to identify the risks accompanying each possible choice, and then to make adjustments to planned activities and deployments as needed, or to make adjustments to the resources or strategies needed to accomplish the goals. Adjustments might also include rebalancing a team, improving interaction with partners, pushing for more resources, or adjusting time lines.[20] At a more basic level, if reaching an initial goal is beginning to appear unlikely or too risky, it may be time to reevaluate and aim for a less ambitious goal that offers a greater chance of success and less risk of calamity.

At the heart of RBD is the need to think a step or two ahead. It involves clearly identifying risk—the potential negative consequences of certain decisions—and the comparable benefits of alternative choices. The experiences the National Aeronautics and Space Administration (NASA) had with the *Columbia* shuttle, which was destroyed on takeoff due to a catastrophic O-ring failure, and with the *Challenger* shuttle, which at launch suffered a tile failure from free-falling foam insulation, are much-studied examples of the need for effective risk management. Agency and independent studies confirmed that while in both cases the specific risk had been identified and understood, the information either hadn't reached or wasn't adequately weighed by key decision makers, who were motivated by the potential effect of calling off a launch or altering a shuttle landing.[21] (Chapter 7 explores the shuttle cases in more depth, along with what they show about the need for the right processes as well as the many issues involved in defining and managing risk.)

The Right Information Technology, Deployed Correctly

Choosing and using the right technologies comprise the third element of the **resources** dimension. How well are existing technologies being used to support and report on program or organizational progress? Is the team identifying and adopting user-friendly technologies that facilitate successful interactions with taxpayers, internal customers, or others who rely on the program or service?

Often the most important decision to make is whether a new IT system is needed or if existing technologies can be adapted to a new problem. It's an important consideration, since acquiring and deploying a new technology is a major project in itself.

There are many examples of existing procedures being adapted to solve new problems. In 2014, for example, the Centers for Disease Control and Prevention (CDC) supplemented already existing airport screening capabilities with specially trained personnel to identify health-related markers in travelers arriving from ebola-ravaged countries.[22] But of course new technologies can be exceptionally effective as well. A new digital application for curbside pickup of prescription drugs at the San Diego Naval Medical Center made it far more convenient for patients to get their prescriptions and helped the center deal with its lack of sufficient parking.[23] (Chapter 3 provides more on choosing and deploying the right technologies.)

Constant Communication with Stakeholders

In addition to balancing stakeholder needs, staying in touch with those stakeholders as a program or initiative is deployed is basic to implementation success as well. This will require listening to and communicating with stakeholders constantly. At the federal level, understanding the breadth and power of the stakeholders involved—and when and how to work with or serve them—is critical.

Anyone working on issues related to Medicare or Social Security, for example, should recognize the strong influence and reach of the American Association of Retired Persons (AARP). If you're working with the Department of Veterans Affairs (VA) and you haven't involved AMVETS (American Veterans, Inc., a privately funded association of service volunteers), you're already behind. Continuing dialogue concerning goals, roles, and relationships, as well as giving progress reports, will help you negotiate possible tradeoffs between what stakeholders want and what the program can actually produce.

For example, when the Obama Administration launched its 2012–13 human trafficking initiative, HHS leaders and the initiative's congressional co-chairs convened at the White House a multidisciplinary meeting of stakeholders, including trafficking survivors, law enforcement, victim services experts, and other advocates. Their input, as well as the involvement of the states, localities, and tribes, helped fashion concrete steps, which were then widely disseminated via the Internet and six national and regional "listening sessions." By the end of the process, a broad stakeholder coalition was moving forward in support.[24]

Of course, stakeholders include a wide array of people and organizations inside government as well, and you need a parallel effort to communicate with them: senior policymakers, including administration leadership; legislative players, including appropriators; oversight organizations such as GAO, inspectors general, and oversight committees; and state and local governments that may actually be delivering the services or administering the program. In the absence of a crisis, this effort can be especially difficult because stakeholder attention is often diverted to other priorities. In *Collaborative Governance Regimes* Kirk Emerson and Tina Nabatchi expand on the value and use of collaborative government networks to handle especially "wicked" public sector challenges.[25]

Bringing these interest groups into the effort early can help you understand their priorities and allow you to find common ground that will in turn help the players support the program goals. (These issues are explored in more depth in chapters 5 and 9.)

Force Multipliers

The final component of solid implementation is what can be called "force multi-pliers," which can enhance the effective use of the other tools of Phase 2. Some-times these force multipliers consist of specialized personnel who can provide beefed-up service to key customers or groups.

For example, the DOD has deployed specially trained expediters to handle prob-lem cases involving military families that run into unusually challenging prob-lems during relocation. Using specialized personnel to divert difficult cases from the normal work process protects response times for everyone else while ensuring that tough cases get the additional attention they need.

At other times, a "force multiplier" might involve using contractors for surge needs or to meet key deadlines. For example, when deadlines loomed for tax-payer registration under the Affordable Care Act and the web-based solution was still under construction, HHS turned to the Department of Agriculture's National Finance Center (NFC). NFC used its call center and a preexisting expansion con-tractor to directly call individuals who were eligible for national health care and handle these populations' call-based registrations.[26]

Finally, and unsurprisingly, one of the most useful force multipliers is technol-ogy, including low-cost, easy access applications that give clients direct access to information previously reserved for program personnel only. These apps provide both higher customer satisfaction rates and increased efficiency gains when they allow customers to do much of the work themselves.

PHASE 3: PLAY A SMART DEFENSE

There's an old adage that "the best defense is a good offense." The truth is that in the federal sphere you have to play both well, which is why a solid plan for de-fense is equally important. Things rarely (or never) play out exactly as planned, especially within the complex bureaucratic and highly challenging politicized environment of the federal bureaucracy, with its numerous moving parts and powerful players.

Sometimes the media, an oversight organization, or even key stakeholders will cause complications. At other times the basic environmental factors might shift or anticipated resources might not materialize. Anticipating, understanding, and being ready to respond to challenges and problems is essential to a solid defense.

Key elements of a smart defense—that can be particularly helpful when facing the conflicting goals ever present in the federal sphere—must include anticipative and adaptive strategies, a conciliatory and noncombative approach, and pre-planned maneuvers. A smart defense includes eight key components:

- Identify and neutralize opponents
- Avoid arguments and defensiveness
- Co-opt the "opposition"
- Build in defensive capacity
- Use criticism to argue for resources
- Be ready to pivot
- Negotiate when necessary
- Pick your battles

Identify and Neutralize Opponents

From the start, you should explicitly identify potential opponents to your initiative. You're always going to run up against those who, to be generous, may have something other than your best interests at heart, who might want to criticize your progress or denigrate the results. A sound defensive strategy will enable you to head off interference—or worse, sabotage—or at least help you be prepared for it.

For instance, it may be that people are opposed to the program for reasons having nothing to do with you or your management team. Perhaps they feel the program goals are either too modest or too ambitious. Perhaps they wanted to run the program themselves. Perhaps they want to hold you responsible for results even when you couldn't muster the necessary resources.[27] The key here is to have an explicit defensive strategy for anticipating, understanding, and, if possible, neutralizing or buffering opposition.

For example, with the appearance of Title IX of the education amendments of 1972, the landmark civil rights legislation prohibiting discrimination in higher education on the basis of gender and thereby requiring athletic funding parity for women at publicly supported schools, it became clear that pushback would arise from representatives of established, big-money men's athletic programs. Anticipating that opposition, HEW's Office of Civil Rights (OCR) identified a group of influential sports figures who also happened to be the fathers of some top collegiate women athletes; their influence and public support for their daughters was used to diffuse opposition and move policy.

Of course, how much you can realistically hope to "neutralize opponents" depends on the nature of the issue and the power held by the opposition. Broad and powerful opposition to major changes, like those encountered by Califano in his anti-smoking campaign or the recurring kind that results from major policy differences between political parties, can require patience and realistic expectations. In *Federal Management Reform in a World of Contradictions* author Beryl Radin concludes that it is best to look for incremental, modest solutions in addressing major challenges, given the inherent "contradictions" in the federal system.[28] Incremental strategies—such as implementation of less-threatening interim alternatives, use of media and thought leadership activities, or even explicit acceptance of more modest goals in return for support—will often find the most success in the face of powerful opposition.

Avoid Arguments and Defensiveness

Behaving in a defensive way compromises your ability to be the reasonable, rational voice in any debate or conflict. Sometimes defensive strategies are preemptive, as with the Califano and Title IX examples. Other times they are deployed in response to criticism or opposition. When the GAO, an inspector general, or a congressional oversight committee weighs in, for instance, it's generally not to heap praise on your performance. Or perhaps you're getting hammered by the media or an official in the administration or on the Hill.

In such cases it is, perhaps paradoxically, *very* important *not* to appear defensive. The best defense begins by stressing that everyone involved wants to achieve a positive result (even if that's not true!). Remember that the person at the table who listens attentively and respectfully to all sides in a disagreement and then identifies the most reasonable path forward holds the power position.

In his recent book, *A Journey through Governance: A Public Servant's Experience Serving under Six Presidents*, Bill Morrill calls this the "consigliere" role. He used the strategy constantly and to great effect throughout his career at DOD, OMB, and numerous cabinet departments to craft otherwise-impossible political coalitions around major federal achievements.[29]

As assistant secretary for planning and evaluation at HEW, for example, Morrill obtained support for controversial welfare reform, social services, and civil rights expansions during the Nixon and Ford administrations by "leading with data and defending with analytics rather than emotion." Usually the last to speak, Morrill often reserved for himself the "summing-up and next-steps" role. (See chapter 5 for more about the consigliere role.)

Fighting critics in a head-on way simply prompts new and more aggressive responses and gives the media story or congressional oversight reaction added "legs" in a Washington environment that loves controversy. There are better defensive strategies.

Co-opt the "Opposition"

Critical stakeholders can sometimes be pulled into the fold if you show an appreciation and understanding of their criticisms and seek their help. As for dealing with the media or oversight groups, there's real truth to the old adage, "Never pick fights with people who buy ink by the barrel [or pixels by the trillions]." Depending on the nature of the criticism (or attack), you may have a range of strategies, from accepting the criticism and offering a plan for fixes to simply ignoring the story and letting the news cycle play out.

In any case, it's vital that you understand in advance what may motivate certain critics and be prepared to make reasonable accommodations. The GAO and inspectors general (IG) exist, after all, to find ways to help make programs and entities as efficient and effective as possible—and to convince agency personnel to accept their advice. The best approach in the wake of a critical GAO or IG report is to find common ground. Time and again, agencies and program advocates have benefited by starting with the premise that they welcome recommendations, though sometimes with added "clarifications" or resources.

In 1998, for instance, a small but influential faction in Congress questioned the National Institutes of Health's $1 billion budget for administrative overhead. Recognizing that this faction was gaining traction, Congressman John Porter (R-IL), who chaired the committee that controlled appropriations for the National Institutes of Health (NIH), did something clever: rather than taking on the opposition directly, he helped secure funding for an impartial study of the NIH's administrative costs.

The study found that, given such a specialized set of research and treatment capabilities, an 8 percent overhead wasn't actually unreasonable, though some areas did offer potential savings.[30] NIH selected the savings initiatives it felt were reasonable and made some trims with congressional support, and the result was the issue dissipated.

Build in Defensive Capacity

In recent years many federal agencies have created offices or designated personnel to address—not argue, but address—oversight reporting and response issues. Often these personnel consist of staff members who formerly worked in an oversight agency and so can quickly establish rapport with it. Integrating this role into their operations actually marks these agencies as willing and eager to improve.

Such offices or personnel also can identify dangers or weaknesses in oversight recommendations, where they exist. Oversight liaison offices in both the DOD and the State Department, for example, have been effective in identifying unintended consequences that well-meaning oversight recommendations can have on US national security vulnerabilities as well as on allies whose security or national interests could be affected. This has the added benefit, of course, of activating "allies" who can be helpful in supporting questioned plans, programs, and resources.

Use Criticism to Argue for Resources

Another key to a solid anticipatory defense is to use any criticism to argue for more and better resources. To do this effectively you must carefully define the resources needed to succeed and then be diligent in tracking and monitoring what you actually do receive. This basic organizational *aikido* allows savvy agencies that are on the receiving end of suggestions to embrace those suggestions and point out that "improvements" require additional resources. Again, always resist the temptation to bluntly defend your position; it makes you look obstinate. Instead, start with the presumption (and the assertion) that your team is competent and can achieve its goals if it is armed with the right resources.

To begin construction of the federally funded "Big Dig" in Boston, local and national advocates pegged the initial cost at $2.6 billion. The Department of Transportation inspector general and other critics repeatedly reported construction and safety challenges as well as a lack of technical compliance by major contractors.[31] Predictably, significant levels of resources were added at many steps along the way as the IG became directly and continuously involved in overseeing repairs and assigning responsibilities.[32]

Be Ready to Pivot

Another key to a solid defense is building your strategy around short-term, midrange, and long-term goals for progress (see dimension four of the success framework). Criticism often comes from a failure to understand that incomplete progress is acceptable at varying points along any program's time line. If you've developed clear progress points for your sprints and are prepared with potential pivot points, you've inoculated yourself from criticism that you're moving too slowly or that results aren't accruing quickly enough.

In 2010, for instance, the newly created Consumer Financial Protection Bureau (CFPB) faced great expectations concerning how rapidly it could start protecting the investing public from predatory practices. Confronted by a critical IG report, CFPB responded with specifics on what it was doing in the short term and what it expected to achieve over time.[33] It was a smart reply that quietly shifted attention from IG criticism about missed targets to what seemed to be CFPB's reasonable goals for progress.

Pivot points also allow you to adjust or totally change goals when resourcing proves inadequate to the challenge. If the team simply doesn't have the skills, knowledge, or resources to do a thing well and the situation can't be fixed, it may be time to scale down expectations and adjust output and outcome goals to realistic levels. The wisdom of "incrementalism" has a long and illustrious history in public management, including a classic Charles Lindblom article ironically titled "The Science of 'Muddling Through.'"[34] Incrementalism may not be the "popular" thing to do, but it is far better than going over the cliff!

Negotiate When Necessary

Despite one's best attempts at compromise and conciliation, intractable opposition is inevitable in our divided government and diverse stakeholder environment. Sometimes you can do better by waiting for conditions to change; sometimes getting "half a loaf" might be the best you can get. The key is to focus on the most important goals—and on understanding if the opposition's minimum acceptable conditions violate those goals. Don't forget to leave your ego at the door in order to achieve important program goals.

Adopting a mediator's approach also can help: focus privately on what each side truly must have and what each would be willing to give up to get it. There are tools that can help do this, from enlisting the aid of trusted third parties to obtaining specific waivers, altered time lines, or unwritten or unpublicized agreements. President Kennedy's use of informal communication channels and secret agreements to remove US missiles from Turkey in resolving the Cuban missile confrontation are examples of such negotiation tools at a grand scale.

Pick Your Battles

Finally, pick your fights carefully. Not all criticisms need to be rebutted. My experience in testifying as GAO's assistant comptroller general helped me realize that in the context of congressional hearings, representatives and senators are frequently communicating with their constituencies rather than speaking to the witnesses at the table. In many cases it is smarter (and more strategic) to listen quietly and take the momentary heat than to debate with a representative who has an audience or targets beyond those in the room.[35]

Putting It All Together

So how can federal practitioners use the **Four Dimensions of Success** to assemble all these techniques into a cohesive operating plan? In 1981 Charles A. Bowsher, GAO's new comptroller general, proved to be unusually successful in balancing **goals, stakeholders, resources,** and **timeframes**. Arriving with the ambition to dramatically expand GAO's expertise from fiscal audits to a focus on program effectiveness, Bowsher knew he had to change GAO's hiring and promotion patterns. Furthermore, oversight committee feedback made it clear that Congress was cutting its own staffing levels and GAO would have to cut as well. In addition, the dozens of congressional committees receiving GAO's roughly seven hundred annual reports had privately indicated that they needed higher-quality work with faster turnarounds. The average wait time for a GAO report was nearly a year.[36]

Bowsher framed a plan that explicitly defined short-, medium-, and long-term goals (the three elements of the **timeframes** dimension) and identified specific activities supported by resources and tools for each timeframe. The near term would be dominated by visits with the executive branch, national thought leaders, and congressional committees (i.e., "**stakeholder** analysis"), as well as internal skills analyses and quality assurance activities.

The agency developed a longer-term **resource** adjustment plan to reduce staffing needs through more strategic use of technology during audits and program reviews. More efficient technology-enabled reporting processes were planned in order to improve reporting timeframes, a key output goal for stakeholders.

Bowsher also committed to an agency-wide performance-based personnel model aimed at garnering skills in newer program evaluation capabilities and moving fresher, younger talent up the ranks more quickly.

And, in perhaps the agency's riskiest move, significant staff reductions would be achieved by closing half of GAO's forty field offices. This last step was placed in the long-run timeframe so that leadership could first increase headquarters skills, change procedures, and adopt more computer-based data sources rather than relying on so many field visits. This strategy allowed key members of Congress to become more accepting of staffing cuts in their districts. Enabled by technology, higher skill levels, and more efficient data-driven processes, outcome effectiveness could improve despite (and in some cases enabled by) downsizing.

All **Four Dimensions of Success** illustrated in Figure 1.1, and most of the elements within each, came into play for the transformation at GAO. A full year of **stakeholder** analysis started the process within the congressional and executive branches and media audiences. **Input goals** were adjusted based upon a realistic negotiation of changes in all three **resources** elements—people reductions, reporting process reforms, and major technology improvements. **Output goals** expressed to specific committees on major issues of importance were negotiated. Implementation was split into three five-year **timeframes**, which matched the comptroller general's fifteen-year term of office.

The multiphased **timeframes,** with **goals** and **resources** that were explicitly adjusted over time, provided an added benefit: it helped GAO obtain the funding it needed for building the technology and skills that would increase effectiveness, a logical sequence of action on which most key **stakeholders** could agree.[37] According to Comptroller General Bowsher,

> It is essential for new leadership to spend time getting to know the organization and key appropriators—to make agreements with key congressional and executive branch leaders that can get their support for building the right capability over time. We did that at GAO by breaking the task into key timeframes and goals. Good leaders focus on learning the organization first, then on what investments are needed to get the needed talent, build the right infrastructure and technology capabilities and show results over time.[38]

Managing for Results

One professor at the Harvard Business School started his course on stocks and financial markets by declaring that making money in the stock market is simple: "Buy low and sell high." Easy to say, not so easy to accomplish. Defining success often can be characterized similarly: establish goals, line up resources, define actions, and execute faithfully. Or, as engineers might say, "Plan your work and work your plan."

This, too, can be easier to articulate than to accomplish. The **Three Phases of Action**, however, provide a coherent (if not always simple or easy to achieve) framework for thinking about how to structure a program or work through an implementation campaign successfully: **create your offense, execute effectively, play a smart defense.** Successful federal managers take the time to clearly define achievable goals and related input-output-outcome equations, they understand the critical constituencies and stakeholders, they deploy the basic resources and tools well, and they establish strategic but sensible timeframes. They also recognize the importance of managing the interdependencies between all of these. To organize and manage these in the practical and often rough-and-tumble political world requires effective offensive and defensive strategies and some specific implementation maneuvers.

The following chapters examine more specifically the application of these strategies, tools, and tactics to major federal functional areas with the goal of building the strongest possible foundation for success in the federal realm.

Notes

1. Steven Levy, "The Day the World Shuts Down," *Newsweek*, June 1, 1997, http://www.newsweek.com/day-world-shuts-down-173474; "Y2K: Overhyped and Oversold?" BBC News, January 6, 2000, http://news.bbc.co.uk/2/hi/talking_point/586938.stm.
2. US President's Council on Year 2000 Conversion, "The Journey to Y2K: Final Report of the President's Council on Year 2000 Conversion" (2000), 3.
3. Ibid., 1–3.
4. Elizabeth Shogren, "Whole Nation on Y2K Alert: Every State, Federal Emergency Staff on Duty December 31," *Seattle Times*, December 29, 1999, http://community.seattletimes.nwsource.com/archive/?date=19991228&slug=A19991229010300.
5. President's Council, "The Journey to Y2K," 19–22; Lou Carlozo, "A Minor Pest? World Buzzes On with Few Y2K Glitches," *Chicago Tribune*, January 11, 2000, http://articles.chicagotribune.com/2000-01-11/features/0001110274_1_y2k-bug-y2k-glitches-computers.
6. Peter Kendall and Cornelia Grumman, "Cost of Y2K Is Just Being Computed," *Chicago Tribune*, December 26, 1999, http://articles.chicagotribune.com/1999-12-26/news/9912260213_1_y2k-lou-marcoccio-money.
7. President's Council, "The Journey to Y2K," 7.
8. Clay Johnson, in discussion with the author, December 2014; Peter H. Daly, Michael Watkins, and Cate Reavis, *The First Ninety Days in Government: Critical Success Strategies for New Public Managers at All Levels* (Boston: Harvard Business School, 2006), 13–14, 34.
9. Jeffrey L. Pressman and Aaron Wildavsky, *Implementation: How Great Expectations in Washington Are Dashed in Oakland*, 3rd ed. (Berkeley: University of California Press, 1984), xvi–xvii, 188–90.

10. President's Council, "The Journey to Y2K," 4–16.

11. Stephen Goldsmith and William D. Eggers, *Governing by Network: The New Shape of the Public Sector* (Washington, DC: Brookings Institution, 2004), 68.

12. President's Council, "The Journey to Y2K," 8, 10.

13. Johnson discussion.

14. For more on performance measurement and the relationships between inputs, outputs, and outcomes, see Harry P. Hatry, *Performance Measurement: Getting Results* (Washington, DC: Urban Institute, 1999).

15. "Arnold Jackson," Census Newsroom Archive, last accessed June 6, 2015, https://www.census.gov/newsroom/releases/archives/bios/arnold_jackson.html.

16. Arnold Jackson, in discussion with the author, August 2014.

17. Kenneth Ashworth, *Caught between the Dog and the Fireplug, Or How to Survive Public Service* (Washington, DC: Georgetown University Press, 2001), 2–5.

18. Jackson discussion.

19. "An Update on the High Speed and Intercity Passenger Rail Program: Mistakes Made and Lessons Learned," *Hearing before the Committee on Transportation and Infrastructure, United States House of Representatives,* 112th Cong. 6, 13 (2012) (statement of the Honorable Ray LaHood, Secretary of Transportation, Washington, DC), http://testimony.ost.dot.gov/test/pasttest/12test/lahood6.pdf.

20. Deloitte Development LLC, "Nine Principles of a Risk Intelligent Framework for Risk Management—A Briefing for Federal Executives," 2012, http://www2.deloitte.com/content/dam/Deloitte/global/Documents/Governance-Risk-Compliance/dttl-grc-puttingriskinthecomfortzone.pdf.

21. NASA Accident Investigation Board, "*Columbia* Accident Investigation Board Releases Final Report" vol. 1 (Washington, DC: Government Printing Office, 2003), 195, http://spaceflight.nasa.gov/shuttle/archives/sts-107/investigation/CAIB_medres_full.pdf.

22. "Enhanced Ebola Screening to Start at Five US Airports and New Tracking Program for All People Entering US from Ebola-Affected Countries," Centers for Disease Control and Prevention, October 8, 2014, http://www.cdc.gov/media/releases/2014/p1008-ebola-screening.html.

23. US Navy Medicine Information Systems Support Activity Public Affairs, "NAVMISSA Helps Prepare Pharmacy Phone App for Prescription Ordering" (Washington, DC: US Navy, October 19, 2012), http://www.navy.mil/submit/display.asp?story_id=70254.

24. "Coordination, Collaboration, Capacity," Federal Strategic Action Plan on Services for Victims of Human Trafficking in the United States 2013–2017 (Washington, DC: President's Interagency Task Force to Monitor and Combat Trafficking in Persons, 2014), http://www.ovc.gov/pubs/Federal HumanTraffickingStrategicPlan.pdf.

25. Kirk Emerson and Tina Nabatchi, *Collaborative Governance Regimes* (Washington, DC: Georgetown University Press, 2015), 6.

26. "Helping Government Deliver 2: The Obstacles and Opportunities Sur-

rounding Shared Services," Partnership for Public Service and Deloitte Development LLC, March 2015, 8, http://www.google.com/url?sa=t&rct= j&q=&esrc=s&source=web&cd=2&ved=0CCUQFjAB&url=http%3A%2F %2Fourpublicservice.org%2Fpublications%2Fdownload.php%3Fid%3D477&ei= QFVaVceVB42uogTjroDoDg&usg=AFQjCNHXaaLYq1D-Dt1Ib4Wd2gy0W9yl1g.

27. Ashworth, *Caught Between*, 18–20.

28. Beryl A. Radin, *Federal Management Reform in a World of Contradictions* (Washington, DC: Georgetown University Press, 2012), 179.

29. William A. Morrill, *A Journey through Governance: A Public Servant's Experience Serving under Six Presidents* (New York: Cosmic, 2014), 146–47.

30. "Arthur Andersen Delivers Mixed Review of NIH Administrative Acumen," *NIH Catalyst* (January–February 1998), http://www.nih.gov/catalyst/back/98.01 /arthur_anderson.html.

31. Robert Poole and Peter Samuel, "Transportation Mega-projects and Risk," *Policy Brief* 97 (2011): 2–4, at http://reason.org/files/transportation_mega_projects_risk _big_dig.pdf.

32. Robert Cerasoli, "Central Artery Tunnel Project: Management Issues and Recommendations 1993–2000," Massachusetts Office of the Inspector General (2000), https://ia802502.us.archive.org/4/items/centralarterytun00cera /centralarterytun00cera.pdf.

33. Board of Governors of the Federal Reserve System, "Opportunities Exist to Enhance the Board's Oversight of Future Complex Enforcement Actions," Office of the US Inspector General, Report No. 2014-SR-B-015 (2014), http:// oig.federalreserve.gov/reports/board-future-complex-enforcement-actions -oversight-sep2014.pdf.

34. Charles E. Lindblom, "The Science of 'Muddling Through,'" *Public Administration Review* 19, no. 2 (1959): 79–88, http://www.jstor.org/stable/973677.

35. Morrill, *Journey through Governance*, 126–27; Ashworth, *Caught Between*, 11.

36. US General Accounting Office, "Excellence through the Eighties: Report of the Comptroller General's Task Force on GAO Reports" (Washington, DC: General Accounting Office, 1982), 17–18, http://www.gao.gov/assets/590/586020.pdf.

37. Charles Bowsher, in discussion with the author, October 2014.

38. Bowsher discussion.

Empowering Your Most Valuable Asset—Your People

On April 23, 2014, CNN broke the news that at least forty veterans had died while waiting for appointments with physicians in the Phoenix Department of Veterans Affairs (VA) healthcare system. While the specific charge proved hard to substantiate, six months of reporting on lengthy wait times at VA centers across the nation made it amply clear that the agency had big problems.[1] Yet the VA had received $57.4 billion in 2014 to provide medical care to veterans, with an established goal of providing appointments within fourteen days.[2] Furthermore, the VA's own metrics didn't show any problem with wait times.[3]

In the real world, though, thousands of veterans were experiencing unacceptably long wait times for appointments.[4] And as the media kept digging, it found multiple instances of unofficial waiting lists of veterans who were waiting to make it onto the "official" list the VA used when reporting wait times.[5]

What was the problem? Too few facilities or doctors? Inadequate triage? Was it a technology problem or a process glitch? Ultimately it became clear that both the growing backlog and the "cover-up" had multiple causes, all of which were related to motivating people or meeting their needs, employees and veterans alike.

First, the crush of new arrivals in the wake of the wars in Iraq and Afghanistan was straining VA's healthcare resources to the breaking point.[6] According to former VA chief financial officer Todd Grams, the VA needed thousands of new doctors and nurses to meet its performance goals in the face of the avalanche.[7]

Perversely, however, evidence emerged that the "gaming" of wait-time data was a direct and chosen response to the fact that shorter wait times were a high-priority goal for then–Secretary of Veterans Affairs Gen. Eric Shinseki.[8] Having started as an aspirational "stretch goal," reduced wait times became a metric tracked by organizational units and, eventually, a personal performance goal for many VA employees.[9]

At the same time, however, employee requests for additional resources went unheeded.[10] It was a situation ripe for trouble: federal staffs, while motivated, had been given goals they simply couldn't achieve with the resources available to them.

To meet goals and save face with senior managers, VA personnel found a way to cope: "unofficial" holding lists that kept the official numbers looking good. When these revelations surfaced, the investigations began and the secretary himself ended up resigning.

The Importance of Motivating and Empowering

This chapter is devoted to the art of motivating, empowering, and managing federal personnel—the key asset underpinning organizational success—by capitalizing on the public sector's "helping" mission. The discussion includes essential mentoring approaches and the power of building teams; it illustrates career progression, from early gains of technical skills to interpersonal and leadership skills more relevant at senior levels; and it describes tools and techniques especially important as new generations enter with more education and less patience for bureaucracy. The discussion concludes with some advice on creating incentives for top performance and, as an approach of last resort, directly addressing performance disappointments.

In government—as in every walk of life—*nothing* is accomplished without capable people who are motivated and empowered to succeed. Even the best technology only works because of skilled designers. Success hinges on understanding what people or programs want or need and motivating people to deliver it. This seems obvious, of course. But failing to do either well can lead to disaster. No matter what the organization, the process, or the technology, if we don't get the "people thing" right, nothing will work.

Any book on organizational success will tell you that your people are your most important asset. According to Deloitte Consulting LLP Human Capital director Patrick Nealon:

> The challenge is to clearly *articulate a future state* that people understand as something good and are motivated to achieve, and help them figure out *how* they can do it well. Too often federal leaders simply define goals and direct action toward them. But success demands leadership in execution, with specific attention to motivating and enabling personnel.[11]

A 2014 Deloitte report on twelve dominant human resource trends puts this into a broader context, citing "the power of purpose" as a major motivator for today's workforce, not just the federal workforce, and for millennials in particular.

These are talented people who "want to join organizations whose work engages their interests and deserves their passion."[12] If that's true in the private sector, think of the advantage we have in the federal sector, given its lofty goals (notwithstanding sometimes imperfect execution). This is consistent with what others have written about why people work for government and the power of engagement, especially in the public sector.[13]

While the literature on public service motivation is predictably complex,[14] virtually all of the leaders and employees interviewed for this book agree that the primary motivation for federal employees is the calling to public service.[15] This is the key to overcoming the snarls and complexities of federal work, and our job is to motivate and support federal employees by appealing to their dedication to national purpose and the often-critical value of their missions. Most federal employees had this motivation when they signed up. Most *still* have it.

Challenges

Of course, even a manager who is capable of meeting this standard still faces huge challenges, given the federal government's sheer size and complexity. Unfortunately, we tend to depersonalize our most valuable asset in federal settings. We call them "civil servants" or "human capital," as if they were indentured serfs or dry goods rather than actual men and women. That's a big mistake, especially within the federal government, because the more impersonal parts of federal service, like the massive and cumbersome formal personnel and performance systems, are strong *de*-motivators. The personal touch, whether helping one on one or in teams, "speaks" more to the individual gratification that comes from making government work for the people. Successful federal managers know this and use it at both individual and team levels to meet important needs.

The motivation for public service too often is undercut by politics. Some candidates for office and elected officials have criticized government in general, and federal workers in particular, as part of their platforms or strategies.[16] Media coverage and reports from the Office of Personnel Management (OPM) have documented how this criticism undercuts confidence and morale across the broad swathes of rank-and-file employees who are drawn to public service, especially when combined with the impact of multiyear pay freezes, service furloughs, and automatic reductions from sequester.[17]

Yet another challenge is the civil service system itself, created in reaction to the so-called spoils system of the nineteenth century. Career civil service protections and procedures solved many problems when they were created, but the system rewards longevity and seldom rewards performance. It does make it easier for some to sleepwalk through their careers, counting down the days and hours before retirement. It makes accountability hard to enforce and discourages the risk-taking needed to achieve important goals.

Yet there are many examples of successful leaders who motivate individuals and teams with a well-articulated vision and give them the help they need to take on tough jobs. Former HEW secretary Joseph Califano, for example, created specific management goals for each of HEW's operating divisions, including the Food and Drug Administration, the National Institutes of Health, and the Centers for Disease Control and Prevention. He also chaired quarterly performance reviews with senior managers to examine their progress (or lack thereof) toward the president's goals. Califano's approach made clear the importance of shared goals and team spirit—and connection with the boss.

In another administration years later, George W. Bush convened a series of high-level meetings with agency leaders as part of a drive to establish performance initiatives across the federal government. His first meeting with government officials was straightforward: he divided the agencies involved into red, yellow, and green, depending on their progress. At the end of the meeting the president complimented the greens individually; told the yellows he expected progress reports by the next meeting; and, turning to the reds, told them that if they were still red when they reconvened in six months they would not be serving in the administration any longer.[18]

Califano and Bush illustrate key premises of success in the federal realm: managers must provide incentives at both the *personal* and *team* levels and they must focus simultaneously on the goals of their supervisors and executives (managing *up*), their agency peers (managing *across*), and their subordinate staffs (managing *down*). Pay for performance and other strategies can help, to be sure. But success in federal management is principally driven by individual and team success. We will take them in turn.

Individual Skills Growth

Of course, having visionary goals and motivated people isn't enough. A third element must also be brought to the task: an understanding of what is expected of them at each stage of their career.

Pastor Clarence Crawford's ministry assists disadvantaged people and ex-offenders in Prince George's County, Maryland. His goal is to help them gain the skills needed to transform their lives and gain economic self-sustainability by becoming successful entrepreneurs. He calls it "teaching 'em to fish."

Crawford's background is worth a second look. After his first job as a local police officer, he entered a federal career that took him to the IRS, GAO, and the federal senior executive service, ultimately becoming associate director for management at OMB and then chief financial officer (CFO) for the US Patent and Trademark Office and then OPM. Crawford has seen career development in two very different contexts. Yet he's seen a clear pattern in both. "Technical skills are essential to early success," he says, "but give way to 'softer' skills, as you move up the chain of command, to the social skills needed to lead people and build teams. Most executives whose careers get derailed failed to understand and master the social skills required at more senior levels." Yet people don't automatically learn these skills on any given federal career path; they must seek them out or find mentors who will teach or model them.[19]

This progression of skills as applied to federal careers is illustrated in Figure 2.1.[20] In the early stages of a professional career, technical knowledge and skills are the most important element. They are what "get you in the door" in our qualifications-oriented civil service system. It could be program planning and analysis, construction management, or engineering or technology skills or abil-

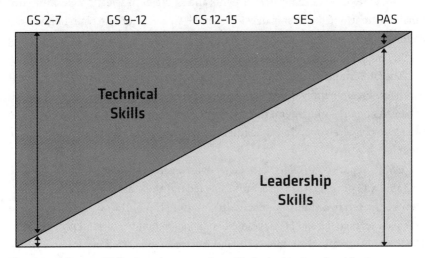

Figure 2.1 Career Skills Development from Technical to Leadership
Figure by Clarence Crawford.

ities, for example. "They make up 80 to 90 percent of a person's solution set for hiring and success in the early years," says Crawford.

As one's career progresses, success relates more to mastering the complex social skills needed to be a successful leader within the federal sphere. But these skills aren't really taught in schools of public affairs or administration. As one moves into a supervisory, managerial, or, ultimately, a senior executive role, the proportions reverse, and social, organizational, and interpersonal skills and behaviors become paramount. These include:

- builds relationships
- motivates and inspires
- politically insightful
- negotiates well
- flexible and able to compromise
- understands risk
- constantly communicates
- persuasive

Certainly, many of these elements can be found in federal performance standards. The Office of Personnel Management identifies five core qualifications and twenty-three core competencies required for entry into the senior executive service that are "used by many departments and agencies in selection, performance management, and leadership development."[21] These include, in plain English, the ability to lead and build coalitions, being political savvy, possessing negotiating skills, and having a willingness to be flexible.

The OPM standards capture many of the social skills in the list of eight, albeit with less focus on individual relationships and motivational and communication skills. As one rises in federal management, these softer skills become critical to success. If you're not an "adult learner" *and* a competent mentor, it's going to be tough going.

OMB's deputy controller, Mark Reger, whose career success has been based on his ability to develop trust across multiple federal and state assignments, characterizes the top two skills for **successful relationship building** as *understanding personal perceptions and biases* and *maintaining mutually respectful personal relationships*. Never attack or unnecessarily criticize anyone. "You never know where they'll end up," Reger says.[22] Perhaps in a position with direct influence over your program, for instance.

Deloitte's Patrick Nealon highlights the importance of setting and communicating an inspiring vision that is tied to goals important to the nation. These are key to **motivating and inspiring** and also for stimulating personal and professional growth.[23] Encouraging active two-way dialogues around important goals can also be powerful in motivating personnel to feel part of the solution.

Seven-term Republican Congressman and former chairman of the US House of Representatives' Oversight and Government Reform Committee Tom Davis characterizes **politically insightful** as a combination of learning what matters to the constituencies in his colleagues' districts, on the one hand, and listening respectfully to senators and congressmen across the aisle, on the other.[24] Davis crossed the aisle on numerous legislative initiatives, including several major federal technology and management reform statutes, and was able to **negotiate** with intensely partisan Democrats such as Jim Moran and Henry Waxman. Davis paid close attention to what Moran and Waxman wanted from legislation and helped them get a good deal of it. Davis's ability to be **flexible** made him a particularly effective dealmaker. But Davis coupled this with a personal touch, supporting his colleagues' families and community sensitivities. He could be seen on the eve of Yom Kippur walking through the Capitol Building with "a basket of fruit for my friend Henry, before he starts his fast."[25]

Davis's highly visible gestures across the aisle certainly posed some personal **risk**, given the extremely polarized politics of Capitol Hill. But two more of Davis's strengths arguably bolstered his standing: he constantly **communicated** his legislative goals to his constituents and he **persuaded** his colleagues on both sides of the aisle to tackle big jobs in the name of public service.

Federal leaders should practice and ultimately master all eight of these skills, and then build team loyalty and even affection by helping others acquire them—in essence, by helping them become better versions of themselves.

Building Teams

The ability to build teams boils down to one familiar word: *leadership*. Leadership, according to Colin Powell, requires you to *give your followers what they need*. It sounds simple, but the point is important enough to repeat: you can't lead if they won't follow. But they *will* follow if you genuinely provide for their needs.[26] Former HHS secretary Donna Shalala broadens the issue even further. In a 1998 article in *Public Administration Review*, Shalala devotes four of her "Top Ten Lessons" for managing public sector bureaucracies to the importance of enabling and attending to your people: choose the best, enable and fight for them, stitch together the right teams, and recognize the needs of career civil servants.[27]

In explaining his success with the 2010 Decennial Census, former director Arnold Jackson candidly notes that what really threatened the mission wasn't the much ballyhooed failure of contractor-developed handheld computers the canvassers were supposed to use. The real threat was that the stakeholders who were supposed to be working together to organize the effort simply weren't. They all represented so many different organizational viewpoints that each wanted a different approach.[28] The field personnel wanted to collect data in a way that was different than the central office had planned. Budget personnel wanted less-expensive methods, while program leaders believed that stronger efficiency measures would introduce unnecessary risk. Commerce Department leaders focused on what would reflect best on the administration and were particularly sensitive to the fact that census undercounts could change the balance of political power in some districts.

Resolving these competing goals proved difficult, as the various stakeholders saw little reason to compromise. But as crisis loomed, Jackson followed the famous political adage about not wasting a good crisis. He gathered all the players in a room and appealed to their mutual interest in not being part of the first decennial census to fail. He told them they were there to discuss common goals and engage with one another directly in order to develop compromises that recognized everyone's needs. And he told them they were going to stay in that room as long as it would take.[29]

Groundbreaking agreements followed, including the acquisition of $4 billion in added funding for an identified $2 billion gap, with the difference to be held as a "risk pool" and returned as "savings" if not used. Using input received from census leaders, the technology contractor made sweeping personnel changes to better assure successful performance and mutual success.

The key to the success of this team-building imperative was ensuring a group stake in the outcome, an effort that required a level of personal trust built up only by working face-to-face over long hours and weekends.

In most cases, it is also important to give the whole group the charter and accountability for success. Team and group rewards are highly desirable in the federal environment, as elsewhere, but can be difficult to apply through the formal reward structure. While the notion of group rewards was raised during the debate on the Civil Service Reform Act of 1978, nothing was ultimately written into law. Even in the absence of cash awards, however, team recognition is highly desirable, so cobbling together individual awards may be necessary.

Of course, teamwork helps in most complex efforts. In the federal environment, with its diffuse authority and multiple stakeholders, it's essential. Given the absence of a single command-and-control hierarchy, it's important to explicitly understand and address the needs and expectations of personnel in three directions: with your boss and other executives above you, whose support is essential; with your peers in the bureaucracy, the ones whose cooperation you rely on every day for help and support; and, of course, with your subordinates, without whom nothing gets done. This is managing up, across, and down.

Managing Up, Across, and Down

Most things look different depending on your point of view. Successful managers make a point of seeing situations from multiple perspectives and managing accordingly. What do you need from your superiors, peers, and subordinates to achieve your goals? What do they need from you?

Managing Up

Managing up—tending to what you need from your superiors and what they need from you—can be a tough challenge in a high-visibility environment. Former New York City Police Chief William Bratton freely admits that his highly public and ultimately fatal (for his job) feud with Mayor Rudolph Giuliani was the result

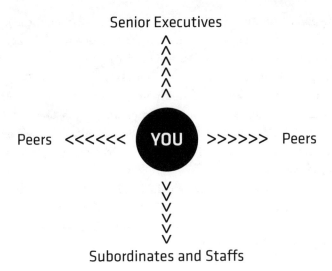

Figure 2.2 The Importance of Managing Up, Across, and Down

of his failure to manage up.[30] He was so busy pushing his data-driven policing agenda that he wasn't paying attention to the needs of his boss. "To drive change you need a relationship with your boss," agrees former VA CFO and IRS chief of staff Todd Grams, "and his backing when things get dark."[31]

For federal managers, the relationship is particularly tricky in that we sometimes serve political appointees, who often assume office with little experience in—and varying degrees of sympathy for—the projects and programs under their control. Of course, career managers have something to offer: new bosses need a significant amount of support and assistance from an ally. Why not the career manager? But whether one's superiors are political appointees or career workers, focusing on *their* definition of personal success is always the first key to "managing up."

The first thing to do, of course, is listen (always a good rule anyway). Understanding your boss's priorities and melding yours with theirs works much better than trying to get them to see things your way. Of course, it's also wise to understand your boss's preferred work patterns: some want structured briefings, others favor more informal discussion.

The second key is to understand that your boss has to manage up as well. Everything you provide, whether it's background information or key recommendations, should be considered in light of how it will ultimately play for him or her with the secretary, the White House, the media, or the Hill. Remember also that you can make successful ideas "theirs" and problems or challenges "yours." It's the quickest, most reliable way to win loyalty and trust. People will remember and appreciate you for it.

At one point while at GAO, for example, Charles Bowsher, the comptroller general, started expressing some concerns about the quality of the agency's reports. Too often, he noted, the evidence didn't fully support the conclusions and the recommendations didn't adequately address the problems. Plus, his boss, Congress, wanted the reports completed more quickly.

Rather than pushing a top-down plan for improvements, however, Bowsher created a task force of GAO leaders with significant ties to key stakeholders, including to leaders on the Hill. This task force tackled both the quality and timeliness concerns.[32]

Based on the analysis of the team (which I chaired), GAO embarked on an improvement plan to be defined and led by the newly created Office of Quality Assurance. Having the GAO's long-term career leaders take ownership of the improvement initiative ensured their buy-in and helped the agency achieve real change in a difficult environment.

Managing Peer Relationships

Managing "across," or laterally, is a teamwork issue. Whether it's with an IT unit, a personnel office, or a controller with money you need, success will depend on getting critical support from peers within your organization who you don't manage and can't control. They need regular recognition and, despite what they might say, few of them want you to be recognized before or above them. Being a team player means helping them with their problems and asking for their help with yours. Honest praise for work well done goes a long way toward creating long-term allies. In the GAO task force example mentioned earlier, giving praise and recognition to peer-leaders across GAO was critical to institutional success. The peer-leaders had to own the results to "sell it" to their divisions and congressional sponsors.

Also, don't be shy about horse trading: "I can help you at GAO because my sister works there. Can you help me with this budget problem, since your son works on the appropriations staff?" Trades and connections can be very useful.

Working for Employees

Compared to managing up or across, federal management literature pays much more attention to employee management, or "managing down." In Bob Lavigna's recent book, *Energizing Government Employees*—based upon Lavigna's experience as a personnel director at both the federal and state levels—"employee engagement" is highlighted as the key to managing down. Keep in mind the call to public service, and frame the challenges and expectations in those terms.[33] Getting caught up in pay-for-performance systems and "management by objectives" unfortunately makes it easy to forget the higher calling. In analyzing the wait-time failures at the VA, for instance, it's clear that employee incentives were focused much more on quantitative metrics than on the underlying and truly noble mission of helping veterans.

The team dynamic is all-important. Sometimes you actually get to see a successful team-based effort in real time. Some years ago, during a GAO conference held at the Westfields Conference Center in the suburbs of Washington, DC, a huge and heavy ceiling-tracked partition in the ballroom slipped its groove. It hung dangerously as federal workers below scattered. A siren rang and *every* employee of the hotel, from truck drivers and chambermaids to the CEO, converged on the ballroom. Massive ladders being carried by dozens of people appeared, and with the help of these hundreds of men and women the partition was back in place within five minutes. The watching feds applauded, and everyone went back to their regular assignments.

The Westfields general manager said his staff looked forward to and, in fact, practiced "all-together calls," the important things they could do as a team. It was all the better if customers observed these events. Post-event recaps reinforced their success, including "snacks on management," thanks expressed to everyone, and a call for suggestions for the future.

Of course, not every supervisor between you and the staff will be supportive and skilled in carrying your messages and motivating your staffs. You may need to work around difficult bureaucratic layers using a combination of broadcasting messages, leading group meetings with direct reports and below, and counseling with intermediaries about the message(s) and their important role in achieving the goal.

Using location, timing, and even food and drink to build camaraderie can help a lot. When Deloitte sought new space for its expanding federal practice, I made an early decision to move the office from Reston, Virginia—near many of our partners' homes and families—to downtown Washington, DC. To me it seemed an obvious decision; after all, that's where our customers are. To the partners whose commutes were quadrupled and office size was quartered, it was a near tragedy.

The downtown move eventually worked out, but not until we acted on advice from Gene Procknow, who was later named *Consulting Magazine*'s 2011 public sector consultant of the year and who was clearly wiser than I: "How many bottles of wine have you opened with your partners on this?"[34] (Chapter 12 presents more wise Procknow Personal Pointers.)

It may not always be obvious to federal managers, but staff perceptions of leadership and team play can turn on questions as basic as where you're going to meet, at what time, whether food or drink will be offered, and whether there should be a "power position" at the table (and, if so, who should hold it). Such considerations are so important, in fact, that a key elective in my Harvard MBA program was taught by a professor from the university's Psychology Department. Dubbed "Managing Two-Person Relationships," the course focused on when to stand and where to sit and how to pick the right environment for any discussion—when it should be done over lunch or cocktails and when it should take place across a big desk.

When Dan Tangherlini became administrator of the GSA (the US General Services Administration), he inherited customary executive-suite offices that were separated from peers and lower-level employees. Borrowing an approach adopted by New York mayor Michael Bloomberg, Tangherlini's first move was to create a large "bullpen" for the top GSA leaders to facilitate communication and, more important, show the staff and public that he expected his management team to work together.[35]

GAO's comptroller general uses a small dining room to host agency leaders and staffs when he wants to signal that GAO is an ally, not an enemy, despite the tough message he may have to deliver. Smart supervisors learn that it's wise to come out from behind their desks when they want to convey sensitivity or support. They also know it's wise to stay behind them when they need to assert authority.

Another key to managing down is viewing your job as bigger than just keeping staff focused and motivated. You are a *mentor*. Your staff's career growth is another often-overlooked key to leadership and to successfully managing employees. In the words of Clarence Crawford, "Teach 'em to fish."

Mark Reger at the OMB points out that management success requires more than picking the right people; you have to motivate them as well, and it's wise to match what your employees want to do with what the organization needs them to do. Personnel whose individual goals aren't consistent with organizational success are going to bog you down. Reger views it as part of his job to motivate staff to be enthusiastic about agency goals and identify areas of personal employee growth that may fit with specific assignments.[36] It's a constant building of skills, knowledge, and confidence in support of your agency's overall goals.

Sometimes, it's simply a matter of leading by example.

At the Social Security Administration's Office of Family Assistance, our primary mission was to develop regulations for federal welfare funding. The person drafting the regulations was clearly struggling. The first draft was too complex and poorly written. My boss asked if this person's performance could be used to fire him.

We actually started the separation process, but I still had an important set of regulations to hammer out. I decided to stay at work one night with pen, scissors, and tape (yes, we're talking a while back). I asked the staffer to work with me; he had some proven technical expertise I needed. By 2:00 a.m. we were done, with a new and much better set of regs in hand. The staffer expressed surprise at the level of editing and refinement. "I have always just written it," he observed, "had the clerk type it up, and sent it to the *Federal Register*." No drafts, no rewrites, no second reads. Wow. He didn't need a new job, he just needed to learn how to write complex rules. And he needed a mentor.

This story illustrates a final rule of managing down: always be ready to help employees learn how to do their jobs and how to reach their goals. Disappointing results, such as a failed website deployment or faked waiting lists, often can be traced in part to management's unwillingness or inability to address whether and how employees can do what they are being asked to do, leaving staffs to "figure it out on their own." Figuring it out on their own is rarely the right answer, and it sure isn't leadership.[37] But it can lead to disastrous employee "work-arounds," like those illustrated by the VA case described earlier.

Managing Performance: The Good, the Bad, and the Ugly

One of the key findings of the recent Deloitte report on major human resource trends is that "performance management," as such, is broken.[38] Successful enterprises replace such systems with effective coaching and personal development.

Make It Personal—Inspire, Mentor, and Model

Understanding and motivating people on an ongoing basis has little to do with a system that marches subordinates into the head office once a year and gives them a "meets," "doesn't meet," or "exceeds" expectations rating. Indeed, many professionals in the talent field believe that there is no perfect performance management system and that many do more harm than good.

A leader's job is to inspire, mentor, and model. Managing performance should be seen as a very personal thing. The fact of the matter is that the formal performance reward system is largely set by civil service rules and union contracts; there's little you can do to change it. What leaders *can* do, however, is encourage top performers while trying to help poor performers improve with informal coaching and support.

Make the Right Match

In terms of any given project, obtaining good support is first about job match. Is the candidate up to the expectations of the job? Should expectations be adjusted to fit available skills? It's always surprising to me when supervisors dealing with performance issues begin with annoyance or outright anger. The *first* consideration ought to be the question of compatibility: are your employees positioned where they can play to their strengths each day? When a job match simply seems like a bad fit, can it be fixed by altering job functions or by swapping roles with another individual?

Sometimes, you can make fixes without even adjusting a formal position description. At Social Security, for instance, we found that analysts who were skilled in quantitative economic analysis often weren't well suited to hearing criticisms submitted by interest groups during the "request for comment" phase. We chose to leave the hard economics to those individuals and moved the discussion portions to other employees with stronger interpersonal and listening skills—all within the same job descriptions. Job satisfaction and performance went up for both groups.

Clearly Define "Good Performance"

Regardless of how employees are evaluated, whether formally or informally, a key consideration needs to be clarity in defining and communicating performance expectations. Deloitte's Patrick Nealon points out that one of the most visible problems with the typical performance system is the failure to clearly define "good performance" and communicate that definition to staff members.[39]

In creating formal performance goals, major success factors for a good manager include having a good alignment of goals with capabilities and resources, coaching and mentoring, and making a personal commitment to each employee's success. Again, if an employee is struggling, lend a personal touch as mentor and coach. Just as every good doctor first suggests other remedies besides surgery, personnel experts recommend trying to figure out "fit" before taking more formal action.

Match the Job with the Person

At both Social Security and GAO, I found that some people who were highly competent at the agency's core functions didn't have the writing skills to craft SSA regulations or GAO reports. In both cases we created a small cadre of skilled writers to support and assist our more technically skilled staff, and we accepted that "adjustment" cost as far better than moving or losing competent personnel.

Motivate

There are other little things a supervisor can do to build meaning, and therefore motivation, into everyday work. People often simply don't recognize how important their contribution is to a social security recipient, for instance, or a supplemental security income recipient with physical or mental disabilities. Occasional field trips into the real world can work wonders in developing this recognition.

When Bill Leighty, former chief of staff to Virginia governors Mark Warner and Tim Kaine, was asked to take over the state's pension system, he made a point of connecting frontline workers with the customers they served. He wanted them to clearly understand that they were doing more than just processing cases and issuing checks—they were having a significant impact on people's lives.[40]

Understand the Personal Perspective

At times, of course, no amount of jiggering, coaching, or communicating can turn an employee's performance around. Even in those cases, though, it's never a good idea to simply start the "formal" performance improvement process (the one that leads to the "formal" firing process). If an employee simply isn't cutting it, it's important to talk with him or her informally at first. There may be challenges in that person's life you simply didn't know about. Or they may not clearly understand the work expectations.

Often in the course of such conversations employees will point out ways to improve, which is a far more elegant solution than a formal "improvement plan." Michael Gelles, a Deloitte insider-threat specialist with more than fifteen years of experience at the Naval Criminal Investigative Service (the real NCIS), believes that many supervisors simply don't know about their subordinates' real skills and that conversations about "missed expectations" can highlight those skills.[41] According to Gelles, Generation Y in particular responds well when offered the opportunity to work on positive change. The secret is to craft your approach around the question, How do *you* think we can achieve better results?

Formal Action, If You Must

Truly bad performance requires action. Demotion or reassignment, while unpleasant and often time consuming, are arrows in your quiver.[42] The fact is, no one likes coming to work when they know they are in over their heads. And while most people will object to being demoted or reassigned, at least initially, many come around later as they realize they're actually happier in a better-matched new role. Plus, the civil service's salary protections make the economic consequences of downgrades often more tolerable.

At GAO we sometimes encountered employees who were simply not cut out for program evaluation or financial audit work. "Theresa," a GS-12 evaluator on a team responsible for reviewing agency IT implementations, was clearly dragging down her whole group, even making it the target of congressional complaints. After numerous failed attempts at counseling, we reassigned Theresa to an internal nonsupervisory technology support function and reduced her grade to GS-9. While it was painful, Theresa accepted the demotion—and it was certainly preferable to being fired. One day, as we passed each other in the cavernous hallway of the GAO's Washington headquarters, she motioned me aside and said, "I thought you'd want to know that even though I still think I was doing fine as a GS-12, now I actually feel good at the job every day, which is worth the thirty-five hundred dollars it cost me to drop two grades. I'm hoping that my good evaluations are lining me up to a GS-11 job my supervisor thinks I can do."

Support Your All-Stars

Of course, as a manager it's more fun and exciting to encourage top performers rather than deal with performance shortfalls. Successful leaders spend much more of their time on encouraging and supporting high performance than on managing "problem" employees.[43] By increasing expectations for top performers you offer them the opportunity for rapid growth and room to innovate. Creating an environment that supports and encourages innovation isn't easy in the fishbowl world of federal management, to be sure, but great leaders and managers have found ways to create and maintain top-performing teams.

The US Postal Service, for example, uses creative approaches with contractors to jointly invest in innovations that can enhance mail handling and customer service. Annual awards given by the postmaster general, as well as modest innovation pool funds contained in some contracts, support the public-private teams that top the list of innovative ideas. (Similar motivational strategies are described later, under Offensive Strategies.)

It's a "Next Generation" World

The twenty-first-century workforce is highly connected, tech savvy, and demanding when it comes to job satisfaction and finding passion and purpose. For federal supervisors this can be a major advantage, since it fits nicely with what public service can offer—and the reason most people get into this business in the first place. Yet harnessing and capitalizing on this advantage can be challenging in an environment steeped in the centuries-long accretion of federal rules and processes.

Michael Gelles, who also is a psychiatrist specializing in employee management and motivation, defines changing workforce demographics as the *top* challenge to federal managers, as "boomers" give way to successive waves of GenXers, GenYers, and now millennials. Gelles believes that GenYers, in particular, are better educated than previous generations but also less experienced and less imbued with an abiding faith in bureaucracy.[44] Teaming them with boomers provides excellent results and complementary experiences for both, not to mention a way to provide continuity as retirements continue to increase. With so many employers, both public and private, competing for top talent, it's critical that federal managers do everything possible to create a workplace that offers the challenge, flexibility, and motivation needed to attract and inspire new generations of federal workers.

Workplace Flexibility

There's no longer much debate that workplace flexibility is essential to recruiting and retaining today's workers. In today's high-flex, high-tech world, the "office" can be located anywhere. For millennials this is virtually required in order to capitalize on an already integrated, technology-dominated skill base and lifestyle. The challenge is to properly manage performance in this environment. (See chapter 1 for more on the concepts of "inputs," "outputs" and "outcomes." Flexible operations require us to clearly understand and distinguish between them.)

For example, it's far better for taxpayers—and far more motivational for employees—to use outputs and outcomes as performance goals. The current crop of new workers has little interest in input measures, like how many forms they reviewed by 5:00 p.m. To them it makes more sense to be held accountable for—and inspired by—outcomes they can directly correlate to societal goals. This should be the case with all workers and all work, of course, but it's especially important in a highly flexible, mobile work environment. The greatest challenge to workplace flexibility in the federal environment is the need to shift from an input-oriented supervisory approach—hours worked, arrival and departure times, fund expenditure rates—to a focus on outputs and outcomes.

It is also important to recognize just how harmful it can be to use input goals to manage people or their performance. Input measurement approaches reflect the dominant role that appropriations have played in the perception of "success" in the federal government: the more funding you have, the more successful you are. They also reflect the historical command-and-control approach to federal supervision, where "senior" supervisors check and monitor the presence (or absence) of "junior" personnel.

The hunt for talent and increased productivity has rendered the command-and-control approach obsolete. Who cares how much time an IRS auditor spends in her office? What's important is how many returns she is able to review and how many dollars she is returning to Uncle Sam.

This example raises an important point concerning the risks inherent in managing by outputs and outcomes. It's essential to build *quality*-related expectations into the goals as well. We want our IRS examiners, and all other federal professionals as well, to treat people equitably and courteously. It is not just a matter of hitting their "numbers."

For researchers, policy analysts, or supervisors of large teams, however, output or outcome standards can be more difficult to devise. But starting with modest negotiated goals based upon discussions with staffs and stakeholders is a smart way to begin.

Note that "flex-work" does not mean that employees get to decide when and where they will work without regard to issues such as IT security and customer service. As assistant comptroller general at GAO, I supported a relatively liberal flextime policy and discovered that many employees chose to shift their workday so that it started very early. They were doing so for sensible reasons: beating the rush hour, being home when the kids arrived from school, and so forth. Unfortunately, Congress, the GAO's key "customer," works a relatively late day, sometimes beginning at 9:00 or 10:00 a.m. and running well into the evening. When a member of Congress or key staffer calls at 4:00 p.m. and gets no answer, that isn't a good thing.

The answer was not to abandon flextime wholesale, but rather to figure out how to make it work. Most GAO review teams worked consistently in one policy area and thus had regular contact with a handful of congressional committees and their staffs. Personal relationships built up over time allowed our team leaders to negotiate informally with key committee staff members on availability and methods of contact. We also developed informal arrangements whereby our staff would cover for one another during off hours. As technology has advanced, handheld access to cell phones that can manage emails, calls, and text messages anywhere and anytime has further expanded the tool kit for work flexibility.

At Social Security, by contrast, staggered work hours allow clients to get in touch with staffs from early morning to as late as 10:00 p.m., sometimes through call centers with rolling eight-hour shifts. For example, employees in one call center work from 2:00 p.m. to 10:00 p.m. Eastern Time to accommodate the East Coast's after-dinner demand. When wait times exceed a certain threshold, the SSA offers "callbacks" at customer-convenient times.

But there are clearly times when employees need to be in the office, whether it's to meet with clients or to work closely with fellow staffers. Creating a coherent strategy supported by goal-oriented performance expectations will make it easier to determine when the staff needs to be present in the flesh and when they can weigh in from the ether. Customers and key stakeholders sometimes need face-to-face contact. Furthermore, the critical issue of federal data security sometimes requires government facility protections.

It's important as a manager, then, to designate the times when everyone knows to be in the office. There's really no substitute for face-to-face teamwork when it comes to brainstorming, solving complex challenges, or reinforcing motivation and a sense of camaraderie. Periodic Apple FaceTime™ video calling sessions can work in some cases, but having something like "everyone in on Thursdays" can also be a valuable strategy.[45] Of course, "face-to-face" doesn't necessarily equate with "in official government space," unless sensitive information is to be discussed. Otherwise, meeting at a coffee shop works just as well and can be a nice break for staff.

One note of caution regarding informal settings, though: when the topic or information is sensitive or important, formality is best. I paid a price some years ago for giving a disappointing performance rating to a GS-15 employee at a nearby McDonald's restaurant. Years later, when he became special assistant to my boss (the commissioner of Social Security), he repeatedly reminded me of that episode. He disagreed with the evaluation itself, of course, but he also felt that my delivering the news at a crowded fast-food restaurant had been callous. He was right about that.

Digital Freedom

The explosion of digital tools and apps has enormously increased the potential for flexible work patterns. Younger staff members usually adopt new technologies and tools with astounding ease and often without formal training, learning on their own or with the help of colleagues, friends, and family. Managers, on the other hand, sometimes view social media such as LinkedIn and Instagram as distracting rather than enabling. This is a mistake. As leaders we need to harness this digital freedom in a way that both makes us more effective and provides our customers with easy access to services and information.

Of course, numerous high-profile data leaks have painfully illustrated the need for proper security; as I write this, Washington is still reeling from the recent theft of the personal information of millions of federal employees. Nevertheless, the proper use of IT-enabled systems and processes offers exciting opportunities throughout the federal government.

In 2012 the White House formally recognized the need for greater digital engagement by launching the Digital Government Strategy (DGS), which Chief Information Officer Steve VanRoekel called "a coordinated, information- and customer-centric approach to changing how the government works." Under the DGS, federal agencies must support the nation's large and growing population of "digital natives"—those who use the Internet and mobile devices daily, for work and for play, and who expect and *demand* the ability to interact with government in this way as well.

For example, the Environmental Protection Agency's Developer Central provides access to the agency's data for students and professionals who want to build applications. The Pentagon, meanwhile, is developing ways to deliver important battlefield information to frontline fighters via personal apps. And one high-visibility intelligence agency's daily briefing has moved from paper to a secure tablet format that allows leaders to both drill down instantly on topics of interest and also engage with their staffs and other analysts in real time.[46]

Chapter 1 poses the argument in favor of "force multipliers." Digital tools are *major* force multipliers for staff. Digital approaches, moreover, can help agencies realize significant economies. "BYOD," or bring your own device—once unheard-of in government—is allowing federal employees to work more creatively and with much more frequent and informal interactions (again, with the proper safeguards). It also opens new doors for telework and flextime. (The chapter on technology examines digital trends in more depth.)

Recruiting the Best

One would think that today's high-tech environment would make recruiting top talent easier. Somewhat paradoxically, however, is that the web actually poses a challenge to efficient recruiting. A colleague I ran into recently said one agency had opened an online position description for an "entry analyst" with flexible requirements. It received *sixty thousand* applications. Clearly there has to be some sort of fair but efficient sorting and screening process for online recruiting, or it can become counterproductive.

Software can come to your aid. A good consultant, moreover, can also help create screening tools that pass legal muster while quickly and efficiently identifying quality candidates. Of course, the consultant will start by challenging you to be as specific as possible about whom and what you really need. That in itself winds up being an important component of your screening procedure. If you absolutely require highly specific skills and abilities, applicants can screen themselves, which will cut down on the avalanche of applications.

Some of the skills being sought are those specific to working in the federal government, including experience with complex sets of strategic relationships. Does an applicant have experience in managing multiple, sometimes opposing stakeholder groups? Can the applicant build relationships with critical oversight and review organizations? It's important, too, to recognize that different areas of federal practice have different cultures. Success in the world of health care may require entirely different skills than those needed in higher education; it's important to be specific.

In the federal environment even the most specialized jobs can require critical "soft" leadership and relationship skills. President Kennedy, when asked why he had named his just-out-of-law-school brother Robert as US attorney general, responded jokingly, "I can't see that it's wrong to give him a little legal experience before he goes out to practice law."[47] Clearly the president's choice was risky. It smelled of patronage and insularity. Only the president could get away with this sort of risk, and these days perhaps not even the president. But Kennedy, in addressing the question more seriously, held that his brother had the very characteristics discussed in this chapter: negotiating and consensus-building skills and the political acumen and sensitivity needed to manage diverse stakeholders.

The Department of Justice was packed with people experienced in all facets of federal law; the president needed a loyal lieutenant who could harness and steer that inherent experience to advance his agenda. Robert Kennedy's personal motivations and performance goals were tied to the president's. He was also clearly someone the president could trust.

President Kennedy, of course, didn't have to post the position, nor did his brother have to compete for it. But the Senate votes its consent for such appointments for much the same reason as normal hiring criteria are used: to ensure a basic level of job match. A legitimate and legal set of selection criteria did exist, even if in a highly political context, and Robert was confirmed and "hired."

Hiring someone you know, or someone whose previous performance and experience have already impressed you, can be a smart recruitment tactic. This is why it's always wise to "put the word out" about an opening, especially a higher-level one. A government lawyer once reminded me that it isn't illegal to have people in mind for competitive positions, to consider their qualifications when you write the position requirements, or even to notify them when the job is posted. As long as you're writing the requirements based on program needs and you are willing to consider other candidates before selecting the best one, you're in the clear.

This sort of "relationship recruiting" offers the best combination of a genuine candidate search with the desire to reach out to those in whom you have confidence. In a 2014 speech to the National Academy of Public Administration in Arlington, VA, OPM Director Katherine Archuleta put it well by saying that increasing competition for top talent "has changed the equation. We cannot post our needs and wait for talent to find us. We have to go out and find the top talent and show them that a federal career will be enriching and exciting."[48]

Outlanders Are People Too

People are people even when they exist outside your organization, such as customers, stakeholders, oversight officials, and consultants. The better you can relate to them on a personal level, the more smoothly things will go. When asked to define the qualities that helped her succeed, former Homeland Security undersecretary Janet Hale immediately cited the work she had done to build personal relationships with interest groups, stakeholders, and career staffs. In managing the creation of the new Department of Homeland Security (DHS) in 2003, which consolidated twenty-two individual and intensely independent organizations, Hale made a point of getting to know every one of them, including their external interest groups, their alliances, and the varying ways in which they defined success.[49]

As assistant secretary at the Department of Health and Human Services, Hale employed similar skills to successfully deploy a new financial system, as well as other challenging initiatives. Interestingly, Hale isn't actually known for being delicate. She succeeds by focusing clearly and astutely on individual needs and motivations and incorporating others' goals into hers.

Whether they're hard chargers or pussycats, successful federal leaders are marked by an innate understanding of the importance of alliances in moving policy and programs forward. Mark Reger's mantra, throughout a successful career at state and federal levels, including at Treasury and OMB, has been to "be nice to everyone since you don't know where people will show up."[50] Todd Grams, who was successful in multiple federal leadership roles, including at OMB, IRS, and VA, urges managers to support outsiders who can "go to bat for what your program needs."[51] As far back as 1949, Norton Long wrote of this as well in his classic article, "Power and Administration."[52]

The message is clear: in dealing with oversight, stakeholders, state and local governments, private firms, and other external groups, success requires a focus on what will make them your allies and supporters.

Key Takeaways

Government leaders need to motivate and empower based on important federal missions and the desire to accomplish those goals. It's not always easy, but there are some approaches and tools that can help.

Create Your Offense

1. *Motivate and Manage from the Organization's Mission and Vision.* Communicate the vision clearly and relate it personally to team performance. Whether you're managing up, across, or down, with high performers or low, with employees, consultants, stakeholders, or oversight committees, try to understand the personal interests and motives of *every person* key to your success. Clearly communicate to each what you want to achieve and how *his or her personal success* can be achieved as part of your team. *Always* play to the primary personal motivation of federal practitioners: service to our country.

2. *Use Mentorship to Promote Individuals' Growth.* Traditional learning and development programs simply aren't dynamic enough. Work with your teams on understanding the nontechnical skills needed to succeed in the federal environment, including the social ones: political insight, ability to negotiate, ability to understand and balance risk, persuasion, motivation, relationship building, communication, and compromise.

Demonstrate these qualities to your staffs and mentor them as you help them move up the ladder from the mid-grades to the SES level. Create career models that will help identify potential leaders early on, and then challenge them with training and experiences that stress teamwork, clear communications, risk-based decision making, and adaptability. The Defense Department, for example, requires that leaders at all levels, uniformed and civilian, be capable of understanding complex security threats, of making split-second decisions under pressure, and of motivating and mobilizing personnel in complex and ambiguous environments. DOD invests heavily in developing well-rounded leaders who understand its requirements for success.[53]

3. *Rethink Recruitment and Retention.* Unlock the power of social media and highlight the importance of the federal mission with an explicitly market-oriented, media-savvy approach. Build relationships with schools or organizations that are training or employing the kind of staff members you seek, and try to cherry-pick them rather than relying on mass recruitment campaigns.

At GAO, for example, we assigned a key leader to each of the US colleges and universities targeted for talent acquisition. They taught classes, got to know students and professors, and generally showed potential recruits what an exciting and fulfilling employer GAO could be. Again, "purpose" is a motivator for young talent, so use your mission to "sell" federal service.

Adopt strategies that build new relationships and open new channels for acquiring talent. Joint ventures, contracting, short-term consultancies, relationships with think tanks, and other cooperative endeavors are excellent ways to find new talent, and even allow you to "try it before you buy it." Similarly, talent communities within your organization—those informal voluntary groups of similarly trained individuals who share a common functional or customer interest or passion—can keep *current* personnel engaged and growing. AT&T's talent community, for example, attracts potential team members by providing a forum to talk about mobile computing and telecommunications in a lively, engaging way.[54]

Execute Effectively

1. *Help Define How the Team Will Meet the Goal.* Starting from mission motivation, match individuals and teams with job requirements, then help them define *how* they will get the job done with available resources. Does the team and it's personnel have the skills they need? Will the team need force multipliers? Is there a decision-making process in place for "pivots" when situations change, as they always do?

2. *Use Every Available Tool and Technique to Communicate.* Frequent and informal interaction and communication help everyone stay in touch and keep team momentum going.[55] Feedback on progress toward important goals and how each

person is contributing are strong motivators. Of course, everyone must come together in person at certain times, for decision making, motivation, or celebration. Avoid physical barriers such as huge square tables or desks, in favor of more communal spaces that signal a common set of goals. Remember, there's a reason why those knights of long ago preferred a round table. When a staff check-in is needed, join them where *they* work rather than in *your* space.

3. *Encourage New Approaches to Work Time and Location.* Don't be shy about trying new ways to get the work done. Be open to flexible schedules that don't jeopardize the mission but do create a better work-life balance for your employees. This isn't just formal federal policy.[56] It is also a *very* effective motivational technique that focuses the team on outputs and outcomes rather than on hours worked. When innovative work methods are identified, such as meeting outside the office for lunch or using new technologies to communicate with customers, encourage *others* to spread these practices across the organization.

4. *Focus on "Best Performance" Rather Than on "Problem Performers."* Spend a lot more time on the top 10 percent than on the bottom 10 percent, and on improving the people in the middle 80 percent.[57] Communicate informally and regularly with team members on performance and progress. In fact, informal contact should be the *primary* method of feedback, with any formal reporting or assessment process simply documenting what the employee already understands.[58] *Listen* to the people who do the work and align their jobs with project goals and their personal aspirations, adjusting assignments where possible. Watch for the "innovators" and give them space and encouragement to find new ways.

Play a Smart Defense

Playing defense shouldn't involve a negative or defensive mind-set. It simply requires managers to anticipate challenges that may arise and create strategies to meet them. Three elements are important to a smart defense:

1. *Stay Ahead of the Trends.* Understand the business trends that can affect your people and the work they do. There are profound effects, for example, on front line staff located in social security or postal service field offices as their respective customers—who are getting increasingly skilled and technologically proficient—prefer direct-entry access from home. Oversight and analytical organizations, such as inspectors general and offices of planning and evaluation, require dramatically new skills as web-based research tools replace desktop analytics.

Depending upon the size and mission of your organization or enterprise, it can be worthwhile to designate at least one "innovator" who will maintain a robust dialogue with staffs and leaders concerning trends and changes on the horizon. Such an individual can help ensure that the focus on the future doesn't get lost.

Consider designating a specific individual to be an advocate for employee involvement and motivation—and for necessary changes to the status quo. When GAO moved from its audit-based approach to a program evaluation approach, for example, it found it valuable to designate one person to identify, advocate for, and demonstrate innovative study methods, such as adding database analysis to GAO's usual focus on fact-finding through interviews. This met with predictable resistance from managers raised on older methods, so the comptroller general hired an innovation leader from a highly regarded research institution to bring us fresh skills, tools, and techniques.

2. *Address Performance Disappointments Quickly and Effectively.* Not everything goes as planned in terms of organizational or personal success. Tactically, the best organizational defense begins with learning the personal needs of key employees and stakeholders—and their personal definition of a "win." Be cognizant of when the performance of the enterprise begins to diverge from the interests and needs of stakeholders. If your people don't want to or can't reach the goal, make the needed changes or adjust the goal. Being explicit about any shortfall will help you move the effort back on course or introduce a compromise. Often underperformance is best discussed in advance and in private with the individuals or team in question, before it becomes a visibly contentious issue.

3. *Give Credit Generously.* Buy agreement, if needed, by giving credit to the judgment and skills of others. Key players and stakeholders are usually more able to accept compromises when the fix is framed as one resulting from their insights or actions. This is a worthwhile tactic when the media asks you to explain why a key initiative isn't achieving the goals so proudly established by the White House or in a secretary's press room. I'm reminded of a colleague, more senior than I was, who could help me accomplish just about anything, once I convinced him that it was his idea all along.

Conclusion: "Close Enough for Government Work"

GAO put federal human capital management on its high-risk list in 2001—and it's still there.[59] Given the severe limitations of formal federal processes for staff improvements (including the often-hated annual performance evaluation), *go personal*. Remember to motivate from and with the mission, and be there to assure that skills and resources can accomplish the goal. Make sure those on your staff know how they're doing on an ongoing basis, and that you are invested in their success.

Always make it clear, from your words and your actions, that "close enough for government work" is meant to be high praise. As Bob Lavigna writes in *Engaging Government Employees*:

> Although the etymology of this expression is not entirely clear, one explanation is that it originated during World War II, when the industrial sector began to produce large quantities of war-related materials for the federal government. At that time, so the story goes, "close enough for government work" meant that government had the highest and most exacting standards. If the work could pass government inspection, it could meet any benchmark. In other words, "finally, it's close enough for government work."[60]

Notes

1. Scott Bronstein and Drew Griffin, "A Fatal Wait: Veterans Languish and Die on a VA Hospital's Secret List," CNN, April 23, 2014, http://www.cnn.com/2014/04/23/health/veterans-dying-health-care-delays/.
2. US Department of Veterans Affairs, FY-2016 VA Congressional Budget Submission (2016), Volume II Medical Programs and Information Technology Programs, VHA-3 and Mike Brunker, "Performance Mismanagement: How an Unrealistic Goal Fueled the VA Scandal," *NBC News*, June 25, 2014, http://www.nbcnews.com/storyline/va-hospital-scandal/performance-mismanagement-how-unrealistic-goal-fueled-va-scandal-n139906.
3. Department of Veterans Affairs Office of Inspector General, "Review of Access to Care in the Veterans Health Administration," Report No. 05-03028-145 (May 17, 2006), http://www.va.gov/oig/54/reports/VAOIG-05-03028-145.pdf.
4. Mark Thompson, "VA Appointment Delays Keep Getting Worse," *Time Magazine*, June 9, 2014, http://time.com/2850879/va-appointment-delays-keep-getting-worse/.
5. Ibid.
6. Richard Oppel, Jr., and Abby Goodnough, "Doctor Shortage Is Cited in Delays at VA Hospitals," *New York Times*, May 29, 2014, http://www.nytimes.com/2014/05/30/us/doctor-shortages-cited-in-va-hospital-waits.html?_r=0.
7. Todd Grams, in discussion with the author, November 2014.
8. Department of Veterans Affairs, "Access Audit: System-Wide Review of Access" (June 2013), 17, http://www.va.gov/health/docs/VAAccessAuditFindingsReport.pdf.

9. Grams discussion.

10. Richard Oppel Jr., "Some Top Officials Knew of V.A. Woes, before the Scandal," *New York Times*, December 25, 2014, http://www.nytimes.com/2014/12/26/us /politics/high-level-knowledge-before-veterans-affairs-scandal.html?ref=topics &_r=0.

11. Patrick Nealon, in discussion with the author, October 2014.

12. Cathy Benko, Robin Erickson, John Hagel, and Jungle Wong, "Beyond Retention: Build Passion and Purpose," *Global Human Capital Trends: Engaging the Twenty-First-Century Workforce,* ed. Cathy Benko, Robin Erickson, John Hagel, and Jungle Wong, 79 (West Lake, TX: Deloitte University Press, 2014), http://dupress.com /wp-content/uploads/2014/04/GlobalHumanCapitalTrends_2014.pdf.

13. See, for example, Stewart Liff, *Managing Government Employees: How to Motivate Your People, Deal with Difficult Issues, and Achieve Tangible Results* (New York: American Management Association, 2007), 10–11; Robert J. Lavigna, *Engaging Government Employees: Motivate and Inspire Your People to Achieve Superior Performance* (New York: American Management Association, 2013), 2–4.

14. See, for example, James L. Perry, "Symposium on Public Sector Motivation Research," *Public Administration Review* 70 (September-October 2010): 679–718, doi:10.1111/j.1540-6210.2010.02195-02199.x.

15. Approximately forty interview discussions.

16. Eric Katz, "What a Rand Paul Presidency Would Mean for Federal Employees," *Government Executive*, April 7, 2015, http://www.govexec.com/oversight/2015 /04/what-rand-paul-presidency-would-mean-federal-employees/109513/; and "Scott Walker: 'Plenty' of Federal Agencies Have 'Lived Past Their Usefulness,'" *Government Executive*, July 27, 2015, http://www.govexec.com/oversight/2015 /07/scott-walker-plenty-federal-agencies-have-lived-past-their-usefulness /118618/.

17. US Office of Personnel Management, "OPM Releases 2013 Federal Employee Viewpoint Survey Government-Wide Results," news release, November 8, 2013, https://www.opm.gov/news/releases/2013/11/opm-releases-2013-federal -employee-viewpoint-survey-governmentwide-results/; and Lisa Rein, "Wave of Retirements Hits Federal Workforce," *Washington Post*, August 26, 2013, http://www.washingtonpost.com/politics/wave-of-retirements-hitting-federal -workforce/2013/08/26/97adacee-09b8-11e3-8974-f97ab3b3c677_story.html.

18. Tim Young, in discussion with the author, January 2015.

19. Clarence Crawford, in discussion with the author, June 2014.

20. Figure 2.1 and book text make reference to the most commonly used federal white-collar career classification system, OPM's General Schedule (GS). The General Schedule has fifteen grades—GS-1 (lowest) to GS-15 (highest)—based on level of difficulty, responsibility, and qualifications. Federal personnel more senior than GS-15 generally are part of the Senior Executive Service (SES), a separate classification system for federal executives and leaders.

21. Office of Personnel Management, "Guide to Senior Executive Service Qualifi-

cations" (September 2012), http://www.opm.gov/policy-data-oversight/senior
-executive-service/reference-materials/guidetosesquals_2012.pdf.

22. Mark Reger, in discussion with the author, September 2014.

23. Nealon discussion.

24. Tom Davis, in discussion with the author, October 2014.

25. Ibid.

26. Colin Powell, 15th Annual CFO Vision Conference, Deloitte Development LLC, Washington, DC, September 2011.

27. Donna E. Shalala, "Are Large Public Organizations Manageable?" *Public Administration Review* 58 (July-August 1998): 286–87.

28. Arnold Jackson, in discussion with the author, August 2014.

29. Ibid.

30. Bill Bratton, Presentation at *Governing Magazine* 2010 Managing for Performance Conference, Austin, TX, October 2010.

31. Grams discussion.

32. US Government Accountability Office, "Excellence through the Eighties: Report of the Comptroller General's Task Force on GAO Reports" (November 1982), http://www.gao.gov/assets/590/586020.pdf.

33. Lavigna, *Engaging Government Employees*, 4.

34. Joe Kornik, "The 2011 Top 25 Consultants: Gene Procknow," *Consulting Magazine*, May 17, 2011, http://www.consultingmag.com/sites/articles/2011/05/17/the-2011 -top-25-consultants-gene-procknow/.

35. Geoff Whiting, "Tangherlini Looks to Transform GSA," *Fierce Government*, October 15, 2012, http://www.fiercegovernment.com/story/tangherlini-looks -transform-gsa/2012-10-15.

36. Reger discussion.

37. Nealon discussion.

38. Lisa Barry, Stacia Garr, and Andy Liakopoulos, "Performance Management Is Broken: Replace 'Rank and Yank' with Coaching and Development," in *Global Human Capital Trends: Engaging the Twenty-First-Century Workforce*, ed. Cathy Benko, Robin Erickson, John Hagel, and Jungle Wong, 45 (West Lake, TX: Deloitte University Press, 2014), http://dupress.com/wp-content/uploads/2014/04 /GlobalHumanCapitalTrends_2014.pdf.

39. Nealon discussion.

40. Bill Leighty, *Governing Magazine* 2009 Managing Performance Conference, Atlanta, Georgia, October 2009.

41. Michael Gelles, in discussion with the author, October 2014.

42. Liff, *Managing Government Employees*, 17, 73–92.

43. Ibid, 40.

44. Gelles discussion.

45. This book is an independent publication and has not been authorized, sponsored, or otherwise approved by Apple, Inc.

46. Scott Large and Pat Nigro, "Digital Engagement: A Public Sector Perspective," in

Tech Trends 2014: Inspiring Disruption, ed. Bill Briggs, 68 (West Lake, TX: Deloitte University Press, 2014), http://www2.deloitte.com/content/dam/Deloitte/us /Documents/public-sector/us-tech-trends2014-public-sector-perspective-053014 .pdf.

47. "New Administration: All He Asked," *Time Magazine*, February 3, 1961, http:// content.time.com/time/subscriber/article/0,33009,872026,00.html.

48. Katherine Archuleta, Presentation at Fellows Luncheon, National Academy of Public Administration 2014 Annual Fall Meeting, Arlington, VA, November 13, 2014.

49. Janet Hale, in discussion with the author, May 2015.

50. Reger discussion.

51. Grams discussion.

52. Norton E. Long, "Power and Administration," *Public Administration Review* 9, no. 4 (1949): 257–64, ww2.valdosta.edu/~gamerwin/pa/classes/padm7170/Long.pdf.

53. Adam Canwell, Vishalli Dongrie, Neil Neveras, and Heather Stockton, "Leaders at All Levels: Close the Gap between Hype and Readiness," *Global Human Capital Trends: Engaging the Twenty-First-Century Workforce*, ed. Cathy Benko, Robin Erickson, John Hagel, and Jungle Wong, 29 (West Lake, TX: Deloitte University Press, 2014), http://dupress.com/wp-content/uploads/2014/04 /GlobalHumanCapitalTrends_2014.pdf.

54. Lisa Barry, Udo Bohdal-Spiegelhoff, Robin Erickson, and Kim Lamoureux, "Talent Acquisition Revisited: Deploy New Approaches for the New Battlefield," *Global Human Capital Trends: Engaging the Twenty-First-Century Workforce*, ed. Cathy Benko, Robin Erickson, John Hagel, and Jungle Wong, 67 (West Lake, TX: Deloitte University Press, 2014, http://dupress.com/wp-content/uploads/2014 /04/GlobalHumanCapitalTrends_2014.pdf.

55. Liff, *Managing Government Employees*, 47–49.

56. OPM, "Labor-Management Policies: Negotiating Flexible and Compressed Work Schedules," https://www.opm.gov/policy-data-oversight/labor-management -relations/law-policy-resources/#url=Negotiating-Flexible-and-Compressed -Work-Schedules.

57. Liff, *Managing Government Employees*, 40–46.

58. Ibid., 53.

59 Alicia Puente Cackley, "High-Risk Series: An Update," Government Accountability Office, Report No. GAO-15-290 (February 2015), 122, http://www.gao.gov /assets/670/668415.pdf.

60. Lavigna, *Engaging Government Employees*, 47.

Managing the Complex New World of Technology

With the possible exception of Medicare, the most significant advancement in healthcare coverage in our nation's history is the Patient Protection and Affordable Care Act (ACA), enacted in March 2010. The act, among other measures, establishes a national healthcare exchange (website) that could be used to register the millions of individuals who live in the thirty-six states that chose not to establish their own enrollment systems. The deadline for the site's rollout was October 1, 2013.[1] The creation of the enrollment website involved dozens of contractors and almost $1 billion in contract funding. New offices created within HHS assumed responsibility for the ambitious IT system launch.[2]

As almost everyone now knows, the site was not ready by the "go live" deadline. Many people couldn't sign in, and when they could, the site couldn't calculate eligibility accurately or provide descriptions of available plans. The website crashed repeatedly.[3]

The government began a major effort to find and fix problems. Work-arounds were created, most notably call centers and other less-than-cutting-edge technologies.[4]

The problematic launch had some predictable results—besides the obvious, and somewhat gleeful, reaction from the ACA's congressional critics. It ultimately led to the departure of both the secretary of HHS and the prime contractor associated with the program. Huge amounts of additional resources were thrown at the problem, and functionality slowly improved.[5] But clearly the president's keynote initiative did not get off to a good start.

It was hardly the first major federal IT launch or rollout to stumble. Just a few years earlier, a prior administration also had faced significant and potentially disastrous challenges in attempting to move a massive paper-based questionnaire for the entire US population to a relatively well-established handheld technology.

Under its constitutional mandate, the Census Bureau must provide a comprehensive count of the American population every ten years; it has been doing so since 1790.[6] Work on the 2010 Decennial Census began in the early 2000s, and arguably the stakes were just as high as for the ACA. The country depends on the census to drive significant decisions about the makeup of Congress, as well as the distribution of massive amounts of federal funding to the states and local communities.

But as the big 2010 date approached, the count was not going well at all. In an attempt to move away from the paper-based approach of past censuses, the Census Bureau had decided that its door-to-door census takers would use geospatial-enabled handheld devices to collect housing location and individual and household information. While paper would be used for the initial mailings to all known addressees, the census still would require personal follow-ups with a projected 47 million nonresponders, so the handheld devices were viewed as a major improvement in data reliability.[7] Furthermore, the handhelds were to be used to track the movements of the census takers themselves—a group described as the "largest, most transient group of temps ever hired"—to make sure they were actually visiting their assigned dwellings.[8]

Despite years of lead time to design and procure the devices, and the millions of commercially available handheld devices, the bureau's device failed its 2007 qualification testing. Serious contract and management issues surfaced as well. As the days ticked past it began to look more and more like the Census Bureau might be unable to get its act together in time for the 2010 census. Could this be the first time a decennial census failed to make its deadline?

This story, though, has a happier ending than the initial ACA launch story. Faced with a technological and management meltdown, the Census Bureau decided to make significant program management improvements, reduce the scope of tasks to be accomplished by the newly designed handheld device, and abandon it altogether for the high-profile door-to-door collection of nonresponder data, which ultimately was completed with the proven paper-based "technology." The device's function was reduced to the more limited role of validating household addresses, contributing to what officials called "the most successfully implemented decennial census effort" in modern history, due to its record accuracy (an estimated overcount of 0.01 percent) and lower variation in hard-to-count areas than in previous censuses. [9] "[T]he American public can be proud of the 2010 Census their participation made possible," wrote Census Director Robert Groves.[10]

What differentiates the ACA case from the census one? And what can be gleaned from examining successful and failed technology projects that can help technology nonspecialists (i.e., just about all of us) in the federal service succeed in a world dominated by IT? In both cases, the technologies employed weren't groundbreaking and both had the full support of their respective administrations and virtually unlimited funding. Why, then, was one ultimately more successful than the other? How can managers and executives—particularly "nontechnologists"—achieve better success when using technology to implement or improve federal programs?

This chapter includes a review of what makes tech projects successful, starting with the recognition that it's seldom the technology itself. Six factors emerge from the literature and experts: realistic scope, careful acquisition strategy, motivated and experienced talent, adequate timeframe, right resources, and a helping leadership style. Since these are rarely (if ever) available all at once, leaders must make choices in selecting new versus more mature technologies and in prioritizing scope, cost, and schedule. The chapter also includes numerous effectiveness and efficiency tools and strategies available, from combining development and operations to creating a program results office and a sprint-and-pivot approach.

It's More Than the Technology

As Congress's watchdog, the Government Accountability Office reviews federal programs, projects, and policies for efficiency and effectiveness. Dozens of GAO's reports have addressed IT-related initiatives, and only rarely does a GAO report point to actual technological failures as the cause of significant problems. In report after report, the real causes for setbacks or failures are found in basic execution: not setting a realistic plan and adhering to it, not testing adequately and making changes when warranted, or not deploying the fundamental tools and tactics of customer service and program management. These are all basics of success regardless of the technical field.[11]

A renewed glance at the **Four Dimensions of Success** (see Figure 1.1) can help in understanding why managing significant IT projects can be especially challenging in the federal context. Dizzying numbers of stakeholders often wield varying amounts of power and influence over federal program design and execution. Combine this with the myriad environmental and political variables federal leaders must manage, and you have a recipe for real trouble.

Another classic IT pitfall is designers' tendency to proceed on the basis of "the ultimate solution"—the end product and all it promises—and the "overselling" of likely benefits. This is usually prompted by the need to secure significant resources. Yet the sheer complexity of the whole process cries out for short-term goals and the pivot points and incrementalism already discussed; both are lauded in public management teachings as well.[12] If nimbleness is built into your project planning, it becomes much more difficult to criticize your initiative and much easier for you to regroup and move forward with an amended plan of action when needed. (See more on the "agile" method later in this chapter.)

That's a trap officials fell into with the ACA and pivoted away from when designing the census: ACA leaders were totally focused on creating the solution they envisioned within the original deadline and they expressed an often unrealistic confidence in their capability to achieve timely success. Census leaders were flexible in abandoning their initial technology aspirations in favor of a less impressive but more reliable solution.

According to former HHS Assistant Secretary for Children and Families Wade Horn, when it comes to major IT projects,

> there should be a full and open competitive procurement that gets a "best-in-breed" primary integrator with a history of successfully implementing similar systems, and whose contract would give the government "one-throat-to-choke" accountability. Where there are dozens of component contractors and insufficient time for testing along the way, such projects can be doomed from the start.[13]

Horn also points out that technology integration for eligibility systems take a *lot* of time to get requirements stable and individual modules working together, and even more time to get them to provide the "right answers" for eligibility and services. The ACA plan didn't appear to include time for this all-important evolution.[14] As it became clear to insiders that things weren't working correctly, red flags began popping up. They were ignored.[15]

It became increasingly apparent that the ACA rollout was in trouble, but managers began keeping their heads down while also trying to not express doubts that might be viewed as undercutting the administration. And so, rather than alert higher-ups to trouble, key players "soldiered on" to the end.[16]

For ambitious IT projects (or any ambitious project, for that matter) this pattern leads to expensive and sometimes impossible late-in-the-game adjustments, finger-pointing, and, in the case of a huge effort such as the ACA, a bureaucratic and political panic attack that represents the antithesis of best practices.

The vendor contracts for the 2010 Census, by contrast, delineated extensive integration testing and pivot points in the timetable, allowing the bureau to reduce its reliance on the handheld device based upon tests conducted in 2007. To be fair, the bureau had done a decennial census twenty-two times since 1790, so it had both recurring experience and planning time lines that the ACA team clearly lacked. Their experience and planning left plenty of time to recognize and address project staffing and budget shortfalls, which allowed them to deploy the more modest and successful paper-based technology retained from the 2000 Census.[17]

It is important to note that the Census Bureau was also not challenged by the rancorous congressional political opposition attached to the ACA program itself. The acrimony made it virtually impossible for the ACA team to seek or arrive at accommodations about resourcing or time line changes.

In addition to stakeholder and process challenges, *finding and retaining the right people* for the job can be particularly challenging for federal IT projects. Experts in IT deployment have produced a simple triangle that ties together the human aspects of major projects: motivation, talent, and experience (figure 3.1).[18]

As noted in chapter 2, most people who work in the federal government do so because they want to be part of an important mission that helps our citizens. That's true in the IT realm as well, and good leaders know how to get the most out of their teams by nurturing that sense of purpose.

Motivation is, of course, a leadership responsibility, particularly within the public sector, which rarely offers dramatic promotions or performance bonuses for high-level performance. It requires a leader willing and able to take the time and effort needed to find and encourage the right personnel and then make key decisions about scope and cost as well as competing output choices. A "buck stops here" attitude is essential to gaining team confidence, which in turn is key to team motivation.

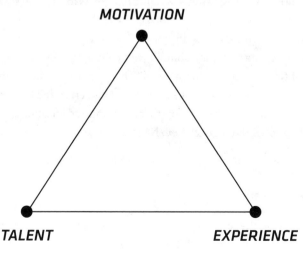

Figure 3.1 The Human Aspect of Major Information Technology Projects

Talent and experience often are perceived as one and the same, but they should be dealt with separately. It's important to ensure your team includes talented IT staff, especially since the inevitable complications will require personnel with the appropriate knowledge, skills, and abilities to accurately analyze and fix problems. But it's also critical to have experience in the particular type of IT being contemplated.[19]

Of course, talent and experience can be supplemented with contractors or consultants where needed and if resources allow. But, again, *both* technical talent and project experience are needed.

What Makes a Deployment Succeed?

In a panel discussion following the 2014 Federal Technology Trends Conference sponsored by Deloitte Consulting LLP, federal and consulting attendees focused on six characteristics essential for successful technology deployments: a manageable **scope** of requirements and specifications; a well-thought-out **acquisition** strategy, in terms of timing and need; a realistic **timeframe**; adequate **resources**; sufficient **talent**; and, last but not least, **leadership**.[20] In the diffuse and constantly shifting federal environment, however, it's unrealistic to expect to get all of these elements. And without explicit adjustments or tradeoffs in your goals, you can expect unrealistic plans and predictable failures.

In 1998, for example, the US National Reconnaissance Office, the agency in charge of intelligence satellites, released a request for two satellites with cutting-edge capabilities that were inspired by shifting threats to national security. Based on the cost estimates submitted, a contractor with little or no satellite design experience was selected based heavily upon price, and given wide latitude for "self-management." In the end, added intelligence collection requirements expanded the scope of the project, putting it years behind schedule and $1 billion above original cost estimates. By 2005 a review board had criticized the program, saying its continuance would require another $5 billion and an additional five years. Director of National Intelligence John Negroponte terminated the program with White House support.[21]

Scope of Requirements

Scope is obviously the most important initial success factor of any new IT program. If leaders are unclear about what they actually expect technology to accomplish for your project, it's entirely possible to have a successful program *design* and program *output* but a massively unsuccessful *outcome*. The federal landscape is littered with the bodies of those who approached advanced technology projects with foggy goals or poorly written requirements and accomplished little beyond giving GAO the chance to write an unhappy report on where the money went.

Before launching *any* IT project, federal leaders must engage the actual users and funders of the project, as well as their stakeholder groups, to identify and help *agree* on expected outcomes. For example, if you're facing a Social Security tech upgrade, have you reached out to actual applicants or recipients as well as to the AARP and the appropriate committees on Capitol Hill? Polling or focus groups can help reach broader audiences. But before you launch, make sure you're focused on the users' *actual* needs and not your (even educated) guesses.

Acquisition

Often the formal contractor requirements issued in IT acquisitions fail to reflect actual needs, whether through vague requirements, bad incentives, or an "arms-length" approach that keeps contractor and customer from collaborating effectively.[22] They also fail to define the short- and mid-term milestones or deliverables needed for success. Compare, for instance, the midterm testing requirements of the census, which revealed problems with the handheld units, to the ACA's "all or nothing" approach. A contract should provide for go/no-go pivot points with clear, sequenced steps that build to the final goal, so all contractors can be held to them.

Another key consideration when using external IT help is whether the talent showcased during the bidding process is actually the group that shows up to do the work. This "bait and switch" in contracting—whereby a team of experienced operatives pitches the job but leaves the execution to lower-level staff—is common enough, though not always a deliberately deceptive move. Sometimes the timeframe extends so far out that key personnel are of necessity assigned to other work. (Some techniques for avoiding or overcoming this problem are addressed in the section **Playing a Smart Defense** later in this chapter.)

Finally, an IT contracting plan should establish clear lines of authority that ensure focused and skilled supervision by government managers and leaders. If a government team lacks the resources or expertise to supervise a contractor effectively, an independent validation and verification contractor can be brought in. In fact, every good contractor dreads situations without adequate skilled supervision.[23]

Timeframes

At minimum, your proposed schedule must provide enough time for the planning, design, development, and testing of any major IT system. According to Janet Foutty, one of *GovCon Exec's* 2015 "Wash100" most influential government consulting leaders and CEO of Deloitte Consulting LLP, this is common with commercial IT projects as well—except for the challenge of the extra-long procurement timeframes involved in federal acquisitions.

"Considering how rapidly technology solutions evolve these days, it's essential to create baseline solutions faster, and then use customer experience and interactions to expand and evolve them," says Foutty. "In the federal sphere, that's really essential to help avoid obsolescence before deployment!"[24] Fortunately, newer generations growing up in the current context welcome the "build it as you go" approach, which is consistent with many familiar applications and game-development strategies that encourage user-developed improvements incorporated into frequent digital updates.

Just as important, as Wade Horn pointed out in the ACA case, is building in enough time to deal with glitches that inevitably surface. Does the schedule leave enough time for each stage? Working backward from a required delivery date without allowing for the complications and setbacks that accompany all large IT projects is unrealistic and unwise. Note again that the decennial census plans involved "go/no-go" prototyping and testing of the technology, with hard deadlines for a course change.

Resources

While the team is nailing down requirements and developing a reasonable timeframe for development, testing, and rollout, it must also consider whether it really has the money and talent to actually *build* it. Unrealistic or inadequate cost planning has been one major and frequently cited problem with large technology projects. In the early 1980s, for example, the Department of Energy (DOE) embarked on a $4.4 billion project to build a superconducting supercollider (SSC) in Texas. The project's costs escalated rapidly, with construction complications and changing design requirements driving the estimated total to $8.2 billion.

Congress canceled the project in 1993 after 20 percent had been completed and $2 billion spent. Four years later a DOE report found that initial cost estimates for the SSC failed to capture the project's actual needs and had assumed foreign funding that never materialized. Most alarmingly, the project had proceeded without a cost monitoring or scheduling system in place.[25]

Certainly, there are times when you have to launch a project with less locked-in funding than you know will ultimately be needed. That's life in the federal government, and sometimes it's even a practical strategy. But hiding likely future costs can be disastrous if it leads to partial progress and no added funding. The 1996 Information Technology Management Reform Act, also known as the Clinger-Cohen Act, established a process for IT project agreement and approval that is intended to ensure adequate resources over the life of a project. Sometimes, however, these agreements lack candor or can seem merely perfunctory steps in the process.

Given our increasingly contentious political environment, it's becoming hard for any federal program to count on stable, predictable funding. But it's still vital (and actually possible) to arrive at major program agreements when dealing with the professional staff and leadership levels.

The closer your relationships with staffs and leadership groups, and the more credible and powerful the stakeholders, the more likely it is that longer-term resources will be sustained. Comptroller General Charles Bowsher, for example, essentially "traded" with appropriators: in exchange for his agreement to accept GAO staffing cuts, he earned their commitment to provide the funds needed for skills, training, and technology upgrades. The agreement hinged on the relationship between Bowsher, Oversight Committee Chair Jack Brooks, and Appropriations Chair Vic Fazio—and the relationships were reinforced at staff levels.

In today's political world, unfortunately, such agreements are getting harder to find. And that's just another argument for building pivot points into your project in the event of sudden funding shortfalls.

Talent

At the January 2015 launch of the National Academy of Public Administration (NAPA) Federal Leaders Digital Insight Study, OMB Deputy Director for Management Beth Cobert identified talent and training as key weaknesses in the federal deployment of digital solutions. "I worry that we do not have the right people or training," Cobert told the audience of mostly federal leaders. Noting that 93 percent of federal respondents to a survey said they embrace digital technology in the federal workplace, she highlighted a still-existing "gap between the will and the skills and capabilities needed." While OMB's new US Digital Service and accompanying GSA staff are working to fill this gap, talent remains a significant challenge.[26]

Ask yourself: Does your team include people who clearly understand the technology being considered? Do you have team members, whether staff or contractors, with experience in this technology? Even strong skills and knowledge may be no substitute for experience.

Leadership (and Accountability)

Since no program or project gets everything its advocates want, even in the private sector, the most important question may be whether the project has a leader willing and able to prioritize needs as circumstances dictate. It can be a matter of negotiating among stakeholders, choosing between often competing needs and goals and deciding which needs can and must be met versus those to be "deferred," adjusting for contingencies such as resource and talent shortfalls and missed deadlines.

Paul Fitzgerald, managing principal of Deloitte Consulting LLP's federal technology consulting practice and a thirty-year veteran in IT, acknowledges this can be very challenging. Fitzgerald says that without such a leader,

> obstacles to success begin to build up noticeably within the first 120 days, and the ability to achieve a successful solution within actual timeframes and resources collapses. Eventually the team grinds to a halt and within eighteen months the project is dead.[27]

Again, the key is to be ready for contingencies beyond your control. There must be a government decision maker who can pivot and change the project and the process as circumstances dictate.

Three Big "Boulders"

In a world of inadequate resources and consistent overpromising, how can managers hope for success on any given project? According to Fitzgerald, there are really three big "boulders" that have to be constantly balanced with one another in technology implementations: *scope* of requirements, *cost*, and *schedule*. Broader scopes with more extensive requirements will obviously require more resources and/or time. If there is less time available, it will require reducing scope or sometimes altering resources to accelerate the schedule.[28]

Traditionally, scope and requirements are established early in consultation with end users and other stakeholders. It sounds straightforward enough, but what typically happens is "scope creep" as a result of changing customer expectations or vague or inadequate initial specifications, which can lead to cost overruns and missed deadlines. Innumerable GAO reports document this pattern, as illustrated in the supercollider case history.[29] It's essential, says Fitzgerald, to determine as early as possible which one of the three "boulders" is *most important* to success.

For the 2010 census the bureau clearly defined schedule as its key factor; the bureau stayed true to its choice by shifting its technology requirements and increasing spending to ensure success. Failing to prioritize this way can leave your team trying to accomplish a big job without having adequate resources or time. You can find yourself trying to achieve results more rapidly without having a corresponding reduction of scope or increase in resources, or trying to achieve the same results with fewer resources. Are you going to hold the line on requirements, cost, or schedule? How are you going to make adjustments in the other two as the project proceeds?

In the ACA case study, the October 1 deadline clearly was the most important of the three factors, and yet schedules were unrealistic and requirements were still being altered a mere two weeks ahead of the deadline.[30] In other cases, critical mission requirements might be the boulder around which your project revolves, so you must develop time lines and resources consistent with those priorities.

The Secure Flight Program of the Transportation Security Administration (TSA), which identifies high-risk passengers for enhanced security screening and lower-risk passengers for expedited screening, is an example of a requirements-driven deployment. It makes sense, given the critical nature of the program's goal: keeping air travel safe. "Flexible" security requirements could be disastrous for the nation and the TSA. Reorganizations, redesign of database mapping capabilities, added resources, and a reengineering of customer interfaces all "flexed" to allow the TSA to launch successfully, but meeting the program's requirements was the most important.[31]

Selecting the Right Technology

Consultants love 2x2 charts such as Figure 3.2 because they allow us to separate the world into four distinct quadrants and easily illustrate the relationship between two variables concurrently. The beauty of such a chart for anyone taking on a major IT project is that it encourages you to make distinctions between traditional and newer business problems; and to compare, for each, the impact of using older, established technology solutions versus the advantages (and risks) of emergent technologies. For a particular IT selection, says Paul Fitzgerald, ask yourself which quadrant you want to be in.[32]

Starting in the upper left corner, the chart guides you to consider applying older, established technologies to traditional problems. This is generally the safest, least expensive, and least risky way to automate or upgrade a system or process because it usually involves applying an existing or prepackaged technology

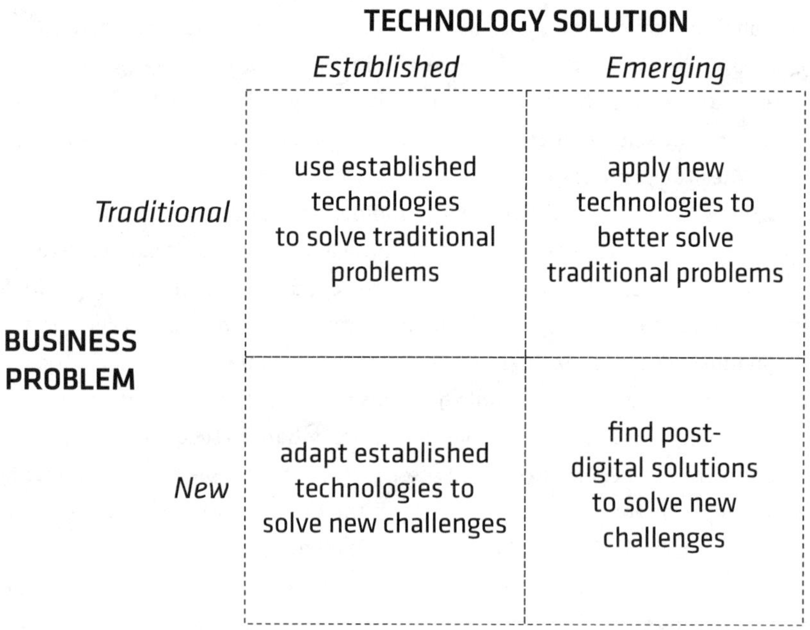

TECHNOLOGY SOLUTION

	Established	*Emerging*
Traditional	use established technologies to solve traditional problems	apply new technologies to better solve traditional problems
New	adapt established technologies to solve new challenges	find post-digital solutions to solve new challenges

BUSINESS PROBLEM

Figure 3.2 Matching a Technology Solution to a Business Problem

to a long-standing problem like a back-office financial or personnel management process or, perhaps, customer service.

Besides its low risk and often low cost, an established technology usually can be introduced into existing operations with minimal workflow disruption and without significant training. Unfortunately, this choice sometimes merely leads to the automation of obsolete operations (known in the business as "paving cow paths") without considering transformation (or even elimination) of the process. In some cases, box one action can lead to missed opportunities and delay of real improvements that might result from more sweeping transformation.

In the upper right quadrant is the application of new or emerging technologies to solve older or traditional problems, which can indeed streamline processes and improve quality. An example would be the use of laser-based handheld devices for facility inspections or cloud-based technologies to store and retrieve massive amounts of information. Such technology can spur a quantum leap in productivity while significantly enhancing the quality and accuracy of the work product.

The lower left quadrant refers to adapting established technologies to address new business goals or challenges. For example, OMB gave taxpayers access to information on federal spending under the 2014 Digital Accountability and Transparency Act (DATA) by using an established, web-based data retrieval system to fulfill the new transparency mandate.

The lower-right quadrant involves finding new technology solutions, usually advancing beyond existing digital capabilities to dramatically enhance how technology solves new problems and new challenges. The work being referred to here is the most innovative, of course, and the most exciting. The use of 3D printing to create highly unique parts, sometimes even human body parts, that can rapidly satisfy customer needs over vast geographical distances is one example of this "new-new" dynamic. "Fast data" is another new-new example. This concept is based on the ability to use data so quickly, as certain events or trends are occurring, that outcomes can be altered. For example, quickly identifying patterns in health data could help us stave off epidemics or hone in on the source of a food-poisoning incident. Real-time monitoring of energy grids can allow quick response to prevent a domino-effect collapse.[33]

There's no magic formula for choosing the "right" quadrant for your program or project. Many considerations are involved in deciding which way to go, including budget, time line, technology options, and user needs and capabilities (e.g., elderly Social Security recipients versus tech-savvy college students).

Key Takeaways

What should federal leaders and managers focus on, in the complex and rapidly changing tech world? It starts, of course, with leadership.

Create Your Offense

1. *Leadership Is Key.* In the federal environment, leadership is especially important in keeping technology efforts focused on mission effectiveness rather than on process alone. The most effective federal technology leaders are dynamic and charismatic. They break down silos, scrounge resources, deploy staff creatively, and do whatever else it takes to achieve their goals.

One example is Coast Guard Rear Adm. Ron Hewitt, who as acting chief information officer (CIO) of the Department of Homeland Security (DHS) helped achieve broad consensus among the eight DHS component technology leaders. Another is the US Postal Service (USPS) CIO James Cochrane, whose roots are actually in mail operations and logistics rather than technology. Both of these leaders are examples of successful CIOs who capitalized on their ability to manage people to get big federal jobs done.

Hewitt's soft-spoken charisma as a leader earned the respect of a federation of formerly independent Homeland Security units. After leading a successful transformation of DHS's IT infrastructure he went on to become the coast guard's chief people leader as assistant commandant, a great commentary on the importance of people leadership in IT. Cochrane covered his USPS conference room wall with dozens of sayings about the importance of teamwork and common goals, which helped shape the culture of those who worked with him. Collegiality is key for federal CIOs.[34]

Perhaps paradoxically, successful federal CIOs also are *disruptors* of the status quo, according to Richard Spires, former CIO for the FBI and DHS and vice chair of the federal Chief Information Officers Council. Spires says technology can be hugely transformative in operations and outcomes, but to be so it must be highly collaborative and have an organization-wide focus on the mission, with sharply drawn and clearly maintained priorities and expectations.[35]

This call for leadership dominated Deloitte's *Tech Trends: Inspiring Disruption Deloitte University* report of 2014, which defines a key CIO goal as "constructive disruption"—with the CIO as a sort of venture capitalist who invests in ideas with the potential to transform the mission.[36] "Where government falls down most," according to Spires, "is in overcoming the risk/failure fears that dominate the career service." Setting up a "skunkworks" that encourages experimentation is one common approach to supporting potentially transformative projects.[37] ("Skunkworks" are addressed in more depth in chapter 8.)

DOE's chief technology officer, Peter Tseronis, gets more specific in defining his mission as Energy's first chief technology officer (CTO): He sees his job as supporting the forward-leaning work of the department's seventeen national laboratories. These labs provide services that include research, strategic nuclear weaponry, and new energy sourcing. Tseronis makes it his business to visit each lab to learn what he can do to support them all. His goal is to identify initiatives that can be launched across DOE and to empower (and provide cover for) early projects by showcasing them in technology summits.[38]

2. *Pick Your Quadrant.* At the start, decide which quadrant on the 2x2 chart in Figure 3.2 best fits your needs. Your choice will be driven by multiple factors, including the six essential characteristics of successful IT projects described earlier.

Other key questions to consider: Do you only need an updated or upgraded solution to an established problem, such as improving employee access to and analytic capacity with an existing database? Are there newer solutions available for solving an existing problem, such as a digital application that provides direct customer access to government information? Would an existing "enterprise system" fit the bill? Are you stuck with outdated systems or procedures that hurt your mission effectiveness and make you incapable of meeting customer expectations produced by the likes of Amazon or Google? What are your budget and timeframe constraints?

All of these questions are obviously important when weighing "which quadrant."

3. *Decide Which "Boulder" Is Most Important—Scope, Cost, or Schedule?* It's critical to begin any project by checking in with all stakeholders, funders, and potential users to develop a plan that realistically balances *scope of requirements, resource costs,* and acceptable *schedule timeframes* for deployment.

It's best to be conservative in setting expectations—discern what you want to do versus what you can do, because they rarely line up exactly. You have to decide which of the three boulders is most important, recognizing that the other two will probably need to be modified as conditions dictate. Build this "recalibration" into standard operating procedures by rolling out the project in measured steps, with pivot points that allow for course correction as you move forward.

Listen to your IT professionals, especially those with experience in comparable deployments. They are the ones who will know all the potholes likely to be encountered along the way . . . and make it crystal clear that you *want* to know these things. A common failing of leaders is that they sometimes don't want to hear about complications or constraints and so they don't have adequate plans to deal with them.

In 2013, for example, a highly visible federal organization decided to use newly accepted rapid development techniques to design digital applications for staff and visitors to self-register for conference rooms, visitors' parking, and the like. The organization, however, declined the advice of technical personnel to build a "road map" that would be used to balance the three boulders: *schedule*, application *requirements*, and fixed *resources*. Predictably, gaps developed between outputs and customer expectations, eventually requiring adjustments in resources and technical expectations. After six months of disappointment and negotiations, technical and program personnel "rebalanced" the program's three boulders by creating a flexible resource approach to making the program work.[39]

Granted, building in a fallback position can be tricky or even unpopular in a politically charged environment, but it often turns out to be the key to success. And, as convenient as they may seem at the time, statements such as, "We'll figure it out when we get there" or "Just get it done" often become traps with consequences that can be far worse than simply adjusting expectations.

4. *Be a "Venture Capitalist."* You'll always face a range of more- and less-risky projects. If you aren't failing from time to time, you probably aren't pushing hard enough for disruption.

This doesn't mean you should be reckless; too many failures can be risky to one's career. But that's why a successful federal IT leader often works on a portfolio of diverse projects, just as a venture capitalist manages a portfolio of investments. It's a demonstrated strategy for overall success, even in the face of individual failures. This multiplicity shifts your attention to a broader base of technology investments and keeps your risks in more reasonable proportion. Be sure your portfolio includes both high- and low-risk projects of varying ambitiousness. Multiple modest project wins can often bring success at lower risk than the pursuit of a single large project.[40]

OMB has gotten on the portfolio bandwagon with its CIO-driven Portfolio-Stat initiative, which created a tool for assessing federal IT investments and identifying opportunities to reduce inefficiency and duplication.[41] A November 2013 OMB report found that twenty-six agencies conducting PortfolioStat assessments of their IT portfolios estimated they could save taxpayers a collective $5.8 billion through fiscal 2015.[42]

5. *Engage Digitally.* One way to massively alter the expense and effectiveness of government programs is a *wider adoption of digital applications.*

Mobile apps are far less expensive to develop than massive software suites and they shift much of the data entry burden to the customer-consumer, most of whom prefer the arrangement anyway. The current development environment makes it possible to create apps quickly and inexpensively and improve them as they get used.

This type of "iterative" development is a perfect fit for both millennial-generation techies and users who tend to get excited about improving the product with their own input. It also helps avoid the IT/acquisition life-cycle challenge noted earlier, which can yield systems that are obsolete upon delivery.[43]

The NAPA study mentioned earlier found strong support for digital technologies among federal leaders. Of all respondents, 93 percent "embrace" it in the workplace, saying, "it has improved productivity and helps serve agency stakeholders. . . . [S]olid majorities report . . . that agencies' investments in it have improved or transformed their operations."[44]

Former IRS Deputy Commissioner Peggy Sherry emphasizes that increased use of digital apps is one of the agency's top goals; she believes it will enable each taxpayer to conduct business with the IRS directly, without human intervention, while allowing the agency to dramatically reduce the cost of its services. Apps such as "Where's My Refund" and "Get Transcript," developed with the help of OMB's Digital Office and GSA's digital fellows, are important milestones toward the agency's self-service goal.[45]

But the NAPA study also identified significant challenges. About a third of surveyed leaders "do not believe their agency is able to procure innovative technology." Only 21 percent believe acquisition can keep up with the pace of technological change. And only 36 percent believe their agency's employees are adequately trained in technology.[46] According to Tim Young, a former OMB deputy director of eGov, overcoming these challenges requires a twofold strategy. First, concentrate on finding the digital talent within your own organization, or hire it, focusing on digital "natives" who have used similar technologies for their entire adult lives.

Second, apply the theory of "diffusion of innovation" to your digital planning. A successful IT initiative should begin by finding and supporting multiple innovative, digitally savvy pioneers—and *not* by asking C-suite executives to lead the way.[47] (See more on diffusion of innovation in chapter 8.)

Anyone who has observed today's digital generation understands just how dramatically the tech boom promises to affect communication and service delivery, even in the stodgy and risk-averse federal environment. While there is still need to provide alternatives for remaining non-digitally-savvy populations, users already expect direct access to federal services and in time they will demand it. Indeed, AMTRAK, Social Security, IRS, and the Postal Service are already in hot pursuit of digital services with the accompanying combination of service enhancement at reduced cost.[48] Put bluntly, the savvy federal IT leader and manager must have a strategy for digital engagement.[49]

6. *Buy It, Don't Build It (If Possible).* Always search for existing applications or providers that serve the right purpose before committing to the development of a custom solution. This is true whether the service is being contracted out or obtained through in-house development; it is especially true for back-office administrative services such as payroll or budgeting, or for standard case-management tasks many agencies have in common. Shared services are critical here (see chapter 4).

For example, existing services or software from a company such as ADP or the Agriculture National Finance Center is likely acceptable for most basic financial management tasks.

But outside services also can offer more specialized help. Census deputy director Nancy Potok sees the issue as one of mission effectiveness:

> Government acquisition processes can be slow, virtually assuring that we would always have the problem of obsolete hardware and software technology, while large-scale commercial services providers are now fed-friendly and allow us to buy the latest approach as a service with little lag time and much less risk of instant obsolescence. Privacy and security concerns, once a roadblock to adoption, are now covered by federal standards such as FedRAMP as well.[50]

Given the sheer variety of commercially available applications, it's surprising how many times federal administrators decide to build something themselves rather than adapting or adopting someone else's technology.

The ACA case offers examples of this inclination, especially at the state level. The states working to create insurance exchanges each struggled to design, build, and roll out their own systems. Predictably, millions of dollars were spent on systems that failed. In the face of failure, a number of states adopted systems that had been created by other states.[51]

Execute Effectively

In May 2014, GAO's director of information technology management issues tes-
tified before the Senate Committee on Homeland Security and Governmental
Affairs on best practices and reform initiatives to improve the management of IT
investments. He identified nine critical factors found in successful federal IT initiatives (contained in Box 3.1) and urged that future programs incorporate them.[52]

These factors reiterate, using slightly different terms and groupings, the three
boulders and six aspects of success. One of the seven projects identified by GAO
as successful, IRS's CADE2, is discussed below.

1. *Prototypes, Pivots, and Sprints.* In 2010 federal CIO Vivek Kundra released an
edict aimed at dramatically shortening IT release cycles to a target of under six
months, with no more than three months for detailed systems specifications.[53]

Avoid the development of major enterprise-wide, multiyear applications, and,
where needed, break projects into incremental shorter-term sprints, with pivot
points for when Plan A isn't going as planned (both supported by the Kundra
report and public management literature).[54] This allows you to adjust resources,
massage stakeholders, and make necessary changes in scope, resources, or timing.

★ **Box 3.1** GAO-Identified Common Critical IT Success Factors

⌒ *Common Critical Success Factors*

1. Program officials were actively engaged with stakeholders.
2. Program staff had the necessary knowledge and skills.
3. Senior department and agency executives supported the programs.
4. End users and stakeholders were involved in the development of
   requirements.
5. End users participated in testing of system functionality prior to
   formal end user acceptance testing.
6. Government and contractor staff were stable and consistent.
7. Program staff prioritized requirements.
8. Program officials maintained regular communication with the prime
   contractor.
9. Programs received sufficient funding.

Source: US Government Accountability Office, "Information Technology: Implementing Best Prac-
tices and Reform Initiatives Can Help Improve the Management of Investments," GAO-14–596T
(Washington, DC: May 2014), 11, http://www.gao.gov/assets/670/663051.pdf; and: "Information
Technology: Critical Factors Underlying Successful Major Acquisitions," Report No. GAO-12-7
(Washington, DC: October 2011), 23, http://www.gao.gov/new.items/d127.pdf.

As the centerpiece of its 1998 business systems modernization plan, the IRS launched the Customer Account Data Engine (CADE) to transform 140 million taxpayer files into modern formats. By 2004, however, CADE was off track, thirty months late, and overrunning the estimated $98 million cost by more than a third. GAO blamed inadequate cost and schedule projections, badly drawn systems requirements, and scope creep.

When Commissioner Doug Shulman arrived in 2008, the project's estimated completion date had slipped from 2013 to sometime between 2018 and 2022, and it appeared to need hundreds of millions of dollars in additional funding.[55] Shulman turned CADE around by reducing its dependence on outside vendors, bringing program management in house, and upgrading the agency's technology leadership.

The revitalized program, rebranded as CADE2, launched successfully on January 17, 2012. The system allows the IRS to update taxpayer information daily rather than through 1960s-era weekly batch processing, and it enables a daily tax refund cycle, putting taxpayers' refunds in their pockets more quickly. Retraining the staff, of course, was part of the challenge, as was coping with daily obstacles and adjustments.[56] GAO attributes CADE2's turnaround to active stakeholder engagement, a skilled and knowledgeable program staff, senior executive support, and adequate funding.[57]

2. *Create a "Results Management Office."* The typical technology project management office (PMO) manages *inputs,* such as hours worked or dollars spent; and *outputs,* such as whether deliverables are arriving on time; but, unfortunately and unwisely, generally not *outcomes.* As a result, most PMOs often don't know whether the inputs and outputs they track add up to a system that actually does what its designers intended and its customers need.

To combat this all-too-common pattern, some federal agencies now use a different take on project management through "results management offices" that focus on the intended *results* of the program or project (lower smoking rates, fewer highway fatalities, etc.). IRS, for example, has used a contractor-managed results management approach since 2010 for the CADE2 program described above.[58]

3. *Build-In Resource Optimization.* The search for IT solutions inevitably involves making choices about resources and determining which budget allocation works best (or what cuts will do least harm if/when necessary). But powerful new analytic tools are available to help optimize the use of program resources.

Consider, for instance, the assessment methodology used by the Army's Joint Improvised Explosive Device Defeat Organization (JIEDDO) to decide which projects to fund in order to best protect combat troops from IED attacks, and the potential applicability of this assessment tool to other program areas.[59] The Defense Health Agency offers another sophisticated yet open-source IT analytics platform, already being used free of charge by the National Oceanic and Atmospheric Administration (NOAA) and NIH. Semantic Open Source Software (SEMOSS) connects multiple large databases and offers tools that help users decide which technologies offer the best result for a particular challenge, particularly low-cost, high-impact options.[60] DOD's Military Health System, for example, uses SEMOSS to flag redundant systems that can be shut down with the least impact on military healthcare.

Of course, these tools can't substitute for the informed judgment of competent leaders. But they can provide essential input for such decisions when multiple databases and systems are involved.[61]

4. *Embrace the Crowd.* One way of overcoming unrealistic time lines or constrained resources can be called "industrial-strength crowdsourcing."

Crowdsourcing is generally defined as the process of soliciting needed information or services from large numbers of people using online or social media communities. Using crowdsourcing can be challenging in the federal sphere, considering data privacy and security challenges.[62] Some federal agencies, however, notably GSA and OMB, are harnessing the power of the crowd to solve problems quickly and inexpensively.[63] In fact, GSA's recent *US Public Participation Playbook* argues that federal managers and leaders should start checking in with the public on a host of program and policy matters *before* launching new programs or services.[64]

GSA's Challenge.gov program, a recent winner of the Kennedy School of Government's Innovations in American Government Award, allows "entrepreneurs, innovators, and the public to compete for prestige and prizes by providing the government with novel solutions to tough problems." Among other products, Challenge.gov competitions have produced robocall blockers and tools to improve employment opportunities for persons with disabilities.[65]

Platforms for collecting employee ideas have been around for almost ten years. In 2007, for example, TSA launched its IdeaFactory to collect employee ideas on process improvements. A ski enthusiast's idea to use "diamond lanes" to expedite experienced travelers, just as "diamond slopes" are reserved for experienced skiers, led directly to streamlined screening for frequent fliers. The Army's Rapid Equipping Force used ArmyCoCreate, a collaborative online platform, to collect ideas from soldiers and civilians for creation of mobile command post vehicles. The winning concept moved from adoption to a physical prototype in sixty days.[66]

A lot of federal IT work involves communicating with key constituencies outside the government, such as farmers on federal crop insurance or college applicants for federal student loans. The growing ubiquity of social media networks provides a new, no-cost vehicle to replace expensive dedicated communications avenues or networks. These ideas need to be approached cautiously—again, due to government's special considerations—but using social media to "spread the word" or "get some help" has to be included in any realistic set of tools.[67] Used wisely these networks can help accomplish big jobs at a fraction of the cost of conventional options. The Smithsonian Institution's Digital Volunteers program, a great example, turned ordinary history enthusiasts into archivists by recruiting more than twenty-five hundred people to transcribe nearly eighteen thousand digital documents in the institution's vast online collection.[68] Now *that's* people power.

5. *Integrate Development and Operations.* The pace of IT evolution means that speed and utility are your primary concern when *developing* applications. But when *operating* IT, stability, efficiency, and response times are what you care about.

It's important to reconcile development's need and desire for rapid experimentation and innovation with operation's need for stability and security, especially with constrained resources. According to *Tech Trends 2014*, the key is to integrate development and operations into a single organization: "When organizations bring these two functions together into a real time Dev/Ops process, benefits can include increased speed and improved quality."[69] This is a particularly valuable strategy when "agile" methods are used, with continuous tinkering and successive improvements.[70]

Of course, changing the way people work can be difficult, and any consolidation should start slowly and with strong leadership support. But it can also produce impressive results. The State of Kentucky, for example, built and launched its healthcare exchange (and met the aggressive federal goals) using this DevOps approach to integrating contractor-developed applications within the context of state-run operations. Kentucky's exchange became a model for numerous other states.[71]

Play a Smart Defense

Because of the lightning-fast evolution of technology and the magnitude of many technical projects, any sound defense strategy should begin with strong project management.

1. *The Right Talent and Plan.* The team must be equipped with the right talent and decision-making power. Pacing the project by using short-term sprints and pivot points is essential. The leader's job is to make sure the talent can meet the milestones and make the key decisions on time—and with the right plans in place to counteract slippage or drift. If not, expectations should be reduced—admittedly tough to do in a politicized environment, but better than hoping for a late reprieve.

Meet with key personnel regularly. Emphasize that bad news isn't just welcome but *vital* to the project's progress and to being able to adjust when something goes wrong, as it always will.

2. *Independent Verification and Validation.* For particularly complex technology contracts, consider using an independent verification and validation (IV&V) contractor. Sometimes criticized as "one contractor hired to watch another," independent verification nevertheless can be critical to a successful large IT launch, particularly if it's low on in-house talent.

For a fraction of the overall contract cost, an independent contractor or consultant can advise on best practices and evaluation standards, can supervise the testing and integrity of reported results, and can make recommendations for problems as they arise. Sometimes IV&V can be provided by nonprofits such as the Rand Corporation or the Logistics Management Institute.

When conflicts arise between IV&V contractors and the prime contractor, and they will, it is essential to make sure they aren't allowed to hurt program progress or team success. Make it clear that the IV&V contractor reports to *you* rather than to the prime contractor. Also, as a defensive play, IV&V also can provide helpful program and technical continuity should it become necessary to change the prime contractor.

3. *Cloud Control.* Cloud-based IT solutions are spreading across the globe. In the federal sphere, adopting cloud services offers important collaborative possibilities among agencies serving the same clients (such as Veterans Affairs and Health and Human Services, for example).[72]

Much adoption of the cloud is occurring *in addition to* existing government on-site systems, rather than as a replacement. Yet the cloud's tested capability and capacity provides an opportunity to eliminate redundancies in locally held data, analytic capacity, backup, etc.

OMB's policies have largely eliminated any risk to agencies from moving to cloud-based services on their own initiative.[73] But because of the continuing evolution of this game-changing technology, everyone should be careful about committing to huge contracts. If the cloud follows the same "utility" pattern as the telephone did, cloud operators may soon offer à la carte pricing and services at considerable savings over large-scale fixed contracts.[74]

4. *Reduce Your Technical Debt.* "Technical debt" is actually a plain concept to understand: it's the money subpar or bad software is costing you. Maybe the cost is due to programming shortcuts or a misfired needs assessment; in any case, technical debt is what must be spent to keep old or inadequate IT systems working well past their "sell by" dates. This debt is paid in the coin of downtime, poor customer service, and higher maintenance, repair, and replacement costs. Channel these resources into more productive uses by slashing your technical debt.[75]

One recent study suggests that an average $3.61 of technical debt exists *per line of code*, or an average of more than $1 million per software system.[76] In 2012 GAO reported that federal agencies spend about 70 percent of their $79 billion IT budgets for operating and maintaining legacy systems, which leaves just 30 percent for new development. While not all of that 70 percent necessarily represents technical debt, it certainly suggests an opportunity to free up funds.[77]

There are two keys to reducing technical debt: knowing where you stand on the magnitude scale and defining the steps to reduce it so as to free capital for productive uses. Enterprise architecture tools and road maps can help when assessing the extent of technical debt. The Postal Service, according to *Tech Trends 2014*, used open-source software to measure tech debt "in terms of reliability, performance, security, and changeability."

Once you've considered your technical debt, there are strategies to reduce it: use standardized systems that minimize separate code and maintenance requirements; document known programming decisions as they are made; and include estimates of technical debt when deciding whether to stick with or dump legacy systems.[78]

Conclusion

The IT side to government management and budgeting is huge, and an especially crucial and challenging area in which to operate. But there are tools and techniques that can help leaders avoid major disasters, putting powerful technology to work for a vast array of projects and teams and, ultimately, the taxpayers. However, IT problems generally boil down to people and the quality of their decisions. If you've got the right people focused on the right goals, you're halfway home. "Wash100" winner Janet Foutty summed up the challenges and the path to success:

> It's never about the technology. It's about sponsorship and clarity of purpose, and about discipline in decision-making, customer needs, execution and training. Much as in the corporate world: but the timeframes are *much* more challenging for federal leaders.[79]

The contrast between healthcare.gov and Census 2010 bears out Foutty's claims. Strategies and techniques focused on fallback positions, realistic time lines, and pivot opportunities offer a solid chance of smoother rollouts. Balancing scope, cost, and schedule—the three boulders—may involve compromises or stopgap fixes and the experience may not be "glitch free." But preparing right will help you *get the job done*!

Notes

1. Daniel R. Levinson, "CMS Did Not Always Manage and Oversee Contractor Performance for the Federal Marketplace as Required by Federal Requirements and Contract Terms," US Department of Health and Human Services Office of Inspector General, Report No. A-03-14-03001 (September 2015), ii, http://oig.hhs .gov/oas/reports/region3/31403001.asp.
2. Ibid., 14–16; William Woods, "Healthcare.gov: Ineffective Planning and Oversight Practices Underscore the Need for Improved Contract Management," US Government Accountability Office (GAO), Report No. GAO-14-694 (July 2014), 9–11, http://www.gao.gov/assets/670/665179.pdf.
3. *Testimony of CMS Administrator Marilyn Tavenner before the House Ways and Means Committee's Subcommittee on the Affordable Care Act Implementation* (October 29, 2013), at HHS.gov, last modified November 1, 2013, http://www.hhs.gov/asl /testify/2013/10/t20131029.html.
4. Ibid.
5. Ibid.
6. Jason Gauthier, "Measuring America: The Decennial Censuses from 1790 to 2000," US Census Bureau (September 2012), http://www.census.gov/history/pdf /measuringamerica.pdf.

7. Sarah Heimel, "Characteristics of the 2010 Census Nonresponse Followup Operation," US Census Bureau, 1, http://www.amstat.org/sections/SRMS/Proceedings /y2011/Files/302821_69162.pdf.

8. Arnold Jackson, in discussion with the author, August 19, 2014.

9. Arnold Jackson discussion; US Census Bureau, "Census Bureau Releases Estimates of Undercount and Overcount in the 2010 Census" (May 22, 2012), http:// www.census.gov/newsroom/releases/archives/2010_census/cb12-95.html.

10. Robert Groves, "How Good Was the 2010 Census? A View from the Post-Enumeration Survey," US Census Bureau (May 30, 2012), http://directorsblog .blogs.census.gov/2012/05/30/how-good-was-the-2010-census-a-view-from-the -post-enumeration-survey/#comment-191355.

11. David Powner, "High-Risk Series, An Update: Improving the Management of IT Acquisitions and Operations," General Accounting Office, Report No. GAO-15-290 (February 2015), 38, http://www.gao.gov/assets/670/668415.pdf,

12. See chap. 1; and Charles E. Lindblom, "The Science of 'Muddling Through,'" *Public Administration Review* 19, no. 2 (1959): 79–88, http://www.jstor.org/stable /973677.

13. Wade Horn, in discussion with the author, January 16, 2015.

14. Woods, "Healthcare.gov: Ineffective Planning," 23.

15. Wade Horn discussion.

16. Ibid.

17. Arnold Jackson discussion.

18. Scott Buchholz, in discussion with the author, June 2014.

19. Ibid.

20. Panel discussion following Deloitte Consulting's 2014 Federal Technology Trends conference, Arlington, VA, June 24, 2014.

21. Philip Taubman, "Failure to Launch: In Death of Spy Satellite Program, Lofty Plans and Unrealistic Bids," *New York Times*, November 11, 2007, http://www .nytimes.com/2007/11/11/washington/11satellite.html?pagewanted=1&_r=3 #step1.

22. Paul Fitzgerald, in discussion with the author, October 1, 2014; Beth McGrath, in discussion with the author, October 9, 2014.

23. Paul Fitzgerald discussion.

24. Janet Foutty, in discussion with the author, December 23, 2014.

25. US Department of Energy, "Summary Audit Report on Lessons Learned from the Superconducting Super Collider Project" (April 1996), 2, http://www.osti.gov /scitech/biblio/231955.

26. National Academy of Public Administration and ICF, "Federal Leaders Digital Insight Study," January 13, 2015, 4, http://napawash.org/images/reports/2015 /Federal_Leaders_Digital_Insights_Study.pdf; Beth Cobert, at NAPA and ICF International Discussion of the Federal Leaders Digital Insight (FLDI) Study, Washington, DC, January 13, 2015.

27. Paul Fitzgerald discussion.

28. Ibid.
29. Cristina Chaplain, "NASA: Assessments of Selected Large-Scale Projects," Government Accountability Office, Report No. GAO-12-207SP (March 1, 2012), http://www.gao.gov/assets/670/669205.pdf; Carol Cha, "Defense Major Automated Information Systems: Cost and Schedule Commitments Need to Be Established Earlier," Government Accountability Office, Report No. GAO-15-282 (February 26, 2015), http://www.gao.gov/assets/670/668718.pdf; David Powner, "Information Technology: DHS Needs to Enhance Management of Cost and Schedule for Major Investments," Report No. GAO-12-904 (September 26, 2012), http://www.gao.gov/assets/650/648888.pdf.
30. GAO, "Healthcare.Gov," 27.
31. Cathleen Berrick, Randolph Hite, and Gregory Wilshusen, "Aviation Security: TSA Has Completed Key Activities Associated with Implementing Secure Flight, but Additional Actions Are Needed to Mitigate Risks," Government Accountability Office, Report No. GAO-09-292 (May 2009), http://www.gao.gov/assets/290/289632.pdf.
32. Paul Fitzgerald discussion.
33. Thomas Been, "Management of Government Technology Annual Summit—Driving Government Innovation: Process and Technology to Achieve Success," Presentation at Potomac Forum, Washington, DC, November 13, 2014.
34. US Coast Guard, "Rear Admiral Ronald T. Hewitt, USCG, Biography," http://www.uscg.mil/history/people/Flags/HewittRT_bio.pdf; Mark White and Brad Eskind, in discussion with the author, October 23, 2014; US Postal Service, "James (Jim) P. Cochrane, Chief Information Officer and Executive Vice President, Biography," September 2014, https://about.usps.com/who-we-are/leadership/pmg-exec-comm.htm#p=1.
35. Richard Spires, Presentation at Potomac Forum, Washington, DC, November 13, 2014.
36. Tom Galizia and Chris Garibaldi, "CIO as Venture Capitalist," *Tech Trends 2014: Inspiring Disruption Deloitte University* (2014), 7, http://www2.deloitte.com/content/dam/Deloitte/us/Documents/public-sector/us-tech-trends2014-public-sector-perspective-053014.pdf.
37. Spires, Potomac Forum.
38. Pete Tseronis, Presentation at Potomac Forum, Washington, DC, November 13, 2014.
39. Bob Capuano, in discussion with the author, March 10, 2015.
40. Kristen Miller and Van Hitch, "CIO as Venture Capitalist: A Public Sector Perspective," *Tech Trends 2014: Inspiring Disruption Deloitte University* (2014), 20, http://www2.deloitte.com/content/dam/Deloitte/us/Documents/public-sector/us-tech-trends2014-public-sector-perspective-053014.pdf.
41. Jeffrey Zients and Steven VanRoekel, "Memorandum for the Heads of Executive Departments and Agencies: Implementing PortfolioStat," Executive Office of the President, Office of Management and Budget, accessed March 30, 2014, 2,

https://www.whitehouse.gov/sites/default/files/omb/memoranda/2012/m-12
-10_1.pdf.

42. David Powner, "Information Technology: Additional OMB and Agency Actions
    Are Needed to Achieve Portfolio Savings," Government Accountability Office,
    Report No. GAO-14-65 (November 2013), 21, http://www.gao.gov/assets/660
    /658883.pdf.

43. Tim Young, in discussion with the author, January 15, 2015.

44. NAPA and ICF, "Federal Leaders Digital Insight Study."

45. Peggy Sherry, "NAPA and ICF Federal Leaders Digital Insight Study," January 13,
    2015; NAPA and ICF, "Federal Leaders Digital Insight Study."

46. NAPA and ICF, "Federal Leaders Digital Insight Study," 9, 11.

47. Tim Young discussion.

48. See, for example, http://www.amtrak.com/get-mobile-application-and-access;
    "My Social Security" at http://www.ssa.gov/myaccount/; and IRS's "Where's My
    Refund" at http://irs.gov/refunds; and http://my.usps.com.

49. Paul Fitzgerald discussion.

50. Nancy Potok, in discussion with the author, November 12, 2014.

51. Jennifer Haberkorn and Kyle Cheney, "$474M for Four Failed Obamacare
    Exchanges," Politico, May 11, 2014, http://www.politico.com/story/2014/05
    /obamacare-cost-failed-exchanges-106535.html.

52. Information Technology: Implementing Best Practices and Reform Initiatives Can
    Help Improve the Management of Investments, Statement of David Powner before
    the Committee on Homeland Security and Governmental Affairs, US Senate, Re-
    port No. GAO-14-596T (May 8, 2014), 9, http://www.gao.gov/assets/670/663051
    .pdf; David Powner, "Information Technology: Critical Factors Underlying
    Successful Major Acquisitions," Government Accountability Office, Report No.
    GAO-12-7 (October 2011), 19, http://www.gao.gov/new.items/d127.pdf.

53. Vivek Kundra, "Twenty-Five-Point Implementation Plan to Reform Federal
    Information Technology Management," Executive Office of the President, Office
    of Management and Budget, Office of E-Government and Information Tech-
    nology, December 9, 2010, 11–12, http://oai.dtic.mil/oai/oai?verb=getRecord&
    metadataPrefix=html&identifier=ADA543512.

54. Ibid.; and Lindblom, "Science."

55. James Thompson, "Fixing the IRS," Government Executive (April 1, 2012), 4, http://
    www.govexec.com/magazine/features/2012/04/fixing-irs/41637/.

56. Kavitha Prabhakar, in discussion with the author, April 9, 2015.

57. Powner, "Information Technology," 19.

58. Diane Murray, "CADE 2 Team Drives IRS Modernization Efforts," View from Ross-
    lyn (April 13, 2012), https://deloittenet.deloitte.com/pc/practicecomm/industries
    /hsg/federal/viewfromrosslyn/lists/posts/post.aspx?id=74; Kavitha Prabhakar
    discussion.

59. Brad Martin, et al., "Assessment of Joint Improvised Explosive Device Defeat
    Organization (JIEDDO) Training Activity," RAND National Defense Research

Institute, (2013), 24, http://www.rand.org/content/dam/rand/pubs/research
_reports/RR400/RR421/RAND_RR421.pdf.

60. Semantic Open Source Software (SEMOSS): Context Award Analytics, http://
semoss.org/.

61. Scott Buchholz and David Sisk, "Technical Debt Reversal: Lowering the IT Debt
Ceiling," *Tech Trends 2014: Inspiring Disruption Deloitte University* (2014), 94, http://
www2.deloitte.com/content/dam/Deloitte/us/Documents/public-sector/us-tech
-trends2014-public-sector-perspective-053014.pdf.

62. *Merriam-Webster's Online Dictionary*, s.v. "crowdsourcing," accessed January 12,
2016, http://www.merriam-webster.com/dictionary/crowdsourcing.

63. Jason Miller, "OMB Crowdsourcing Improvements to Section 508," Federal News
Radio, March 19, 2012, http://www.federalnewsradio.com/517/2792835/OMB
-crowdsourcing-improvements-to-Section-508.

64. See *US Public Participation Handbook* at http://participation.usa.gov.

65. Doug Gavel, "GSA's Challenge.gov Earns Harvard Innovation Award," John F.
Kennedy School of Government, Harvard University, January 23, 2014, http://
www.hks.harvard.edu/news-events/news/press-releases/gsa%E2%80%99s
-challenge.gov-earns-harvard-innovation-award.

66. J. R. Reagan and Eric Bristow, "Industrialized Crowdsourcing: A Public Sector
Perspective," *Tech Trends 2014: Inspiring Disruption Deloitte University* (2014), 51,
http://www2.deloitte.com/content/dam/Deloitte/us/Documents/public-sector
/us-tech-trends2014-public-sector-perspective-053014.pdf.

67. Gregory Wilshusen, "Social Media: Federal Agencies Need Policies and Procedures for Managing and Protecting Information They Access and Disseminate,"
Government Accountability Office, Report No. GAO-11-605 (June 2011), http://
www.gao.gov/new.items/d11605.pdf.

68. Reagan and Bristow, "Industrialized Crowdsourcing," 50.

69. Scott Buchholz, Jon Rice, David Sisk, and Thomas Beck, "Real-Time DevOps: A
Public Sector Perspective," *Tech Trends 2014: Inspiring Disruption Deloitte University* (2014), 165, http://www2.deloitte.com/content/dam/Deloitte/us/Documents
/public-sector/us-tech-trends2014-public-sector-perspective-053014.pdf.

70. Ibid.

71. Ibid., 166.

72. Gregg Bailey and Paul Krein, "Cloud Orchestration: A Public Sector Perspective,"
Tech Trends 2014: Inspiring Disruption Deloitte University (2014), 133, http://www2
.deloitte.com/content/dam/Deloitte/us/Documents/public-sector/us-tech
-trends2014-public-sector-perspective-053014.pdf.

73. Vivek Kundra, "Federal Cloud Computing Strategy," February 8, 2011, 2, https://
www.whitehouse.gov/sites/default/files/omb/assets/egov_docs/federal-cloud
-computing-strategy.pdf.

74. Paul Fitzgerald discussion.

75. Buchholz and Sisk, "Technical Debt Reversal," 89.

76. Ibid., 90.

77. David Powner, "Information Technology: Agencies Need to Strengthen Oversight of Billions of Dollars in Operations and Maintenance Investments," Government Accountability Office, Report No. GAO-13-87 (October 2012), 4, http://www.gao .gov/assets/650/649563.pdf.

78. Buchholz and Sisk, "Technical Debt Reversal," 89.

79. Janet Foutty discussion.

CHAPTER 4

Creating and Leading a Well-Designed Organization

When Charles Rossotti became commissioner of the Internal Revenue Service in 1997, he knew that he was in for a challenge. The number of tax filings had experienced double-digit annual growth for decades, while the complexity of returns had increased substantially. Customer expectations were rising just as IRS responsiveness was falling. As a result of Reagan Administration cuts made in response to a $70 billion budget deficit, IRS walk-in assistance and call centers were drastically scaled back and many offices were closed.[1] The agency's response rate to taxpayer inquiries via telephone had fallen from 58 percent in 1989 to a low of 8 percent in 1995.[2]

Previous attempts to modernize the agency's tax collection system had failed, at a cost of $120 million.[3] In 1997 the Senate Finance Committee conducted a six-month review of the IRS and held its first-ever hearings on the agency, during which Committee Chairman William V. Roth Jr. characterized IRS as "a troubled agency, with widespread and serious problems."[4]

Rossotti was no stranger to dealing with complex organizational challenges. A Harvard MBA with consulting experience, he had been one of Defense Secretary Robert McNamara's "whiz kids" and had risen to become deputy assistant secretary for systems analysis at age twenty-nine. As founder and CEO of American Management Systems, Rossotti was one of the most successful technology integrators in the country, with clients both private and public, including many federal agencies.[5] So it was surprising to many that Rossotti *didn't* approach the IRS's woes principally as a technology issue, especially in the face of the prior IT debacle.

Instead, Rossotti approached the challenge as a matter of organizational transformation. Noting that the agency was "laboring under a 1950s organizational structure and business practices" that lacked a customer-service focus, the new commissioner delayed technology upgrade plans for a year to first address leadership and organizational issues.[6] Backed by bipartisan passage of the Internal Revenue Service Restructuring and Reform Act of 1988, the new commissioner rewrote an outdated mission statement focused on revenue collections to one focused on helping taxpayers as customers: "Provide America's taxpayers top quality service by helping them understand and meet their tax responsibilities and by applying tax law with integrity and fairness to all."[7]

Rossotti instituted three major transformation programs—the Structural Modernization Program, the Business Systems Program, and the Balanced Measures Program—to address structure, technology, and performance, respectively. His vision shifted the agency's organizational structure from one based on geography to one based on customer service. Rossotti reorganized the agency into four units, each charged with "end-to-end responsibility for serving a particular group of taxpayers with similar needs":

- the Wage and Investment Division, to serve 116 million taxpayers with wage and investment income only;
- the Small Business/Self-Employed Division, to serve 45 million self-employed and small-business filers;
- the Large and Midsized Business Division, to serve corporations with assets above $5 million; and
- the Tax Exempt and Government Entities Division, for pension plans, exempt organizations, and government entities.[8]

In addition to these new customer-centric units, Rossotti created a simplified management structure with clear lines of accountability, designated separate leaders responsible for customer service and internal operations excellence, and published the entire organizational structure for all to see.[9]

This restructuring illustrates well how the right organizational structure and incentives can support a customer-targeted definition of success. Rossotti went on to preside over a successful $500 million IT overhaul for the agency.[10]

Not everyone was thrilled, of course. Some observers and employees were critical of the high levels of union involvement and the funds that were spent on consulting, as well as the lack of progress on some budget challenges. Nevertheless, following the IT and organizational restructuring the agency began to recover. Customer satisfaction improved, as did call-center responsiveness. New web-based filing capabilities also helped, and tax collections improved.[11]

What made the IRS transformation successful? Organizational design consultant Alexander Braier, who participated in the effort, says that Rossotti "provided both the top-down vision about restructuring according to customer groups and the organizational leadership experience to be able to align IRS managers and leaders around new performance expectations."[12]

This chapter includes a review of some of the issues that must be addressed and lessons to be learned when designing and maintaining an effective organization, especially the import of customer alignment and having a mission-excellence vision. Key considerations in any decision on whether to reorganize must include overcoming the challenges of "silos" and headquarters/field power struggles in order to obtain vertical and horizontal integration. The chapter includes a discussion on shared services strategies as a way to improve both efficiency and mission focus and concludes with some tips on federal budgeting complexities and the importance of having a strong chief financial officer in the rough-and-tumble world of federal appropriations politics.

Define and Align to Succeed

At IRS it helped that Charles Rossotti was the first commissioner to come from outside the tax world. While it doesn't always work to bring in an outsider, it did give him a broader perspective on both the organizational issues that needed attention and on what had worked in other settings. Rossotti began by defining organizational success and analyzing how the agency's work contributed (or didn't) to achieving it. As former OMB official Clay Johnson (and others) have emphasized, it is "critical to clearly define 'success' for the organization" to be able to focus on what will be considered successful *outcomes*, not just activities or inputs.[13]

Check the Existing Organizational Scheme

Braier explains that the work should begin by determining whether an agency's workflow and staffing do in fact further its business purpose. Are employee incentives established in a way that boosts motivation and morale and improves customer service? If not, change is called for, but it may not necessarily involve major restructuring.

Given the transient nature of federal leadership, it seldom makes sense to spend your eighteen to twenty-four months in charge moving chart boxes around, unless your mission and performance really demands it.[14] Insider threat specialist (and psychiatrist) Mike Gelles says that you usually are better off clearly defining "success" and motivating employees within the inherited structure.[15] Even in war, says two-time Secretary of Defense Donald Rumsfeld, "You go to war with the army you have, not the army you might want or wish to have at a later time."[16]

On the other hand, James Q. Wilson's classic *Bureaucracy: What Government Agencies Do and Why* points out that an organization's structure and incentives tend to define the activities of people within it: "People are the products, not only of their biology, family, and schooling, but of their organizational position."[17] Thus any effort to motivate human behavior *must* consider how structure and process affect it. Successful organizations arrange their staffs in ways that further the organization's goals most effectively.

For example, when the World Bank set an ambitious goal for the elimination of global poverty, it found its efforts being impaired by an organizational structure that heavily emphasized regional management. The bank achieved considerable success by "reorganizing horizontally" and assigning its specialists in areas such as early childhood development and infrastructure to report to global heads for each specialty, a move that dramatically helped it integrate best practices across the globe.[18]

Consulting firms encounter similar issues all the time, and they generally respond with an organizational matrix that calls for some leaders to handle regional issues, some to become experts in functional areas like financial controls or personnel, and some to focus on key industries such as banking, energy, or government.

For the federal government, regional organization is beginning to make less sense in this era of pervasive web and mobile access, supply chains transformed by overnight service, and the emergence of technologies like 3D printing. Social Security offices and regional defense depots may become costly appendages, even though they are difficult to eliminate because of the support of local members of Congress.

I Need a New Structure!

You may decide that your existing organizational structure cannot be saved. One sign: people are succeeding within it *despite* the structure and incentives, rather than being helped by it. So you may be facing the dreaded "reorg." How can you make sure yours works?

Braier identifies five key success factors for an effective reorganization: *a clear business case* for why change is needed; a *motivating vision* of the future; a *committed leadership team* that is "on board" with the change; a *clear road map* and governance model for reorganization; and *incentives for communication, training, and performance* to promote the desired cultural changes. If all five factors (summarized in Figure 4.1) aren't in place, think twice about moving forward with a full-blown reorganization.[19]

The Dodd-Frank Wall Street Reform and Consumer Protection Act, for example, placed significant new controls on the financial services industry in the aftermath of the 2008 banking collapse. As the regulator of commodity trades, the Commodity Futures Trading Commission (CFTC) clearly had to up its game significantly in order to enforce the new regulations and broaden its industry supervisory role.

CFTC's leaders embarked on an organizational transformation to meet the new demands, based on a readiness assessment that identified gaps and a business case for change. The effort was supported by an inspiring vision and ambitious IT plan. But the commission's budget was slashed and key sponsors of the effort left the agency, being replaced by less supportive leaders. Embroiled in constant political battles and without leadership support, the transformation project stagnated. The Partnership for Public Service "Best Places to Work" survey recorded a continued multiyear decline in agency morale, prompted in part by resource pressures from Dodd-Frank requirements. In the 2014 survey results, CFTC appears near the bottom of the pack.[20]

Silos, Horizontals, and Chiefs

Farmers use silos to store grains and other nondifferentiated commodities that can be stacked. If you want to mix the contents of various silos, perhaps for a trail mix, setting them closer together or simply admonishing them to mix won't work. You need some sort of horizontal conveyer to get the job done. Grouping people into silos has the same effect: it inhibits the creation of mixes that satisfy different customers' differing needs in today's collaboration age.

Kimberly McCabe, former CEO of the consulting firm ASI Government, argues that the legacy of organizational silos is the biggest problem federal leaders face in being able to focus their organizations on integrated value for taxpayers. In any vertical agency, no one is clearly responsible for overall program outcomes.[21] Issues that have become more complex and involve a broader range of players now demand more collaborative environments. In this more complex, modern environment, according to Bob Knisely, a veteran of seven cabinet departments and deputy director of Vice President Al Gore's National Performance Review,

Organizational Design Success Factors

Success Factor	When change works . . .	. . . and when it doesn't
1 Business Case for Change	▪ Driven by business strategy and mission goals ▪ Compelling business need for change ▪ Change drivers documented ▪ Data driven ▪ Well socialized with leaders	▪ Not developed or unconvincing ▪ Unapparent business need ▪ Not well understood by leadership/staff
2 Vision for the Future	▪ Tied to business case ▪ Compelling, measurable, simple, easy to understand ▪ Motivates and inspires ▪ Managers/staffs see how their roles will be affected and how they can contribute	▪ Not clearly articulated ▪ Too high-level or generic ▪ Unable to measure progress to vision ▪ Managers/staffs unsure how they will be affected
3 Leadership Alignment	▪ Top leader leads the charge ▪ Leaders and staffs engaged/aligned in vision and design ▪ Those not "on board" are removed/reassigned ▪ Cascading change agents are identified and involved	▪ No visible leadership commitment ▪ Team is split on vision/need for change ▪ Mixed messages to line organizations ▪ Staffs see divided leadership
4 Program Governance	▪ Governance framework defined at top ▪ Detailed road map, smaller linked projects ▪ Established milestones, metrics, and accountabilities ▪ Key performance indicators and reporting ▪ Schedules, costs, issues, risks, and decisions are managed	▪ Projects not integrated at program level ▪ Unclear road map, milestones, targets ▪ Performance indicators not in place ▪ Poor tracking of implementation progress
5 Change Management	▪ Performance incentives adjusted to change behaviors ▪ Communications address "What's in it for me" for employees and stakeholders ▪ Staffs have timely training and tools to succeed	▪ Change is "ordered" from the top ▪ Little or no effort to convince, inspire ▪ Infrequent/inconsistent communications ▪ Little or no training

Figure 4.1 Organizational Design Success Factors

silos inhibit an organization's ability to share, "steal," and build upon solutions developed by other government entities, significantly hampering their ability to innovate.[22]

Focus on Meeting Customer Needs

Fortunately, it is possible to create a "more horizontal" enterprise. Focusing on customer service, as Rossotti did, is one strategy. In some federal entities this creates a wider, flatter organization, as operating divisions receive more autonomy to pursue their individual goals. The Department of Health and Human Services, for example, maintains separate units that are focused on food and drug safety, medical research, substance abuse, disease control and prevention, family welfare, and so forth. Under the Rossotti reorganization, the IRS created semiautonomous enterprises as well, but it united them for coordination and management under a single deputy commissioner.

Wider, more horizontal organizations have implications for leadership, talent, and behavior, and there's a parallel to the difference between professional partnerships and corporations. Partnerships tend to employ broader, flatter organizational structures with less hierarchy and more autonomy for unit leaders. Such units are largely responsible for their own risk management and customer service, and they need fewer approvals for activities such as promotions, market investments, or pricing adjustments. Corporations that process transactions or manufacture products tend to be more hierarchical with less unit autonomy, as innovation is deemed less important than consistency, efficiency, and reliability.

As you may have guessed, I'm partial to more horizontal, less hierarchical organizations because they empower creativity and collaboration; they are also more fun. OMB's relatively flat organizational structure, for instance, gives its employees a great deal of responsibility and autonomy. OMB encourages and *requires* its staff to work independently and creatively.

Neither form of organization, vertical or horizontal, is right or wrong; each has its place. Inevitably, silos build up around whatever groupings an organization creates. As leaders we must determine how our organization should be structured considering the mission, talent, and risks involved, and we must support horizontal integration whenever and wherever we can. It's an important choice because it shapes how we interact with customers and clients every day.

Many mission-focused organizations locate managerial responsibility for important support functions such as IT, finance, personnel, and acquisitions within positions described by their functional role, such as chief financial officers, chief information officers, and the like. Ideally, this helps leaders emerge as experts who know the state of the art in their areas and communicate with others in their professional communities—which are good things, so long as they don't become silos of their own that separate them from the customers they serve.

Regional Relationships

The existence of field offices dates back to the earliest days of US governance, in brick-and-mortar efforts to bring federal services "to the people." Local feds were on hand for a variety of jobs, such as to fill out forms for crop subsidies, answer questions about program benefits, or supervise national parks.

Regional structures, like those employed by large departments such as HHS or DOL, are a somewhat more recent invention and have led to at least one fundamental management question: should regional program staffs report to a regional administrator, whose job is to serve a specific region and manage its stakeholder relationships, or to the program's functional leaders in Washington? During my time managing Aid to Families with Dependent Children (AFDC), the federal cash welfare program, it was consolidated into the Social Security Administration. We needed to decide whether the regional AFDC leaders should report to the SSA leader in each region or to the AFDC's national leader.

Federal departments reflect both models, for better and for worse. The structure should depend on what is wanted and expected from regional program personnel and how much flexibility is ceded to local decision makers. Beware that too much program autonomy may in fact hamper efforts to integrate local services.

As assistant secretary of the Administration for Children and Families (ACF), Wade Horn encountered this issue when he redrew the reporting lines for regional ACF representatives so that they reported directly to Washington rather than to their regional administrators. The goal was to ensure that ACF funds provided to states and their recipients were distributed consistently across the country. Horn had the support of Senate committee chair Ted Kennedy, who, according to Horn, "had gotten tired of having ten different answers to each human development services grant question."[23]

The point is not that direct reporting to Washington is always better. Indeed, regional autonomy and flexibility can be a valuable bureaucracy buster. Certainly, the level of federal agricultural service support needed in New York City is different from what's needed in Kansas City. As with all organizational decisions, decision makers have to consider the best model for the task at hand.

Co-Locate Your Teams

Location can improve effectiveness, too. Washington "veteran" Mark Reger notes that while OMB largely situates appointees and career employees at different locales—the former at the Eisenhower building on the White House grounds, the latter at the New Executive Office Building across the street—the Department of the Treasury integrates them in collocated space. "I like that better," Reger says. "You get teams clear up to the presidential appointees working together."[24] Arnold Jackson, leader of the 2010 Census, attributes much of his team's success to the face-to-face interactions of the key players.[25]

Who Is Running the Show?

Every federal endeavor should begin with a detailed vision of organizational success set by an executive leader. Whether it's George W. Bush's famous admonition to senior appointees that their jobs depended on better agency ratings (see chapter 2) or Charles Rossotti's reframing the IRS's first and foremost mission as customer service, the top leader must define and drive transformation.

This means that the leader must make sure there is sufficient time, resources, and *need* for the project to warrant putting the organization through changes that will absorb massive amounts of leadership's attention. Once that decision is made, the project leader has to motivate leaders and staffs across the enterprise to support the transformation—or it's likely doomed. The vision and the business case must be both compelling and communicated. [26] And if you don't have all of these factors, you may be better off looking for ways to motivate workers within the organizational structure that already exists.

Shared Services

In *Bureaucracy*, James Q. Wilson notes that support tasks, that is, those not in the core mission, demand special attention. "The wise executive," Wilson writes, "will arrange to devolve the . . . tasks onto another agency, or to a wholly new organization created for that purpose. . . . [T]he cost of trying to do everything is that few things are done well." [27]

As chief operating officer at GAO, I moved its payroll administration to the Department of Agriculture's National Finance Center (NFC), one of the federal government's first and largest shared-services centers. GAO was a relatively small organization of about fifty-five hundred people, and it made no sense to use an accounting staff of forty to process our own payroll, especially when an alternative was available. Of course, we had to modify how we did payroll in order to accommodate the NFC's approach. But it was worth it. We redistributed most of the accounting staff to perform unique GAO tasks, plus, when the payroll system crashed or developed a glitch, the problem happened to everyone NFC served, and so fixing glitches was *their* top priority, not ours.

There were some drawbacks, of course. We had to learn a new way to complete time sheets and clean up existing payroll data to bring it into compliance with NFC standards. On the other hand, efficiency gains were made based on economies of scale, and the assistant comptroller general for operations (yours truly) never again had to spend time explaining why payroll checks or W-2s were late.

Most important, however, was the fact that GAO's leaders no longer had to devote time to payroll processes. We could focus instead on mission: the quality and utility of the roughly seven hundred reports submitted annually to Congress, agency heads, and the American people. Of course, "mission focus" and efficiency are the reason so many private sector organizations have used specialized service providers, such as commercial payroll processors or benefits administration companies, for decades. In the federal sphere, however, diffuse authority and the absence of a profit motive have allowed virtually every federal entity to make its own decisions about whether and how to provide its own support functions.

Budget pressures and sequestrations have carved away steadily at federal overhead resources, which in a political environment are easier to reduce than are services to constituents. This has "inspired" leaders to find better ways to manage overhead through the sharing of services, consolidation, or outsourcing. "Unfortunately, we've never made enough investment in federal shared services alternatives," says Jerry Lohfink, former director of the National Finance Center. "We're in a crisis of our own creation, with a deteriorating support base and no federal or commercial strategies for replacing it with better, more rational support."[28]

Federal CFOs appear to agree. In a May 2015 survey by the Partnership for Public Service (PPS) and Deloitte, high-level federal officials cited the lack of adequate cost and quality data on shared services, as well as a need for accountability measures, for the lack of acceptable alternatives. In the absence of better information on cost and performance, many executives remain reluctant to move back-office operations to shared-service providers.[29]

The Efficiency and Effectiveness Imperatives

Why move to shared services? Lohfink cites four reasons: to allow management to focus attention on the mission and customers; to standardize "best" processes; to improve services; and to reduce costs. He believes that providing your own support functions soon will make little sense, given the ever-dwindling resources, but he adds a caveat also reflected in the PPS and Deloitte report: "Begin with your own business case and vision of what *you* want to 'buy,' and then compare commercial and federal providers."[30]

The trick is to find a supplier, public or private, who can assure you that it will stay in the business, maintain agreed-on service quality and cost, and give you priority attention when you need it. "Often the available alternatives can only provide some of what you want," says Lohfink. "Be sure to adjust your 'vision' so as to enter the transaction with realistic expectations."

You will also have to make the *political* case for shared services to your organization. This will require a vision based on mission enhancement and it will require key internal champions and strong leadership to overcome embedded interests and behaviors, according to Bill Beyer, Deloitte's Federal Shared Services lead. "The key is moving quickly to avoid bureaucratic inertia," says Beyer. "If you don't, opponents will have time to muster opposition before the advantages of a shared-service provider become clear."[31]

In 2013, HUD began a multiyear effort to move its human resources and financial management functions to external providers; human resources (HR), for instance, was moved to Treasury's Administrative Resources Center. Travel services followed in 2014, and financial management in 2015. The overall rationale was to enable HUD employees to concentrate on delivering HUD programs.[32]

The Commerce Department embarked on a similar project in 2014. Led by Commerce Secretary Penny Pritzker, the move was intended to enhance service quality with sensible, efficient use of common providers. Deputy Secretary Bruce H. Andrews led Commerce's Department Management Council in a systematic analysis of current services and possible options, ultimately focusing on quality improvements for human resources, finance, acquisitions, and technology. All Commerce entities worked with senior department leaders to determine which functions might be improved using common providers.[33]

Given the current budget outlook, it seems inevitable that more and more common federal functions will be consolidated, especially those that are relatively standard across different agencies. In 2014 the Obama Administration adopted a presidential performance goal to expand the use of shared services to improve federal performance and efficiency. In October 2105, OMB and GSA announced a new cross-federal Shared Services Governance Board, led by OMB, and a Unified Shared Services Management office within GSA, both of which are designed to manage and oversee mission-support shared services expansion in five functions: acquisitions, financial management, human resources, travel, and IT.[34]

The Budget Shuffle

Only within the federal environment could one find a vast document called "2017 Budget of the US Government," replete with multi-pound appendixes and multi-volume analyses, that is *not* the budget of the US Government. This document, of course, is the president's *proposal*. Congressional authorizations and appropriations actually control what agencies can spend.

In recent years, however, rather than pass budgets and appropriations that bring much-needed predictability to agencies' operations, political discord on Capitol Hill has led to expanded use of stop-gap "continuing resolutions" (CRs), which provide money to agencies for limited amounts of time and often make new projects all but impossible. Thus one of the emerging new executive skills in the federal sphere is learning how to manage under CRs, which typically are based on prior-year funding or short-term interim agreements rather than on actual needs.

Adding to the budgeting complexity (and the stakes) is the fact that three fiscal years are in play at all times: the current year, when you are spending appropriated funds; the upcoming year, for which you are battling to *get* funds; and the year following that, which the president's proposed budget addresses. Former Comptroller General Charles Bowsher's advice to those dealing with this complex tangle is worth noting:

> You've got to have a top financial team. They don't have to be high profile, but they have to know the budget process and the appropriators, and you have to work that relationship all the time. That's the key to getting things done in the federal government.[35]

Bowsher advises establishing strong control by your CFO, who should always be the appropriations liaison and lead regarding budget and appropriations matters.

Understanding the personal and political factors that affect budgeting on the Hill and at OMB is very important, says Janet Hale, herself a former OMB associate director and senior budget executive prior to becoming a cabinet-level CFO and under secretary. I, too, have found this understanding helps immensely with difficult funding challenges. Commissioner Rossotti's multiyear IRS systems reform, for example, was supported by an IT investment fund in the 1998 IRS Reform Act that virtually assured IRS of more than $500 million in critical appropriations and also allowed appropriators to retain control of politically essential funding.[36]

It is equally challenging to operate in sequestered environments. Census Deputy Director Nancy Potok points to the wisdom of anticipating multiyear reductions and adapting to them by completely eliminating a service or activity, rather than shaving the commitments to *all* activities. "People won't quibble if you have to drop something entirely," she advises. "Chipping a little off everything just leads to mediocrity across the board and increases the risk of failure."[37]

There are certain tricks of the trade, however, that can buy you a little extra cash. When I was working at GAO, for example, our building had a broken escalator that served the lower floors and needed a $6 million appropriation to fix. The funding for this was included in our appropriation. As the fiscal year went on, however, we needed the money for higher-priority congressional projects. With the agreement of our appropriators, we postponed the repair and budgeted for it for the following year. In the second year, however, higher-profile congressional needs arose again, and a technology upgrade was also required. The escalator repair was bumped once again. This pattern continued for several years. A working escalator is a desirable but nonessential expenditure that can be deferred (we just took the elevator to floors 2 and 3, or used the safe-but-frozen escalator as stairs, and I took to calling it—privately, of course—the "escalator fund"). I'm not sure whether that escalator ever got fixed, but it sure gave us some very useful financial flexibility.

Know the Rules

The federal budget process is described in OMB Circular A-11, a well-written presentation of the official federal budgeting and performance rules and processes. It covers everything from preparation and justification of budget requests to instructions on budget execution and agency strategic and performance reporting.

I recommend that you at least skim through it. Aside from the obvious advantage of knowing how the budget and performance management processes work, you can then employ the following phrase: "I don't think A-11 actually precludes us from doing what I want."[38]

Encouraging Organizational Innovation

Innovative organizational approaches come from collaborative environments that minimize barriers and encourage contacts and conversations across organizational lines. This bringing together of different groups to bear on challenging problems is essential to capitalizing on innovative thinking. Sometimes these can be groups that share a common set of challenges across different clients.

Take, for example, the Consumer Financial Protection Bureau, established under the 2010 Wall Street Reform and Consumer Protection Act, "to make markets for consumer financial products and services work for Americans." Separate CFPB directorates work together on common challenges faced by older Americans, service members, and students.[39] At times the bureau will assemble different units to work together on a specific problem that may require integrated thinking and action.

The Homeland Security Southwest Border Security Initiative, established in 2009 by then-DHS secretary Janet Napolitano with more than $400 million in funding, illustrates a similar approach. The initiative, which targeted illegal traffic in people, drugs, and firearms, was funded through multiple federal departments and border states to work together on projects to strengthen intrusion detection and prevention at ports and border crossings.[40] In *Managing within Networks* Robert Agranoff explores how these types of "public management networks" can make a significant difference in how public organizations can solve more difficult problems.[41] Formal innovation incubators can also encourage collaborative thinking and action—such as establishing protected zones that assemble creative people with various backgrounds and specialties to work together on specific challenges requiring innovative solutions. (Chapter 8 further explores this innovation tool.)

Key Takeaways

I have stressed it time and again, and so have executive leaders, consultants, and management theorists: organizational effectiveness begins with clear organizational goals. *Everything* follows from that.

Create Your Offense

1. *Begin by Defining "Success."* The federal environment can certainly contain multiple and often conflicting definitions of success. Hearkening back to the **Four Measures of Success** (see Figure 1.1), clarity on outcome and output goals is essential to giving your entire organization a common target to aim for and measure against.

Sometimes defining success is somewhat easier, as when a statute is clear regarding purpose. The American Recovery and Reinvestment Act (ARRA), for example, had five explicitly stated purposes: job creation; assistance to those most affected by the recession; investments in science and math training; infrastructure investments that support long-term growth; and budget assistance to state and local governments.[42]

Of course, goals often lack precision and may conflict with one another, and stakeholders seldom agree fully, so arriving at a "consensus" goal agreement is seldom "easy." Even in ARRA implementation, managers had to balance rapid spending with avoiding fraud and abuse. These characteristics of our system certainly make getting goal agreement a challenge, but they can also give leaders some latitude to negotiate definitions of success.

2. *Take the Time to Diagnose Your Troubles.* Chuck Bowsher spent his first full year as comptroller general learning how the organization operated and how it was meeting (or not meeting) its goals before framing a plan for transformation. Few of us have fifteen-year terms of office, but the principle is the same: *assess the current business model*, including workflows, behaviors, leadership, and customer and stakeholder satisfaction, in light of your timeframe and definition of success.

3. *To Reorganize or Not.* That's the question Hamlet confronted when deciding whether 'tis nobler to stay with the status quo or *take arms against a sea of troubles* and reorganize. It doesn't end well for him, but you get the point: there are merits and moats either way.

I've always tried to sidestep major reorganizations. They drain time, energy, and resources; they divert attention from serving citizens and stakeholders; they create morale challenges and logistical difficulties; and they often create new problems. If reasonable success can be achieved by aligning the right people to the right tasks with reasonable risk, and by incentivizing the behavior needed, that's a better short-term strategy. However, if the current organizational scheme forces people to work against it to get important things done, a restructuring may be the best answer.

4. *Create a Vision and Plan for Mission Success.* Charles Rossotti determined that helping taxpayers pay their taxes was the IRS's top mission goal, and he reframed the organization's structure, processes, and technology around that. Centering the vision on mission success rather than on accomplishing internal processes and problems *motivates*. Make the mission vision compelling, clear, easy to understand, motivational, and inspiring. The Social Security Administration, for instance, recently issued its Vision 2025 to help employees, appropriators, and citizens see how SSA can better serve Americans.[43]

Don't forget to create the right plan to achieve the vision, including the necessary activities, resources, and staffing. Resist the temptation to "move on" after the vision and plan are created; manage the organization *according to the plan*.

5. *Create a Bold Shared-Services Strategy.* Mission effectiveness requires *focus*. At GAO, one of my principal jobs was to make sure our senior division leaders, who had oversight responsibility for massive federal departments like Defense, State, HUD, Treasury, and Commerce, didn't have to spend time on procurements, technology, personnel, space, or other support needs. These are important functions—but specialists can do them better.

This requires specialized "chiefs," such as the CFO, the CIO, the CHCO (Chief Human Capital Officer), or, more recently, the chief data officer. Without such designations there's nobody whose top job is to remain abreast of the state of the art in personnel management, purchasing, IT, or finance. It's also worthwhile to consider having an overall operations leader to ensure a continuing focus on supporting mission rather acting in silos.

Outsourcing certain functions is close to inevitable, whether that is to government services centers or to private suppliers. As budgets get tighter and mission expectations continue to rise, it makes less and less sense to have people responsible for national health care, defense, patents, or airport security also handling transactions outside their mission-specific skills. For functions and transactions performed in a relatively standard way across federal agencies, such as IT, finance, procurement, or HR, shared providers are highly desirable.

6. *Find and Support Innovators.* It's essential to explicitly welcome innovative ideas and the people and mechanisms that incubate them. Who are your innovators? How can you ensure they work together on your most difficult problems? What incentives and protections will encourage them? Incubator units are useful, but everyday interactions can be just as important. (Chapter 8 explores the parameters and tools needed to find and support innovators.)

Execute Effectively

Whether you're staying with the organizational scheme you inherited or creating a new one, the right team will make it much easier to achieve your goals.

1. *Use Your Chief Financial Officer.* A CFO knowledgeable and experienced in federal financial management can give you credibility with Capitol Hill, appropriators, OMB, and other oversight organizations. The CFO is also the person who can marshal internal and external support for efficiency and effectiveness measures, organizational restructuring, or investment tradeoffs.

2. *Examine Shared-Services Alternatives.* The CFO, working with the chief information officer and other support leaders, can drive shared-services decisions that are based upon analysis of how the support functions can best enhance mission effectiveness. This should involve an examination of the available alternatives, both public and private.[44]

According to Jerry Lohfink, in the current federal environment a public request for information (RFI) is the best way to begin looking for private-sector suppliers, with human resources being the service most "ripe" for potential outsourcing. Lohfink recommends a three-step approach: develop a vision of what you want; investigate commercial and federal suppliers, with serious attention to what commercial suppliers can provide; and don't forget to reshape your vision to take realistic account of what you can get. A governing structure that can drive strategic decisions and provide some marketplace oversight is also critical.[45]

3. *Create the Incentives That Drive Successful Transformation.* If you believe an organizational transformation is necessary, the tools defined earlier—vision, business case, leadership alignment, program governance structure, and change management strategies—are the key tools you need (see Figure 4.1). Without any one of them your initiative may be doomed. Don't forget to adjust performance incentives to reflect clearly what behaviors need to change, remembering to reward, both formally and informally, the behaviors you want.

4. *Decide Where to Put the Boxes.* Alexander Braier's model starts with an operating audit that establishes where each unit sits in the "ecosystem," who it interacts with, and how it interacts—for example, what has to be done face-to-face and what can be handled electronically. Only then can you begin outlining the skills and relationships your organizational scheme will require. Rossotti, as we saw, decided to organize around customers rather than organizing around geographic areas. The next step, organizing the personnel within the proposed structure, should be based on reasonable spans of control, workloads, and ability levels.[46]

5. Keep It Flat. Your notion of hierarchy will vary, of course, depending upon the amount of authority and responsibility you want your employees to have. Clearly, an organization handling passport policy can be flatter than one handling passport applications. Regardless of the situation, go for the flattest possible structure because it gives people a sense of responsibility and the chance to make a call when it will make a difference and that person can see the customer impact. W. Edwards Deming, who is generally credited with the recovery of Japan's auto industry following World War II, advised Japanese automakers to adopt a much flatter assembly-line structure that gave each worker the right and responsibility to stop the line if an assembly was incorrect. Efficiency, quality, and morale all went up when the workers felt invested in "getting it right."[47]

There's a geographical application to this principle as well. For Wade Horn, requiring field staffs to report directly to headquarters eliminated a layer of bureaucracy and helped focus them on their grant-making responsibilities.[48] I personally would have preferred to manage the AFDC field staff outside of the regional SSA structure, there being little geographic variance in the distribution of AFDC funds to states.

6. Create an Innovation Incubator. Innovation in day-to-day government rarely happens without some specific assignment, sponsor, or enabling body. Sometimes it's a technology-driven "GovLab" enterprise that has a degree of freedom from normal operating procedures and protocols. Or it can simply be a periodic innovation fair or competition that tackles particularly vexing challenges.

Play a Smart Defense

Especially within the budget arena, a good defensive strategy requires some understanding of the motivations of congressional appropriators and administration budget examiners.

1. Know the Politics. Elected officials need to answer to their home constituencies, and providing them a way to do that often takes care of an issue. If there's a serious committee or floor vote at stake, securing allies in the other chamber (e.g., making sure the Senate won't go along if the House votes down the funding) can defuse a problem. Everyone gets what they really want: the offended representative or senator plays to the home district, and can even show the program was stripped from the House budget; and you get to keep the program intact when the Senate refuses to go along.[49]

Having at least one strong supporter for your program on the appropriations or authorizing committee in each chamber is a *must* in today's environment. Of course, the classic way to find these allies is by identifying your program's constituents. If there's a large postal sorting center in a congressman's district, he will generally be on board regarding USPS issues. Senator Y, from a largely rural state, is likely to support agricultural subsidies but oppose more funding for power plants upriver.

Allies like these can be valuable in bureaucratic sparring as well: Wade Horn used Ted Kennedy to trump regional objections to changed reporting structures, even though it seemed like a fairly trivial issue for the senator's involvement. If you can, establish these relationships early so the support exists before problems arise.

Conclusion

In discussing James Madison's 1788 Federalist Paper No. 51, *The Structure of the Government Must Furnish the Proper Checks and Balances between the Different Departments*, James Q. Wilson notes:

> The governments of the United States were not designed to be efficient or powerful, but to be tolerable and malleable. . . . As a result the Constitution is virtually silent on what kind of administration we should have.[50]

In this "malleable" cauldron lie both the challenges and possibilities of effective federal organization. In this day and age, the effort requires managing within the constraints of continuing resolutions and in the face of inconsistent or divergent expectations from stakeholders. Remember: you need a clear, unequivocal definition of success. Restructure the organization *only* when it's essential, and if you do, find ways to enhance the focus on mission. The next chapter addresses the critical roles that communications play in meeting these challenges.

Notes

1. Jorge Cervantes, Maminirina Rakotoarisoa, and Qian Wu, "IRS Customer Service Case Study" Capstone Project, Columbia University School of International and Public Affairs (December 2007), 3–4.
2. Lynda D. Willis, "Tax Administrations: IRS Faces Challenges in Reorganizing for Customer Service," Government Accountability Office, Report No. GAO/GGD-96-3 (1995), 8, http://www.gao.gov/assets/230/221736.pdf; David Attianese et

al., "The 1995 Tax Filing Season: IRS Performance Indicators Provide Incomplete Information about Some Problems," Government Accountability Office, Report No. GAO/GGD-96-48 (1995), 32, http://www.gao.gov/assets/230/222024.pdf; William Bricking et al., "IRS' 1996 Tax Filing Season: Performance Goals Generally Met; Efforts to Modernize Had Mixed Results," Government Accountability Office, Report No. GAO/GGD-97-25 (December 1996), 1, http://www.gao.gov /archive/1997/gg97025.pdf.

3. Ralph V. Carlone, *Report to the Chairman Subcommittee on Oversight, Committee on Ways and Means, House of Representatives—Tax System Modernization: IRS' Challenge for the Twenty-First Century*, Government Accountability Office, Report No. GAO-IM/IMTEC-90-13 (February 1990), 1, http://www.gao.gov/assets/220 /212210.pdf.

4. Jeffrey Corbett and Patrick Kish, *Behind the Offshore Veil* (iUniverse, 2005), 29; William V. Roth Jr., ed., "IRS Oversight: Congressional Hearings" (Collingdale, PA: Diane, 1999), 244.

5. Profile of Charles O. Rossotti, MBA, 1964, Harvard Business School Alumni Bulletin, January 2003, https://www.alumni.hbs.edu/stories/Pages/story-bulletin .aspx?num=2018.

6. Ann Cullen, "How We Transformed the IRS," Harvard Business School, last modified July 2005, http://hbswk.hbs.edu/archive/4674.html.

7. US Internal Revenue Service, "IRS Organization Blueprint," Document 11502 (Rev. 4–2000), cat. no. 27877P (2000), 1–1 and 12–15, http://www.irs.gov/pub/irs -utl/27877d00.pdf.

8. Ibid.

9. Ibid.

10. Internal Revenue Service, "Progress Report: IRS Business Systems Modernization Program (BSM)," Document 3701 (Rev.9–2000), cat. no. 30956R (2000), 25, http://www.irs.gov/pub/irs-utl/bsm-prog.pdf. Internal Revenue Service, "IRS Modernization," National Archives and Records Administration (1998), at http:// clinton4.nara.gov/pcscb/rmo_irs.html.

11. James White and Joanna Stamatiades, "Tax Administration: IRS's 2003 Filing Season Performance Showed Improvements," Government Accountability Office, Report No. GAO-04-84 (October 2003), 16, http://www.gao.gov/assets/250 /240502.pdf.

12. Alexander Braier, in discussion with the author, March 2015.

13. Clay Johnson, in discussion with the author, December 2014.

14. Wade Horn, in discussion with the author, January 2015.

15. Mike Gelles, in discussion with the author, October 2014.

16. "Rumsfeld: You Go to War with the Army You Have," *The Newshole*, July 19, 2007, https://youtu.be/3jPgljRvzQw?t=21s.

17. James Q. Wilson, *Bureaucracy: What Government Agencies Do and Why They Do It* (New York: Basic, 2000), 24.

18. Braier discussion.

19. Ibid.

20. "The Big Picture: Profiles of Notable Movers," Partnership for Public Service (2015), http://bestplacestowork.org/BPTW/rankings/profiles#cftc.

21. Kimberly McCabe, president and CEO of Value Storm Growth Partners, in discussion with the author, January 2015.

22. Robert Knisely, "GAO and the Department of Redundancy," Governing.com, March 2011, http://www.governing.com/blogs/bfc/gao-department-redundancy .html; Robert Knisely, in discussion with the author, July 2014.

23. Wade Horn discussion.

24. Mark Reger, in discussion with the author, September 2015.

25. Arnold Jackson, in discussion with the author, August 2014.

26. Braier discussion.

27. Wilson, *Bureaucracy*, 371.

28. Jerry Lohfink, in discussion with the author, February 2015.

29. "Helping Government Deliver II: The Obstacles and Opportunities surrounding Shared Services," Partnership for Public Service and Deloitte, March 2015, 8, http://www.google.com/url?sa=t&rct=j&q=&esrc=s&source=web&cd=2&ved =0CCUQFjAB&url=http%3A%2F%2Fourpublicservice.org%2Fpublications %2Fdownload.php%3Fid%3D477&ei=QFVaVceVB42uogTjroDoDg&usg= AFQjCNHXaaLYq1D-Dt1Ib4Wd2gy0W9y1lg.

30. Lohfink discussion.

31. Bill Beyer, in discussion with the author, December 2014.

32. "Helping Government Deliver II," 8.

33. Ibid.

34. David Mader and Denise Turner Roth, "Scaling Implementation of Shared Services," whitehouse.gov (blog), October 22, 2015, http://www.whitehouse.gov /blog/2015/10/22/scaling-implementation-shared-services.

35. Charles Bowsher, in discussion with the author, October 2014.

36. IRS, "Progress Report IRS Business Systems," 25.

37. Nancy Potok, in discussion with the author, November 2014.

38. US Office of Management and Budget, "OMB Circular A-11,", accessed May 29, 2015, https://www.whitehouse.gov/omb/circulars_a11_current_year_a11_toc.

39. US Consumer Financial Protection Bureau, "About Us," last modified March 25, 2015, http://www.consumerfinance.gov/the-bureau/.

40. Miguel Salazar and Robert Donnelly, "US Southwest Border Security Initiatives," Woodrow Wilson International Center for Scholars, Mexico Institute, August 2009, http://www.wilsoncenter.org/sites/default/files/SWB%20Fact%20Sheet _0.pdf.

41. Robert Agranoff, *Managing within Networks: Adding Value to Public Organizations* (Washington: Georgetown University Press, 2007).

42. Edward DeSeve, "Managing Recovery: An Insider's View," IBM Center for the Business of Government (2011), 11, http://www.businessofgovernment.org/sites /default/files/Managing%20Recovery.pdf.

43. US Social Security Administration, "Vision 2025," at http://www.ssa.gov /vision2025/.

44. "Helping Government Deliver II," 8; Lohfink discussion.

45. "Shared Services Roundtable," Partnership for Public Service (2015).

46. Ibid.

47. Linda Holbeche and Andrew Mayo, *Motivating People in Lean Organizations* (London: Taylor & Francis, 2009), 1–2; Peter Drucker, "The Emerging Theory of Manufacturing," *Harvard Business Review* (May–June 1990), https://hbr.org/1990 /05/the-emerging-theory-of-manufacturing, accessed May 21, 2015.

48. Horn discussion.

49. Kenneth Ashworth, *Caught between the Dog and the Fireplug, or How to Survive Public Service* (Washington, DC: Georgetown University Press, 2001), 2–5.

50. Wilson, *Bureaucracy,* 376.

CHAPTER 5

Communications— What's the Good Word?

On December 8, 2003, President George W. Bush signed into law the Medicare Modernization Act, creating the first-ever prescription drug benefit for all 54 million Medicare recipients. Calling it "the greatest advance in health care coverage for America's seniors since the founding of Medicare," Bush handed the program's implementation to the Centers for Medicare and Medicaid Services (CMS).[1]

But the legislation establishing the benefit was flawed. In their best-selling book *If We Can Put a Man on the Moon*, William Eggers and John O'Leary describe the "design-free design trap" that legislators had fallen into when they created the added drug coverage without adequate attention to the program's design and implementation. "The Design-Free Design Trap occurs because the work of drafting a bill that launches a major initiative isn't generally treated like the design process it truly is," write Eggers and O'Leary. "The bill gets passed, but the design is unworkable."[2]

In creating a massive marketplace with over a thousand private insurance choices for the elderly, the new law created a major communications challenge for CMS, for Social Security, and for the states, all of which were involved in implementing the program. How could an elderly and often poor population fully understand the choices when, for example, some states had approved more than fifty private plans from which to choose, with different drugs, deductibles, co-pays, and procedures?[3] And, with a new program requiring such complex individual choices, all varying by geography, *who* would provide the information and technical assistance these new buyers needed? Would it be local pharmacies? Interest groups such as the American Association of Retired People (AARP)? Uncle Sam?

Because CMS had collected little information on potential customers during the program's design phase, it had little idea of how to help customers choose and use a plan.[4] What wording would be most effective in helping people decipher the new program and its choices? What media and markets would reach them? In the absence of early and extensive monitoring of users as the program launched (called "feedback loops" in communications parlance), program officials couldn't make real-time adjustments to the messages or media as the massive rollout unfolded.

Through a combination of legislative design flaws and communications problems, the initial launch caused widespread confusion and outright dismay. Given choices among dozens of plans with different features, many people just couldn't figure it out without assistance.[5] Pharmacists, customarily a trusted source of advice for seniors, quickly found themselves spending hours trying to help their customers make complex choices based on what often proved to be misinformation from CMS. And, with striking similarity to what would happen again in a future federal healthcare rollout, people had a hard time getting through to the federal hotline.[6]

One story reported widely by National Public Radio illustrates the chaos well. A seventy-one-year-old Washington, DC, woman with cancer, arthritis, and a heart condition had been buying her eight daily pills through Medicaid for $1.00 each. When she tried to pick up her drugs under the new Part D program, she was told she owed a $250.00 deductible before she could have them, and that her plan required $89.00 monthly dues and $5.00 co-pay per prescription. Unfortunately, *none* of that information was correct. Under Part D, pharmaceuticals for low-income patients maxed out at $3.00 per prescription, with no deductible or monthly premium required.[7] It mattered little whether such errors were caused by disconnects between Medicare and Medicaid databases or were the fault of CMS or even of some pharmacists. Regardless of blame, many stressful hours were spent to clarify entitlements for individuals who needed their drugs.

While CMS didn't build in an early customer feedback loop, it quickly became obvious that the rollout was a public-relations setback. Media reports filed in the wake of Medicare workshops and adult class tutorials reflected major confusion. During the first week the program was live, the Kaiser Family Foundation and the Harvard School of Public Health reported that only 35 percent of Americans aged sixty-five and older said they understood the benefit.[8]

And yet, despite the challenges of the design trap and major launch shortfalls, CMS did a lot right, which ultimately helped the program recover from its initial challenges. As one study notes, CMS signed up fifty thousand groups—from the AARP to local agencies for aging and church organizations—to assist with outreach. It ran ad campaigns featuring celebrities like First Lady Laura Bush. It even made use of family ties, with an ad in *People* magazine urging baby boomers to discuss the new program with their parents.[9]

Not everyone agreed with such positive characterizations, of course, but eventually the messengers and messages caught up with the target population. Complaints about pharmacy problems dropped by 95 percent over a three-month period, and wait times on the toll-free line dipped below two minutes.[10] But none of this happened before the projected $720 billion program found itself mired in serious and highly public communications problems during a presidential election season.[11]

The Medicare Part D launch involved a complex law and benefits structure, a challenging demographic group, and a need for broad, national communications. The following case, however, provides a fairly shocking example of how government efforts can break down over what should be straightforward *internal* communications as well.

Metrics Matter

In 1999, NASA's *Climate Orbiter* reached Mars after a 286-day journey through space. Built to collect information about Mars's climate and relay data from a second vehicle that was also targeted to land on the planet, the trip was intended to investigate the planet's hydrological history and search for evidence of life.[12] Regrettably, a navigational error placed the spacecraft in an orbit around Mars that was much lower than intended. Sucked into the planet's atmosphere, the $125 million orbiter quickly burned up.

How could an agency with an exceptional record of success make such a basic navigational error? It turns out NASA calculated the navigational logistics of the trip in metric measurements, while the contractor hired to build the orbiter had used English (that is, not metric) units. Several independent review boards confirmed the conclusion: the incident reflected a fundamental breakdown in communication between buyer and contractor.[13]

Clearly, poor communications of all sorts can have serious consequences. This shouldn't be surprising, since *nothing* gets done without communication of some kind. Chapter 2 emphasizes that everything gets done **through people**, our most important resource. Just as important, everything gets done **with communications**, our most important tool. The following discussion demonstrates how good communication starts with careful *listening* to stakeholders and customers. Following that, you need a communications strategy keyed to your goals; "feedback loops" to measure how your messaging is influencing behavior; and the right communications styles for maximum impact. The discussion then turns to an examination of the possibilities and dangers of using various media formats and techniques, some of which provide great value when done well but can nevertheless be laden with minefields. The discussion concludes with assessment of the important conventional wisdom on handling bad news, especially getting it all out and moving rapidly to solutions.

Communication Basics

Say the word "communicate" and most of us think of talking *to* some person or entity. "Did you tell the Hill?" This is outward-bound information, as if expressed by bullhorn—or, in today's world, by email, text message, LinkedIn connection, Instagram photo, Twitter feed, and the like. But good communication is as much about *listening* as it is about broadcasting. In *The Seven Habits of Highly Successful People,* one of Stephen Covey's most interesting observations is that one must "seek to understand before seeking to be understood."[14] This, of course, is a core principle of successful customer service as well: to know what a customer (indeed, any stakeholder) wants or needs, you have to listen and understand.

So it is with federal customers as well, especially within the often complex transactional environment. Different federal customers and stakeholders need and expect different avenues and styles of communication.

This isn't substantially different from the challenges private companies face in determining who will be tempted by a new car design or what shows will succeed on cable. But the breadth and scope of government's missions is enormous and often highly complex and federal operations are usually more distant from individual citizens than the services provided by state and local governments. This makes communication with the citizen audience that much more difficult. Furthermore, communication among federal entities can be challenging as well, whether success is defined as preventing nuclear war or calibrating a Mars orbiter.

Defining Effective Communication

Communication can be *inbound*, as when information is being received by a person or entity using tools like surveys or just plain listening; or *outbound,* as when information is being transmitted to others, such as through written or verbal directions or ad campaigns. Communication can be *internal* to an organization or program, as with the Mars orbiter, or *external,* when it is aimed at millions, such as

Medicare recipients. Hearkening back to the **stakeholder** dimension of success, communication can be at the *individual* level, as with your own subordinates, peers, or bosses; at the *organizational* level, as between the Department of Education and Congress; or at the *national* level, as in an effort to reach all taxpayers.

One theme stitched throughout this book applies particularly to communication: if you're not clear about your goal, you're already in trouble. This is true whether you're designing a new highway safety program, working out the parameters of a defense system, writing a contract, or promoting a new way to file income taxes. The communications process *must* begin with clarity of goals; only then should you find ways to measure whether the message is reaching the audience and achieving the goal.[15] So, define your ultimate goal for communication *before* starting to address what the message should be, how it should be communicated, and to whom!

The Art of Listening

"Listening is the starting point and most important part of communications—and the most often overlooked," argues Tracy Haugen, a DC-based consultant in federal communications. Regardless of your goal for a communications campaign, whether internal or external, you must start by asking the target population what they need.[16]

Sometimes the listening part itself actually spurs some of the behavioral changes you seek. The largest recent drop in aviation accidents occurred in the years following 1991, when the FAA asked the industry what should be changed to improve safety; together they have created a joint plan to cut fatality risk in half by 2025.[17] The state of Maine saw even more dramatic improvement in occupational safety using an innovative approach described in chapter 8: OSHA actually asked some top workforce safety *violators* what could be done to improve workplace safety!

Know Your Target Population

Meetings, field trips, focus groups, and formal surveys all can be useful, depending on the size of the target population. When trying to reach national populations, news stories, studies, and public testimony—as well as interest-group publications—provide an excellent starting point for gathering information on stakeholder needs. During this "learning phase," it is very important to determine how your target group takes in information. The mobile and digital media that can be used to reach millennials applying for federal student aid probably won't work as well in reaching social security recipients. Be careful, however, to not stereotype audiences, such as the elderly. In collecting input on what social security should look like in 2025, SSA used public survey instruments augmented by, among other things, crowd-sourced reviews from IdeaScale.[18]

Listening tours are a time-honored and politically savvy way to solicit feedback across broad geographic areas. When Agriculture Secretary Tom Vilsack took office in 2009, he immediately conducted a cross-country listening tour to meet and talk with Agriculture Department local office staffs and individual farmers and ranchers. Preparing for the five-year reauthorization cycle, Vilsack interacted with hundreds of people and groups before framing the department's proposals.[19] These kinds of media-friendly activities offer major public relations benefits and help build grassroots support for what a department might have been planning to do anyway.

More narrow communication efforts, such as internal initiatives, still need to be founded on an understanding of the views of those they are aimed at. Such views can often be tapped in in the context of personal settings, like across a desk or over a beer after hours. Lunch outside the office building can help build trust and woo important allies.

According to Dan Helfrich, a Washington veteran of human-resource consulting and federal CEO for Deloitte Consulting LLP, beginning with direct and truly inclusive interaction provides an added advantage. As he says, it

> sets a tone that *motivates real involvement* from staff, and in broader initiatives even citizen groups. If they feel truly involved, it doesn't just help us find the best solution; it also motivates and energizes people to be "on board" when it's time to implement the new approach.[20]

Get Your Message Across

Turning from inbound information to the challenge of broadcasting the *outbound* kind, the guiding principle is still to start by defining **goals**, particularly desired outputs, as well as critical **stakeholders** and **timeframes** (as discussed in chapter 1). Any successful communications strategy must address all three of these dimensions.

It is especially important to have a timely and clear communications strategy if something big (both good and bad) is coming down the pike—for example, hurricane season, the availability of a new drug benefit, or the closing of a military base. Nobody likes government surprises, and by broadcasting the news at the right time (that is, in advance) you convey that you care about key stakeholders and want to help them be "on top" of any needed actions.

In their book *Achieving Project Management Success in the Federal Government*, Jonathan Weinstein and Timothy Jaques note that "selling the vision" and "setting the context" are vital to effective federal communications.[21] To do this you have to know something about your target audience's media habits and preferences. A major rollout is a risky time to try new media pathways.

For internal communications to leaders—for example, to newly minted presidential appointees—you should tune into their personal communication styles. Does she want large briefing books with reference tabs or would a two-page bulleted list of key points work best? Would a conversation do the job better, versus a weekend's worth of PowerPoint presentations or reading material delivered at 7:00 p.m. on a Friday night?

For external communications, consider whether an interest group might be the best conduit for disseminating information. Perhaps you can put a nonprofit membership organization such as AARP or AMVETS, or a professional society like the National Bar Association, to work for you. In *How Information Matters*, Kathleen Hale posits that government capacity to solve problems is enhanced when agencies create information-based relationships with nonprofits. While her work is based on state and local activities, the best practice tools she uses can be adapted for the federal context as well.[22]

For younger generations, you should ask yourself what new technologies they are using that you should learn to use too? (A later discussion addresses some highly successful communications avenues and techniques that are not yet standard in the federal sphere.)

Show me is better than *tell me*. Most people learn through experience, so they typically learn better from field trips to successful projects or by talking with practitioners who have accomplished similar tasks rather than wading through the minutiae of a program description. For example, when newly named District of Columbia chief financial officer Natwar Gandhi discovered piles of unrecorded local tax returns hidden in the office's closets, he concluded that he needed not just better rules but better-trained and better-motivated employees. He took his revenue personnel on day trips to federal IRS processing centers to show them tax collection processes that were more automated and more efficient, like those he planned to bring to the District. He also was able to show them how much happier and better-motivated IRS workers were when they had been properly trained and fully equipped.

Of course, most traditional personal and organizational communications are verbal or written, but there are plenty of other effective ways to get important messages across. For months before launching its Consolidated Administrative Performance System, for instance, the Department of Education set up a series of campaign-type events in its main lobby, complete with balloons and music timed to staff comings and goings, to get them familiar with and excited about the initiative.

Rewards send important messages about desired behaviors as well, like prime parking spaces (next to the secretary's spot!) for employees of the month, upgraded technology for the best digital idea, or a flextime day for someone putting in a lot of overtime.

Keep in mind, too, that pictures can have major impact. Borrowing an idea from *The Jungle*, Upton Sinclair's 1906 exposé of the meatpacking industry, at GAO we started using photographs in occasional reports covering topics like unsanitary agricultural practices or decaying bridge undercarriages. We got people's attention.[23]

Of course, communication isn't just about words or pictures. Anyone who doubts the power of time and space in communications need only observe a presidential nominee who is kept waiting in an anteroom for hours by a congressional committee chair or senator, while hometown constituents and staffers come and go. As leaders, our actions often have more impact than anything we could write or say.

Pick the Right Message

You can focus the goal of your message by creating a crisp couple of sentences that summarize it. But a compelling message is a lot more than a "should" or "must" missive that directs people to proceed in a specific way.

Be clear about what you want a particular message to actually accomplish. Is it to provide information that Medicare recipients can actually use to pick a drug plan? Is it directions that are understandable to college-bound students who need to fill out FAFSA (Free Application for Federal Student Aid) forms? Or is it guidance on available citizen services and how to access them? Avoid using "fed speak" acronyms or delivering important information via federal industry journals (like the *Federal Register*), which no one outside government even glances at, much less understands.

In defining your messages and their timing, it's important to respect people's time, cautions Tracy Haugen. When you burden target groups, whether internal or external, with superfluous messages or information that is appearing too far in advance of their needs, you train them to skip the message or even resist it when it finally becomes important.[24] Be specific in tailoring information to only what is needed and at the right points in time.

Anchoring messages in common history and tradition can be helpful too, adds Haugen. In recalling the famous Shakespearean quote chiseled on the National Archives building in Washington, DC, "What's past is prologue," she points out that messages are more persuasive if they build on recipients' values, traditions, and prior experiences.[25]

One of the best examples of an effective communication campaign aimed at a change-averse audience was the one launched by the National Archives, which was receiving heavy pushback from staff during a sweeping tech upgrade. Traditionalist archivists were cool to the notion that digital records should begin to supersede paper ones.

The archive's leaders, however, managed to turn their staff around with the message that a key aspect of the archive's mission is *to share* its treasure trove of documents, which had powerful appeal even among the staunchest traditionalists. What better way to share history as broadly as possible than to make the material available online? The genius of the message was that it carried great respect for the archive's traditional role as the keeper of US history but also emphasized its vital role in disseminating that history.[26]

Finally, use humor when appropriate. It, too, can have a powerful effect. When President Barack Obama went on the air early in 2015 to discuss computer security, he made fun of himself and some of the truly awful passwords he had used in the past. It was funny and effective.

Communicate with Stakeholders

The method you choose to communicate depends on your target audience, but you can even make communications with a broad national or organizational constituency feel somewhat intimate. Had Veterans Affairs secretary Eric Shinseki been able to communicate to *all* VA staff his *personal* goals regarding service not just to those with whom he worked closely, and had he then created some clear avenues for employee feedback, he might have received better early warning signs about the challenges his employees faced.

With the advent of digital and social media, there are many additional ways to communicate with major federal constituencies such as taxpayers, social security recipients, and those eligible for subsidized housing or student loans. The limiting factors are one's comfort with the necessary security protocols and our will and ability to use these new tools.

Use Surrogates

Having noted the increasing ease of communicating directly, I would nevertheless caution against overusing mass communications when major and respected surrogates are available to do this heavy lifting. Groups such as AARP for the elderly, AAA for auto-related issues, and business roundtables for broad industry involvement can be your conduit. The caveat here is to consider branding, integrity of messaging, and the existence of multiple organizations that might have a stake in any given issue. Using environmental groups to push a green message, for instance, should be balanced with outreach to interests on the other side of the issue.

Administrations can and do find acceptable partners for controversial messages on most hot-button issues like reproductive health and gun control. The key is to choose them with careful attention to the political implications and then to vet them in full, often through the ranks of the assistant secretary for public affairs or, for particularly sensitive subjects, even with OMB or the White House.

Feedback Loops and Behavioral Change

Engineers build "feedback loops" into things they design to ensure that what they've built actually is having the intended effect. Thermostats have thermometers that tell when the temperature in the room is at the level set. Sensors tell a drawbridge operator when the deck has locked back into place. So it is with communication: it is always wise to build in "social" feedback loops to determine whether the recipients are getting the message and how they're reacting.

One of the most direct ways to do this is via a simple survey. Do state transportation offices understand the steps they need to follow and complete in order to receive infrastructure funding? Have national parks users heard of (or, even better, used) a new mobile app for reserving campsites? According to Jitinder Kohli, who led the Doing What Works project at the Center for American Progress, understanding how to influence behavior and drive change through the federal "ecosystem" is the *top skill* for federal leaders.[27] In other words, effective communication is essential, which is why it's so important to determine whether your message is getting through.

Today there's a growing trend in government toward the use of more sophisticated message testing. Kohli championed the use of research-based tools to improve government when he served as director general for strategy and communications in the United Kingdom's Department for Business Innovation and Skills; today he's a prominent advocate for a technique called "behavioral insight," in which practitioners routinely test multiple messages to gauge which most effectively influences and motivates a given audience.[28]

As documented in a series of studies from Deloitte and Washington's Federal News Radio 1500, behavioral economists have identified a number of ways to change people's behavior through simple shifts in the way questions are phrased or choices are framed, or by changing the wording or physical locations of safety and health-related messages.[29]

Behavioral insights such as these, which have been long understood in commercial sales, first entered the public sector in the United Kingdom, where behavioral economists have, for example, tested differently worded letters to tax debtors (see chapter 8). The language that they settled on boosted voluntary tax compliance from 68 to 83 percent. The UK also tested various messages to get drivers to slow down in areas where children walk or play, and credited the effort with lowering child deaths by 10 percent.[30]

In the United States, state and local governments are dabbling in behavioral insight as well. In Bellevue, Washington, average driving speeds fell by 5 mph after the city attached "YOUR SPEED" feedback signs directly above speed-limit signs, and the reductions continued over time.[31]

At the federal level, OMB responded to an Obama White House request with Memorandum M-13-17, which urges agencies to test and apply behavioral insights to improve performance and increase innovation.[32] Today, federal agencies are using these techniques to improve the effectiveness of Treasury letters sent to delinquent debtors, to reduce caller abandonment rates at the National Domestic Violence Hotline, and to create more intuitive financial disclosures at the Consumer Financial Protection Bureau.[33]

Communicating with the Media

Most federal agencies have media relations officers to help craft an overall media strategy. Entering a media situation without a specialist is like hiking into the jungle without a guide, and about as smart; it's *very* important to partner with a specialist and to take their counsel to heart. They know which outlets and which reporters to trust for fairness and accuracy. Good public relations (PR) officers have established relationships among the key media covering your program or policy area and can work with you to get the word out. By the same token—especially in the case of less-than-good news—a media relations specialist can run interference for you.

The PR specialist also will ensure that you're following internal press policies, which will help protect you if something goes wrong. He or she can "chaperone," if you ask, by listening in on media calls or accompanying you to television or radio station interviews and providing critical "clarifications," both during and after a discussion. A good public information officer (PIO) can help you magnify a great story or minimize a negative one simply by getting the timing and the framing right.

Brave Old and New Worlds of Media

Eileen Shanahan, a former *Washington Star* editor and Joseph Califano's masterful PR officer at HEW, taught me the use of timing and media sourcing. Any good news had to be in Eileen's hands by 2:00 p.m. on Mondays through Thursdays to make the deadline for the 6:00 p.m. weekday news. For really great stories, Eileen would approach the *Washington Post* and offer exclusives with the secretary or a big department name (such as the NIH director or the surgeon general for anti-smoking stories). Bad news went out Friday evenings because fewer people were paying attention and many members of Congress were already headed for their home districts by that time.

But the 24/7 news cycle and the advent of social media have changed the information landscape dramatically. A smart social media strategy allows you to either go straight to the media with strategic dispatches or go right *past* them and directly to the public. If you can't do one of those, you're way behind the curve.

Today's insatiable appetite for information offers unprecedented opportunities to get your message out. The president or the pope or a temporarily famous pop star can reach millions of people with a single tweet. Diana Urban, an old-school veteran representative in the Connecticut Legislature, reports that Facebook posts of her with kids or animals get instant positive responses. She thinks it's one of the main reasons she ran unopposed in 2014.[34]

However, while the variety of media channels can provide multiple avenues for tailored, targeted communications, we face a new world that needs to be approached with care, intelligence, and a clear strategy. In today's environment a mistake can almost instantly become a national or even global affair. The Office of Personnel Management is well aware of these dangers, and recently provided guidance to agencies by defining policies for the use of social media for federal business or on federal devices.[35]

"Think before you tweet or blog" should be tattooed on the back of every federal official's hand, given the public embarrassments we've seen showered on national leaders and celebrities alike. A great American, Will Rogers, said it best: "Never miss a good chance to shut up." That's wisdom for the ages.

A few years back, for instance, one local police department created an Instagram hashtag to allow citizens to quickly and easily post pictures to its social media page. Apparently believing that they'd get a sampling of "cops kissing babies" pictures, what was posted instead was a gallery of officers clubbing and manhandling citizens. It was a stark lesson, noted by other government agencies as well, that social media ought to be the sole purview of a professional, well-run public affairs shop that can provide you with very specific guidance on who can play around with it—and where the boundaries lay.

Some Basic Rules of Engagement

While forward-leaning public officials are reaching out through social media—with varying results—the basic one-on-one media interview is still a staple, so it's important to get some key basics right. One of the biggest mistakes you can make is failing to clarify beforehand the terms of the interview. Will you be speaking *on background, off the record,* or *for attribution?*

On background means you're providing the reporter information on the ins and outs of a given issue or situation. It allows you to influence the media's views without any specific reference to you or the information you've provided. For example, you can explain your reasons for program choices and refer them to a specific report or expert who validates your view. Speaking on background is potentially powerful and comes with very low risk. It's important, though, that your press contact be comfortable with the interviewer's trustworthiness and confirm that the interview is indeed on background, lest you read your free-flowing thoughts in tomorrow's *Washington Times*.

At GAO we often spoke on background with responsible media sources, when asked, because it helped improve the accuracy of reporting on our results. Very few people actually read GAO's reports, but millions, including many elected officials, formed views about our issues from the press accounts of those reports. Helping reporters get it right is crucial.

Speaking *off the record* means that what you tell a reporter can be quoted directly or rephrased but cannot be attributed to you. The reporter can attribute what is said to "a senior agency official" or a "high-level member of the management team," and so forth. A press person should be involved in this dialogue, particularly because everyone in your agency will immediately want to find out who the source was (especially if the facts aren't reported accurately, which is, unfortunately, a common occurrence).

Speaking *for attribution*—or on the record—is generally reserved for officials who are experienced at handling the media. It can be incredibly effective; it's also the riskiest route to take, as persistent reporters will try to get you to say something "newsworthy," that is, controversial or embarrassing. Careful preparation with at least one PR specialist, and perhaps a subject-matter expert from your agency, can help you define and refine key points you want to make and polish the resulting sound bites. Of course, you should try to seem lively, open, and honest. But there are ways to do that without sabotaging yourself.

Jane Norris, a veteran DC reporter and on-air anchor, also has experience as director of public affairs for the Administration for Children and Families and as acting assistant secretary for public affairs at the Department of Labor. "Be authentic," counsels Norris:

> Avoid hubris. Display humility as a public servant, including a calm and friendly speaking voice. . . . [B]e interested and attentive to the interviewer. It's very important to make eye contact, which will help you appear confident, a leader honored to be in public service.[36]

You also have to "craft the interview by weaving the story *you* want," she says. "Don't leave it to the interviewer to control the story you want to tell. *You* have to do that."[37] To do this, you should write down and rehearse your quotes so that they appear spontaneous and convey your message(s). Be careful to provide short, crisp comments so that parts of longer sentences cannot be taken out of context. Make sure your supervisor and whoever has overall media responsibility approve both the appearance and the messaging before they see you in the media or read your comments in print.

Regardless of your environment and the agreed-on ground rules, anything you offer should be *focused on a defined goal*, delivered via a short list of *clear and simple points*, that reflect a *clear understanding of the target audience* and are made in whatever medium is *most likely to further your goal*. Many well-meaning leaders who didn't follow these precepts came to regret it very bitterly indeed. When in doubt, look to less risky strategies, such as standard press releases or media packages, but understand that those may also be less effective ways to get the word out.

One point is, of course, important to all successful communication: be sure the message is carefully crafted and the messenger is carefully selected and rehearsed. Take the time to get it right.

Controlling the Story

At some point in your career you will find yourself on the defensive in the wake of a negative story, whether it's accurate or not. Norris describes one instance at the Labor Department when a politically sensitive employee overtime rule was changed and political opponents were able to put an inaccurate spin on it that the media predictably picked up. "We consistently and immediately responded with corrections every time we saw [the spin] appear," she says, as well as sent letters to the editor, which helped the department regain control of the story. The best response to inaccurate reporting is to respond early and often, to the media as well as to the public.[38]

It's another problem, of course, when the bad news is true. Take, for recent example, YouTube videos of some ill-conceived GSA "conferences" that became lavish events paid for with taxpayer dollars. Two things need to happen in the wake of "true bad news," says Norris. First, don't let it leak out in dribs and drabs. Get to the bottom of the issue and air everything as quickly and as accurately as possible, painful as it might be; it makes you look forthright and in control. Second, fashion a coherent and strong response that shows you take the problem seriously and are taking steps to ensure it will never be repeated on your watch.[39] Regarding the conferences, some Washington insiders complained that GSA

★ **Box 5.1** Lessons from Tylenol

The textbook case of best practice in commercial damage control is still Johnson & Johnson's reaction to the Tylenol poisonings of 1982, when seven people died after ingesting Tylenol that had been tampered with. The company made extraordinary efforts to be open and proactive during the tragedy, offering detailed information on how many bottles were involved and where they were purchased. Tylenol was immediately recalled from store shelves across the country, and Johnson & Johnson guaranteed that the product wouldn't return without reliably tamper-proof bottles. Having quickly and forthrightly dealt with a potentially crippling public-relations crisis, the brand rebounded strongly.[40]

The Tylenol case demonstrates an important communications rule: don't attempt to spin, sugarcoat, or hide bad news. Get it out quickly and fully to protect your own credibility, accompanied by your solution plan, if possible. If your audience has confidence in your facts, they are more likely to trust your solution.

overreacted by aggressively cutting conferences, travel budgets, and so forth, but the black eye eventually became the story of a reformed agency moving forward.

Key Takeaways

In this chapter I have emphasized that one's communication style—such as listening first and conveying a caring and sincere attitude—is just as important as the specific strategies, tools, and techniques used. How you say something often trumps what you say. What is your personal communications style? Can you spot others' styles that work and use them to help achieve your goals? Box 5.2 explores six sometimes-all-too-familiar communications styles and provides some guidance and cautions on using each. Can you locate your style?

Create Your Offense

1. *Adopt a Communications Strategy and Personal Style That Supports Your Goals*. The strategy should define stakeholders, timeframes and message goals. It should address realistic tradeoffs between competing stakeholders and program goals. Your style should be inclusive, forthright, and focused on motivating those you work with and serve.

2. *Always Listen Before Talking*. Use informal conversations, formal meetings, surveys, focus groups, contacts with interest groups, and more to ensure that you

understand the issues and interests surrounding any given decision or initiative—*before* you offer your feedback or decision.

3. *Tailor Your Message and Medium for the Target Audience.* Who do you want to reach and how do they absorb information? Adapt to *their* ways of taking in information. Pay attention to all three levels of communication: individual, organizational, and national.

4. *Communicate a Vision of Success.* Tie your messages to the culture and prior successes of your audience, and to its pride as a population group (such as veterans) or pride in mission, if internal.

5. *Include Nonverbal Communications,* such as events, perks, and celebrations. Figure out how to "catch their attention."

6. *Get to Know the Media Professionals* who can support and protect you. Develop relationships with them, and through them with good media contacts— again, *before* a crisis.

Execute Effectively

1. *Be Clear about What Message You Want to Communicate, and Why.* This should form the basis of your communication strategy and actions. Providing information should never be its own goal. What do you want the target audience to do with the information: select a plan? evacuate the coast? understand their rights?

2. *Use Listening Tours and Other Broad-Based Information Collection Tools* to get a complete understanding of how internal and external constituencies feel about your issue or initiative and what they think should be done. Repeat back to them what you have heard—both during any initial face-to-face communication and as part of communicating your eventual decision—to assure them they have been heard. They will more easily accept your decisions, even if different from their recommendations, if they are convinced you took their perspectives seriously. Often it helps to explicitly explain the compromises you made between legitimate but competing stakeholders and program goals.

3. *Do a "Traceability Matrix."* This matrix is a table that records the input you received from each stakeholder group as you move forward collecting views on a program or policy. The matrix also should include stakeholders' principal positions, the things they consider essentials as opposed to "nice-to-haves," their communication desires, and their expectations for results.[41]

4. *Create a Communications Guide for Your Project.* The guide should include a section on the use of communication during crisis management. A great example

Communication, whether internal or external, is definitely influenced by personal style, and successful federal leaders have employed a vast and often entertaining variety of every kind. Each has strengths and weaknesses, and they can be combined creatively to help deliver your message effectively.

★ ★

★ The *preacher* steps up to the pulpit and delivers the sermon to the flock arrayed before him, revealing the "Lord's word" as taught and interpreted by him. The message is about what's _____ right and just. At the end there's a group "Amen."

★ The *cowboy* gets up on his high horse with spurs ready to assure he has command. He holds the rope just right as both horse and steer dart, seemingly uncontrollably, around the ring. _____ He has twenty seconds to rope, drop, tie, and raise his hands to show all that he has won.

★ The *strategist* has a plan, even if others don't yet see it. Information will be collected, goals refined, and stakeholders considered. Steps will be defined to achieve the goal; costs _____ will be nailed down; and, with a little luck, a good decision will be made. Her strategy will mobilize adherence to the plan.

★ The *politician* supports the new direction but needs some changes to sell it back home or to the opposition. She determines what deal can be made and who it must benefit. Agreement is reached in time to be interviewed on the evening news, with details to be _____ worked out later.

★ The *hammer* makes it clear that he knows what to do and that everyone should get in line and be rewarded for following his directions. Metrics and a performance dashboard will _____ help assure they hit their targets.

★ The *consigliere* is always the last to speak. Listening intensely, she finds a wise resolution that most can agree upon. If the plan is predictably imperfect, it can be adjusted later. _____ What's important is finding common ground and moving forward, together.

Six different styles, but by no means a comprehensive list. None is right or wrong. We've all seen examples and combinations, sometimes highly successful and sometimes appallingly damaging.

They vary along four basic dimensions: some rely more on collecting *inbound* information, others on communicating *outbound*. Some are more decisive in settling on the *best solutions*, others on using the *right processes*. Some are *pioneers* eagerly looking for new pathways and ideas, others more cautious *traditionalists*. Some get *ego* gratification from personal accomplishment, others partner with and *empower* colleagues. Depending upon the task and the circumstances, different combinations are called for. We need them all.

★ If you need someone to repeatedly remind the team, the agency, or the department of the "right" path and to provide inspired leadership in that direction, find a preacher. Strongly self-assured, preachers are usually more focused on outbound information than on listening; generally they are not the pioneers in new ways of thinking; you might want to add a strategist or a politician to the mix.

★ If you need someone to grab the reins with singular conviction and chase down a specific target without worrying much about process or conversation, find a cowboy. It can be good to team cowboys with consensus builders or politicians to help broaden the view and facilitate acceptance.

★ If you need someone to instill confidence in overcoming a complex challenge, find a strategist. They are good team builders and communicators, though they can sometimes be a tad indecisive. Pair a strategist with a hammer to rebut naysayers, or to refocus the strategist herself.

★ If you need someone to spur sensitive policy changes, including legislation, find a politician: not necessarily a literal "politician," but someone skilled in the art of working with and balancing among different stakeholders and constituencies. Many presidential appointees qualify for this duty, especially at the deputy secretary level. Whether it's a quiet compromise to fix a technical problem or boldly pushing a program through Congress, politicians know how to navigate the system.

★ If you need someone to focus on and fix a single recurring problem, find a hammer with knowledge or skill tuned to that problem. If it's a human resources problem, find an experienced HR system fixer; for financial management, use a CFO hammer. The danger is that, as the adage goes, to a hammer every problem looks like a nail, so it's important to pick the right hammer for each specific need. Hammers can team well with strategists to broaden the focus or with consiglieres to smooth the way to collective solutions.

★ If you need someone to build a team around a problem, find a consigliere. A consigliere listens without taking sides and can piece together a team's best ideas using a participatory process. The danger is that you may end up with a solution that is more popular than effective and the whole process may take a while. Success often depends heavily on whether the consigliere exercises enough personal or positional power to push people toward the "right" solution.

is the Substance Abuse and Mental Health Administration's primer published in the aftermath of 9/11, from which the "Top Ten Tips" are excerpted in Box 5.3.

5. *Use "Behavioral Insights" to Test and Refine the Most Effective Messaging*, and use feedback loops to determine whether your message is getting through accurately and having the desired impact.

Play a Smart Defense

1. *Be Forthcoming When Fielding Questions, Both Internal and External.* When you don't know the answer, say so; if possible, offer to try to find it out. Get bad news out as soon as possible, on your terms, preferably with a get-well plan or timeframe.

2. *Prepare a "Change History" for Every Communications Initiative.* Most initiatives have been tried before, in some form. Explicitly chronicling previous efforts will help you understand why they failed so you can figure out what to do differently.[42]

3. *Deploy Your <u>Best</u> Communicators Publicly in Crisis Periods.* Don't just throw your information officer or the program manager into the fray to absorb incoming volleys. Rehearse the message of candor and recovery.

★ **Box 5.3** Communicating in a Crisis: Risk Communication Guidelines for Public Officials

---

⌐ *Top Ten Tips for the Savvy Communicator*

1. First, do no harm. Your words have consequences—be sure they're the right ones.
2. Don't babble. Know what you want to say. Say it . . . then say it again.
3. If you don't know what you're talking about, stop talking.
4. Focus on informing people rather than impressing them. Use everyday language.
5. Never say anything you're not willing to see printed on tomorrow's front page.
6. Never lie. You won't get away with it.
7. Don't make promises you can't keep.
8. Don't use "no comment." You'll look like you have something to hide.
9. Don't get angry. When you argue with the media, you always lose . . . and lose publicly.
10. Don't speculate, guess, or assume. When you don't know something, say so.

Source: US Department of Health and Human Services Public Health Service, "Communicating in a Crisis: Risk Communication Guidelines for Public Officials," 2002.

4. *Never Lie or Guess.* In communications, your credibility is your most valuable asset. If you don't know something, say so.

Conclusion: Communications—Your Most Important Tool

You *have* to be able to communicate well to lead successfully in the federal sphere. This requires you to understand how to receive and send information effectively, who to engage, and which media to use. Create feedback loops to accurately assess whether your message is getting through and whether or not you need to make adjustments using behavioral insights and other strategies. Begin with a clear goal, using simple messaging targeted for specific audiences and the media that reach that audience. And handle the press in ways that serve *your* goals, not theirs, which is part art and part survival technique that requires patience and practice.

For all the attention paid to *how* to communicate well, however, having the right message is still all-important. Ronald Reagan, broadly dubbed "the great communicator," expressed this sentiment in a statement that demonstrates the use of imagery to reinforce the underlying message of mission and dedication:

> I wasn't a great communicator, but I communicated great things, and they didn't spring full blown from my brow; they came from the heart of a great nation, from our experience, our wisdom, and our belief in the principles that have guided us for two centuries.[43]

Now that's communication!

Notes

1. "Remarks by the President at Signing of the Medicare Prescription Drug, Improvement and Modernization Act of 2003" (Washington, DC) December 8, 2003.http://www.ssa.gov/history/gwbushstmts3.html#12082003.
2. William D. Eggers and John O'Leary, *If We Can Put a Man on the Moon: Getting Big Things Done in Government* (Boston: Harvard Business Press, 2009), 54–55.
3   Ibid., 53.
4. Joe Fahy, "Confusion, Frustration Abound as Drug Program Gets Under Way," *Pittsburgh Post-Gazette*, November 6, 2005, http://www.post-gazette.com/pg /05310/600360.stm.
5. Robert Pear, "Confusion Is Rife about Drug Plan as Sign-Up Nears," *New York*

Times, November 12, 2005, http://www.nytimes.com/2005/11/13/national/13drug.html?pagewanted=all&_r=0.

6. Julie Rovner, "Problems Plague Rollout of New Medicare Drug Plan," NPR's *Morning Edition*, January 11, 2006, http://www.npr.org/templates/story/story.php?storyId=5148817.

7. Ibid.

8. Pear, "Confusion Is Rife."

9. Kimberly Palmer, "Countdown," *Government Executive*, October 1, 2006, http://www.govexec.com/story_page_pf.cfm?articleeid=35238.

10. Peter B. Bach and Mark B. McClellan, "The First Months of the Prescription-Drug Benefit—A CMS Update," *New England Journal of Medicine* (2006): 2312–14, http://www.nejm.org/doi/full/10.1056/NEJMp068108.

11. Ceci Connolly and Mike Allen, "Medicare Drug Benefit May Cost More than Reported," *Washington Post*, February 9, 2005, A01.

12. Douglas Isbell and Don Savage, "Root Cause Analysis: Mars Climate Orbiter," NASA, Mars Climate Orbiter Failure Board, Report No. 99-134, November 10, 1999, http://schools.birdville.k12.tx.us/cms/lib2/TX01000797/Centricity/Domain/912/ChemLessons/Lessons/Measurement/measurement1.pdf.

13. Ibid.

14. Stephen R. Covey, *The Seven Habits of Highly Effective People Personal Workbook* (New York: Simon & Schuster, 2003).

15. Clay Johnson, in discussion with the author, December 2014.

16. Tracy Haugen, in discussion with the author, March 2015.

17. Tracy Haugen, in discussion with FAA, March 2015. See also Alison Dequette, "Fact Sheet—Commercial Aviation Safety Team," FAA, January 28, 2015, http://www.faa.gov/news/fact_sheets/news_story.cfm?newsid=18178.

18. Tracy Haugen discussion.

19. Ibid.

20. Dan Helfrich, in discussion with the author, January 2015.

21. Jonathan Weinstein and Timothy Jaques, *Achieving Project Management Success in the Federal Government* (Vienna, VA: Management Concepts, 2010).

22. Kathleen Hale, *How Information Matters: Networks and Public Policy Innovation* (Washington: Georgetown University Press, 2011), 5, 107–21.

23. US Government Accountability Office, "Physical Infrastructure: Crosscutting Issues Planning Conference Report," Report No. GOA-02-139 (2001), http://www.gao.gov/new.items/d02139.pdf.

24. Tracy Haugen discussion.

25. Ibid.

26. Ibid.

27. Jitinder Kohli, in discussion with the author, August 2014.

28. Ibid.

29. Sanaj Choudhury, "Behavioral Insights for Healthy Behavior," Federal News

Radio 1500, August 13, 2013, http://www.federalnewsradio.com/?sid=3422976&nid=1179.

30. Sarah Williamson, "Behavioral Insights for Transportation," Federal News Radio 1500, August 19, 2013, http://www.federalnewsradio.com/?sid=3422992&nid=1179.

31. Ibid.

32. Sylvia M. Burwell, Cecilia Munoz, John Holdren, and Alan Krueger, "Next Steps in the Evidence and Innovation Agenda," Office of Management and Budget, Report No. M-13-17 (July 26, 2013), https://www.whitehouse.gov/sites/default/files/omb/memoranda/2013/m-13-17.pdf.

33. Ibid., 7.

34. Jonathan Walters, in discussion with Diana Urban, November 2014.

35. Communications and Public Liaison and Office of the Chief Information Officer, "Social Media Policy," http://www.opm.gov/news/social-media-presence/social-media-policy.pdf.

36. Jane Norris, in discussion with the author, March 2015.

37. Ibid.

38. Ibid.

39. Ibid.

40. "Case Study: The Johnson & Johnson Tylenol Crisis," Crisis Communication Strategies, http://www.ou.edu/deptcomm/dodjcc/groups/02C2/Johnson%20&%20Johnson.htm.

41. Tracy Haugen discussion.

42. Ibid.

43. G. Edward DeSeve, *The Presidential Appointee's Handbook* (Washington, DC: Brookings Institution Press, 2009), 45–47.

CHAPTER 6

Getting Value from Contracting

In June 2011 a House subcommittee with jurisdiction over the US Department of Labor held a hearing called *Investigating Financial Mismanagement at the US Department of Labor*. While there were sharp and predictable disagreements along party lines over the apportionment of blame between the Bush and Obama administrations, there was no argument over Labor's ten-year effort to replace its financial systems: it was an expensive and embarrassing failure, capped by the agency's inability to obtain a clean audit on time for 2010 as required under the Chief Financial Officer's Act of 1990.[1]

The agency's initial $35 million contract for installing a new financial system, called "an unmitigated disaster" by one congressman, yielded a product that had to be shelved. The next effort, which cost $25 million, failed to complete software installation and training in time to prevent the audit embarrassment.[2] The GAO criticized this second contracting attempt for its poor needs assessment and inadequate testing.[3] Yet the initiative involved the implementation of industry-standard commercial software by a respected, experienced contractor. How could things have gone so wrong?

The program faced challenges from day one. The contract was awarded by the department's CFO, who lacks direct budget or acquisition authority, through a separate procurement organization within the department and under specifications approved by the CIO. Multiple DOL power centers and decision makers were involved. Agencies within DOL, such as Occupational Safety and Health, Mine Safety, Labor Statistics, Employee Benefits, and Veterans Employment all had to be convinced to pay for the "upgrade" and there was little agreement on the need for or terms of the new capabilities.

The DOL's CFO and contractor, in turn, often debated the contract's terms.[4] Three additional contractors were brought in: one as project manager and "enterprise architect"; a second to support strategy; and a third to validate contract progress and provide independent verification of results. Questions arose regarding how to keep the project on track with the baseline schedule and plan. The Office of Management and Budget got involved to monitor adherence to the terms of its "Exhibit 300" requirement, which contains DOL's justification, planning, and implementation commitments for the project. Without strong agreement on needs and priorities, in the end the funding dried up and the contract was phased out six years and $35 million later. A new Labor CFO began an entirely new procurement effort a few years after that.[5]

While the DOL example illustrates a specific procurement experience, the same broad acquisition strategy issues arise when major challenges are facing an agency. For example, in the 1990s the Internal Revenue Service faced some complex program challenges. Declining taxpayer compliance rates and lengthy response times to taxpayer queries were hurting the agency's image and prompting questions in Congress, which had just shut down the agency's contracts for system upgrades after almost a decade.[6] GAO put IRS's tax modernization effort on its high-risk list.

This was the picture facing Charles Rossotti when confirmed as IRS commissioner in 1997. With an antiquated IT system cracking at the seams, Rossotti knew he needed a replacement. One question was whether to simply refine the existing specifications and seek yet another technology contractor or take on more of the change internally and use separate contracts for specifically defined parts of the work. In other words, whether to contract *out* or contract *in*.

In theory, at least, there were advantages to be gained either way. A single contractor would give the agency a "single throat to choke." But by acting as its own general contractor, IRS would have full control of overall agency transformation needs to be met and would be able to directly coordinate the effort from inside by tightly defining specifications for specific contractors.

Given his background as the CEO of a major technology company, Rossotti was comfortable with the notion of handling transformation in house. He built an internal leadership team consisting of experienced IRS hands and new talent, and he set up a performance management system to monitor and report on progress.[7] He also turned to Mitre Corporation, a nonprofit federally funded research and development think tank, for help in defining specific needs in key areas. By the end of Rossotti's five-year term as IRS commissioner, the agency had well under way the system it had needed for a long time; new Internet-based services were being rolled out and taxpayer approval ratings—especially from electronic filers—were trending upward.[8]

The question of whether to contract "in" or "out" isn't really an either-or decision; it's more a matter of when and how. When should you call in an outside contractor? How will you align agency and contractor goals to ensure that each party is utterly clear about its respective requirements and responsibilities?

The Department of Defense, of course, has weathered comparable acquisition challenges, with tales of cost overruns and schedule slippages appearing in numerous press accounts over the years. GAO put DOD contract management on its "high risk" list in 1992, and despite some recent improvements, it's still on the list.[9]

But DOD has certainly seen many important successes as well. In 2012 the Defense Information Systems Agency (DISA) sought a contractor to modernize its financial system and bring it into compliance with audit requirements. DISA's one-year, $28 million fixed-price contract achieved what comparable enterprise-wide contracts had taken five years or more to accomplish, including the replacement of programs written in antiquated or obsolete programming languages.

It is important to note that the DISA comptroller had unquestioned accountability and authority that was supported by the DISA vice director and with DOD-wide assistance. The agency did its homework on the necessary business process changes, including intensely vetting requirements with users before specifying those requirements in the contract. It established a leadership team and executive steering committee that included client stakeholders and strong functional knowledge of DISA's business processes. Perhaps most important, DISA and the contractor held each other to a commercial mind-set, with speed to market and rapid decision making as top concerns. The new system went live in October 2013, barely a year from its inception, and it came in under budget.[10]

There are mission examples of DOD contracting successes as well. The Surface Ship Torpedo Defense (SSTD) system, a joint US-UK project in the late 1990s, involved the development of leading-edge sensors and countermeasure hardware that are towed behind surface ships to detect, track, and divert incoming torpedoes. Hosted in the United States, the project codified its requirements through early memorandums of understanding among all parties. Funding and management skills were integrated (e.g., a US program manager and a UK deputy). Government laboratories conducted the project trials, which gave credibility to the results. Two highly regarded defense contractors were selected to develop prototypes, with the production contract awarded to the better one based on test results. Rare levels of government-industry partnership grew over the duration of the program, allowing for a modular production that both vendors could support. The SSTD was deployed on schedule and on budget and hit its performance marks; today torpedo countermeasures are deployed on every US naval ship.[11]

In this chapter I discuss important considerations for when to contract, and on determining the right requirements, team-building, and contracting approaches—the major keys to success—when you do. I discuss the importance of differentiating consultants from contractors and of working closely with both, which is encouraged even in our rules-dominated federal system. And I describe how to set up value-based techniques for aligning contractor and government incentives. The chapter concludes with advice aimed directly at consultants and contractors on how to maximize the value we can provide to federal buyers.

Do You Need a Contract?

The starting point in determining if you need a contract, of course, should be in deciding how to strike a balance between in-house and contracted functions. If you need specialized skills or resources not currently available among in-house staffs, contracts can be essential and can provide great value. Broad transformations, like fixing DOL's financial management inadequacies or IRS's performance problems, usually require more comprehensive acquisition programs that define the roles that contractors will play and the needs they will meet. Situations calling for contractors generally fall into one of four categories:

- *commodities, hardware,* and *preconfigured solutions*
- *urgent surge* or *emergency needs*, as when the federal HealthCare.gov website went down and the administration had to quickly establish a beefed-up call center to implement the Affordable Care Act
- *recurring tasks,* such as payroll processing or IT support
- *specialized consulting skills* in areas such as technology, organizational effectiveness, or process reengineering, or for tasks such as case management, financial management, or human capital management.

Considerations for Leaders

Knowing which of these categories reflects your project needs is important because it will drive your all-important definition of success and will specify the value you expect to receive from the contractor you engage to help achieve it. Surge needs, for example, are almost always driven by a short-term event requiring fast action. In surge cases, ginning up new full-blown contracts usually doesn't make sense, and it's better to use existing arrangements that provide relevant experience and expertise (discussed later). Longer-term transformation projects or reforms, on the other hand, often require full competition for contract awards in order to ensure the best matches for complex needs.

Next, you must ask whether you are hiring an implementation contractor, a consultant, or both. If you need someone who can deliver defined products or services and your requirements are clear and specific, you need a contractor. If you need a different kind of help, the kind I call a "trusted business advisor," then you need a consultant. The trust part is important: it's a personal relationship that ultimately rests on your willingness to hear the unvarnished truth, including candid insights on your team's limitations. Such consultants may be hired as part of the service contract or may be hired separately—neither is a terribly expensive option, since typically you're looking for quality advice in relatively small doses.

Trusted advisors often can provide help without billing you separately for their time if you're buying broader services from their company. In other cases, federal or nonprofit entities such as Mitre or other federally funded research and development centers can provide specialized advice without going through a competitive procurement process.[12]

A third point is the need to be very clear about your requirements and the ways in which they are defined for potential contractors. What are your outcome goals for the program, and which outputs and outcomes will you assign to the contractor? Alignment between your goals and the contractor's requirements is a basic tenet, yes—and it's one of the most common differentiators between procurement successes and failures. Good contractors will happily work with you to define your ultimate goals and their part in reaching them; ambiguity about what's actually being purchased is probably the most common cause of friction with clients.

Next, be sure that any contractor you consider has the experience to do the job—and a temperament and style that fits well with your team. This may sound obvious, but federal buyers often get so lost in the maze of contracting rules they don't hire the company with the best fit for the job. Procurement rules are rightly intended to protect taxpayers from favoritism, excessive costs, and inadequate solutions. Unfortunately, in practice the rigidity of the system tends to add massive levels of complication and higher costs without actually ensuring the best solution at the best price.

And yet there are plenty of examples of successful federal acquisition programs and contracts, some huge and some mundane. What they all have in common is leadership and management focused on three basic factors: clearly defining the right **requirements** (specifications); creating the right **team** of members, from both the agency and the contractor, with the right skills to achieve the needed outcome(s); and choosing a **contracting approach** that defines and aligns incentives to create true value—that is, achieve desired outcomes that meet taxpayer needs at a reasonable price.

At GAO, for example, when the time came to replace the laptops of the agency's evaluators, we knew we were making a decision that would profoundly affect work quality and efficiency for a long time. The assistant comptroller general for operations (that was I) designated himself as the one who would approve the specs *and* pick the winner. This wasn't because I had any special knowledge of laptops nor any preconceived notion of what we should buy; I knew the experts could advise me on the technical points. No, it was because I understood this was a key leadership moment for GAO's operational capabilities. Our evaluators needed the best product available for them to do their work over long periods of time—and I believed we could get it.

Few outside the federal government understand the importance of the two roles of requirement approval and vendor selection. Since I knew the decision would determine how our evaluators and auditors worked for at least the forthcoming five years, "future proofing" by selecting very high-end requirements was important. A range of factors could be considered in this decision, cost being one of them. In my view, though, no factor was more important than getting the technology our people needed to do top-quality work, with the ability to upgrade as technology evolved.

Of course, we had the benefit of expert evaluators' reviews of bids, and their views of "best value" tradeoffs (what functionality might be worth added costs). We also allowed bidders to go beyond our basic tech request. This was an unusual move, but it turned out to be a wise one because some bidders proposed added capabilities that would be very useful even if not absolutely necessary. It also led to lively and productive discussions, both internally and with contractors, about value and price. In the end we got great equipment at an excellent price—and not from the lowest bidder, by the way. In procurement parlance, it was clearly the *best value* for the GAO and the taxpayer. But it's discouraging how often the protective, legalistic approach to acquisitions gets in the way of common sense and proved experience. It often requires leaders to buck the system to get the best value.

So how do you make a maximum impact in this environment? Much has been made of the complexity of federal acquisition regulations, and with good reason.

Many rules were established in response to single isolated events and then were baked into government-wide practice whether they made sense or not.

But "rules" sometimes turn out to be less than binding. Viewing every rule as written in stone is the habitual behavior of the overly cautious. As a leader, obviously you cannot ignore procurement policy outright. But it's always worth the effort to push back if needed, and even get an outside legal opinion when that can help increase flexibility. At all times leaders should provide cover and support for any staffer pursuing legitimately innovative ideas.

It is also important to have two teams working together—engaging early and often with senior contracting staffs internal to the government and with outside contractor staffs as well, before and after the contract decision, to make sure the program can pivot when outputs need to be rethought. Don't believe the myth that you have to stay "at arm's length" at any time other than in the formal bid stage, which is certainly made clear in OMB's 2011 "Myth-Busting" memo that encourages increased industry-federal communications (discussed later).

During the 2010 Decennial Census, for example, Commerce Secretary Carlos Gutierrez met with the CEO of Harris Corporation, the handheld technology vendor, to reaffirm that Harris was committed to the program's success. Census lead Arnold Jackson assisted Harris's senior vice president to change the composition of the contractor team itself and to ensure that the handhelds were ready for numerous support roles after they were abandoned for direct canvassing. It is hard to imagine that the successful census would have been possible without the federal and Harris teams working together.

Considerations for Managers

First and foremost, when working with contractors you have to **get the requirements right**, with careful attention to detail. Too many federal contracts are cut-and-paste jobs using language from related or prior procurements. There is often useful language to be borrowed from these models, of course, but it's no substitute for spending meaningful time with the ultimate end users to make sure project outputs will actually meet their needs.

You also have to **choose the right procurement vehicle**. Professionals know precisely what this means: a single-award, "full-and-open" competitive procurement process will yield different results than a multiple-award blanket purchase agreement or a task order in force under broad GSA supply schedules. Do you want one contractor or several? Fixed price, by the hour, cost-plus, or a mix? How do you build in incentives to ensure the contractor's deliverables actually meet your needs?

Remember that *you* must **build the team**. All successful procurement activities involve effective teamwork among government contracting, legal, and program management personnel. Yet this key element is often weak or missing. Keep the team focused on the goal: a quality outcome that provides the best value to taxpayers.

Get the Requirements Right

In a December 2014 interview, former Defense Department chief management officer Beth McGrath defined *clarity of purpose* as the most important element for successful acquisitions. Asked what could improve federal acquisitions, McGrath said, "It boils down to having strong leadership and accountability, alignment to mission, stakeholder engagement, and perhaps most important, clarity of purpose." For McGrath, this means interacting with critical stakeholders to define and ultimately agree on their actual needs, then ensuring that every business case *precisely* addresses those needs, and not with generalities such as "increase efficiency and save money." You need clear output and outcome expectations, with performance measures embedded in the contract. Specificity is the key. For example, are you looking to improve customer service through shorter response times, higher accuracy, or both?

Getting the "overseers" into the mix is a good idea as well. Make sure to involve the individuals or groups who will ultimately report on whether your program is meeting its milestones. McGrath says this is helpful in two ways: their insights can be incorporated into creating meaningful performance standards, and their involvement turns them into "enablers" who can help "by breaking down bureaucratic barriers that could have slowed down the program as it moved through the various government policies and procedures."[13]

Pick the Right Contract

Today, federal purchasers have access to a broad range of formats and vehicles, including both prequalified master contracts for hardware purchases as well as technical expertise. GSA's Professional Services Schedule, for example, provides easy access to a wide variety of business consulting, financial, and audit services, while its "IT Schedule 70" can be used for technology products and services. And then there are the very handy "government-wide acquisition contracts" (GWACs), which are fast and flexible contracts that can be used to purchase everything from complex defense hardware to statistical support and strategic planning services.

It is often better to use an established vehicle of this kind rather than a full, open procurement process that takes much more time and labor and is more vulnerable to legal challenges. These limit the competition to a select group of qualified suppliers for greater efficiency. And some schedules allow for a less formal process, like short written proposals, interviews, and oral presentations.

"Best-value" competitions have been popular for decades because they allow both the government and the contractor community to propose and consider a range of capabilities, usually at variations in cost, to create the "best value" for the taxpayer. It's frequently worthwhile for everyone, since it gives the buyer flexibility while allowing contractors to be more creative .

Recently, lowest price technically acceptable contracts (LPTAs) have gained some traction due to budget pressures. The LPTAs, however, are a slightly more sophisticated variant on the old low-bidder approach that fell out of favor years ago. Using an LPTA means that all bidders are assessed on a basic threshold of technical acceptability and, among those found even minimally acceptable, the lowest bid wins. This technique does simplify contractor selection when a specific minimal item or action is desired (like commodities or basic transport) and a need can be objectively defined; but the LPTA process limits the government's ability to buy better performance even at nominal added cost. It's a risky option, considering that a minimally "acceptable" proposal could come in pennies cheaper than a smarter, better one.[14]

Unsurprisingly, vendors and suppliers who compete mainly on price often prefer LPTA contracts; this is true of some purchasers as well, especially those who can specify with certainty the needed quality level and want to keep the procurement process judgment free while reducing workload and risk of protest.[15] Under best-value one can still pick the lowest bidder, but had the GAO project described above used an LPTA, it would have bought a much inferior product at a slightly lower cost.

Then there's the question of whether to use a firm fixed-price, a time-and-materials, or a cost-plus contract. When you can define your outputs with precision, a firm fixed-price contract makes sense. The contract covers what is specified, subject to "clarifications," at the price bid, regardless of the contractor's costs or most unanticipated complications. But it can be a challenge to work cooperatively with contractors if the fixed-price contract specs aren't clear or if unexpected events substantially change the work scope.

The time-and-materials contract is often called the "labor-hour" contract, since the labor portion of the contract is based on hours spent (hence the acronym LH/TM). An LH/TM contract offers a fixed hourly rate for each skill that is provided but allows the contractor and the buyer to work together more flexibly. This feature has great advantages, especially if you're unsure of just how much work needs to be done and you want to be able to expand or redirect resources. However, LH/TM contracts don't inherently address the issue of *outcome* or *output* achievement. The contract covers input measures—such as hours of work or cost of materials—rather than progress toward a desired outcome. While LH/TM contracts provide valuable flexibility and certain deliverables, they don't fully align outcome goals with contractor performance.

Cost-plus contracts also provide flexibility, since they commit to payment for actual contractor costs for whatever resources are used plus a prenegotiated fee. If requirements change, resources can be changed accordingly. Performance incentives can be built into the fee agreement based on almost anything, from judgmental evaluation ratings by the government, to progress on delivery dates, higher-quality deliverables, or cost savings. The challenges that accompany cost-plus contracts are similar to those associated with LH/TMs. Since payment is based mostly on inputs, a cost-plus contract doesn't easily reward outputs or outcomes even though adding incentive and award fee options can partially fill that void if designed well (this is one advantage over LH/TMs). Also, it can be more difficult to get highly skilled or specialized contractor talent using a cost-plus contract since negotiated fees are generally lower than the premiums such talent command under fixed-price or commercial arrangements.

The most appropriate contract in *any* situation is the one that establishes an agreed-on defined outcome and best aligns your interests and incentives with those of the implementing contractor. Sometimes fixed-price engagements framed around carefully defined requirements and best value can ensure this alignment. In other cases, hourly agreements or cost-plus arrangements can provide the flexibility needed to work together without the "dreaded" changes in scope.

Create the Right Acquisition Process

Successful contracts, like most other endeavors, involve key players sharing a common understanding of "success" and operating as a team, i.e., having aligned goals. It is also important that all players share in accountability; the credit or blame for an outcome must be borne by all. "Arms length" doesn't work any better in government contracting than it does in family life.

Here we can take a leaf from private-sector playbooks. Successful companies don't pay more than they should for products or services because they won't survive if they do. The higher the stakes, the more invested they are in partnering with reliable suppliers who share their goals and perform accordingly. When a particular contract is important to achieving ultimate success, quite often one will find very personal, board-level interactions to show that "we're in this together." Amazon likely would not pick a technology partner using an LPTA contract on thirty-day turnaround or put such contracts out for competitive bid every year.

Unfortunately, in our federal fishbowl it's hard to establish enduring relationships, especially since the contracting process is so rule-bound and litigious. There are contractors out there that challenge awards as a form of sport. It's a high-stakes sport indeed, especially in the area of defense, with its multiyear, multibillion-dollar contracts.

Considering the regulations, subordinate interpretations, agency-specific codicils, GAO opinions, and court rulings, federal procurement can seem completely inflexible and even hostile to common sense. In reality, there is enough flexibility to build and incentivize your teams, both internal and external, based on close working relationships and agreed-upon outcomes. It's essential to use that flexibility wisely.

Longtime consultant Kimberly McCabe has strong feelings on the topic. Having served a three-year tour of duty in US Army management, including as acting deputy for the Office of Business Transformation, to then become CEO of ASI Government, Inc. (arguably the most prominent provider of independent federal acquisition strategy support), McCabe believes that acquisitions must adopt *value* as the target and embrace *collaboration* as the way to get there:

> We have moved from the industrial age through the information age and are now in the collaboration age. So, the future of acquisition includes creating incentives and measures that ensure procurement and program personnel work as teams *horizontally* across organizational units, to collaborate on acquisitions—and succeed in delivering outcomes—together.[16]

Making the teams *jointly* accountable for value, that is, including program and contracting staff as well as contractors in the effort, can be the key to success, according to McCabe: "Leadership has to provide 'championship' and 'top cover' for those working horizontally in federal organizations that are generally organized vertically and functionally." Noting movement in this direction already under way in OMB policy and at the Department of Homeland Security, McCabe says that cross-functional training and actions to combine contracting and program personnel into a single organizational unit are examples of helping staffs overcome entrenched silos and focus on customer value.

Time and again, successes in the federal sphere demonstrate the importance of informal contractor-government interactions, market surveys, studies of previous efforts, and broad dialogue before locking in decisions. It's not only permitted but encouraged by the Office of Federal Procurement Policy.[17] Get program people, purchasers, and lawyers all involved. Educate them on what you want to accomplish and discuss your options with them *before* you issue a request for proposal or sign that contract.

The Defense Advanced Research Projects Agency (DARPA), the Pentagon's advanced research arm, regularly reaches out to potential partners through "industry days" designed to highlight its strategy and goals. The events help contractors fit their efforts and ideas to DARPA's interests and provide venues for them to have one-on-one meetings with key officials. Contractors also are encouraged to submit short summaries of their own ideas to gauge agency interest before committing the time and resources needed to draft a full proposal. If DARPA officials are interested, they will solicit an abstract with more detail and potentially request a full proposal thereafter.

To make the process even more collaborative, RFIs and draft RFPs now are often floated to a broad range of potential bidders, which lead to multiple opportunities for meaningful discussion of the contingencies that may arise as part of the project. Having lived on both sides of the government-contractor divide, I'm often astounded at how little common understanding the sides have regarding the risks and consequences of various steps.

Talking with contractors also allows you to see which ones fit best with you, strategically and culturally. Finding a contractor that shares your value system—and that you can work with—can be a godsend. One of the best ways to do this is through "orals," which requires a live presentation of the proposal, with questions and answers. The format provides an excellent opportunity to ensure the alignment of goals and operating styles. Federal agencies have personalities and so do companies. Every major procurement event (and most minor ones too) should include oral conversations with the potential contractor team—including the people who will actually be doing the work, not just those who are "selling" the service. Do you share a common vision and style? Can the contractor team explain how it will deal with the risks and pitfalls involved?

Contrary to popular belief, frank discussions with contractors can continue throughout the formal procurement process. Federal procurement experts confirm that discussions with program personnel can occur at specific points on specific issues throughout the process, so long as the proper protections to ensure fairness are in place.[18] The terms and rules vary depending upon whether a formal solicitation has been issued, and what type that solicitation is. But OMB's Office of Federal Procurement Policy (OFPP) clearly endorses the validity and value of enhanced communication in its 2011 memorandum "'Myth-Busting': Addressing Misconceptions to Improve Communication with Industry during the Acquisition Process."[19] Know that you will get pushback about this. The prevailing wisdom calls for *arms-length* and *quiet periods*, especially among those who define "success" as avoiding a protest or demand for explanation. It might be smart to keep a copy of the OFPP memo in your hip pocket.

To achieve a successful procurement, a contracting officer should be involved with your program team throughout the acquisition program to assure that he or she is tuned into the economic and competitive environment associated with the contract, understands what's important to include in the buyer requirements and contract terms, and is able to balance technical issues with price, given the goals.

In recent years the responsibility for key tradeoff decisions has tended to shift from program leaders to contracting officials, probably due to general financial pressures. This can create a misalignment of program needs and personal incentives. Good contracting personnel are dedicated to ensuring the integrity and cost effectiveness of the decision. Program personnel share that incentive, too, but they also have a longer-term interest in the actual program *outcome*, so they are best positioned to make the call on ultimate value-cost tradeoffs.

Aligning Contractor and Government Goals

Good contracts provide the right incentives to ensure that both parties understand how the buyer defines "value" and how they will share the downside pains and upside rewards of the results. Finding the right risk-sharing balance is important. Ensuring that contractors have enough "skin in the game" enhances performance; too much risk discourages contractor participation, reduces competition, and sometimes leaves government "holding the bag" when contractors fail.

Many federal contracting schemes are allowed to include award and incentive fees for performance or cost savings. Yet many (perhaps most) federal contracts don't use them. Awards and incentives should relate to more than financial performance, perhaps covering faster delivery, shorter downtimes, higher customer-satisfaction ratings, etc. It's probably unwise to offer incentives that bend performance out of predictable pathways—such as a contract that significantly rewards speed over quality, for instance. But some form of an incentive structure should usually be in play. At a minimum, incentives force both the government and contractor personnel to think through what *really* matters among the multiple performance goals—rather than simply listing deliverables—and they must agree, before signing on, that both sides will do what it takes to reach them.

Value-Based Arrangements

In the private sector, common practice increasingly links contractor payment with client success. One major consulting firm, for example, has more than $1 billion in commercial contracts that depend on specific outcomes for the client. Commercial enterprises even provide capital in value-based arrangements, "fronting" the cost of the work in return for a share of savings or revenues realized or for payments based heavily upon specific outcomes.

According to OFPP, such arrangements can be made by federal entities, such as "share in savings" guidelines or under the Sustainable Energy Improvement statutes.[20] Yet relatively little use has been made of value-based arrangements in federal contracts. This is ironic, to say the least, in an era of less discretionary funding availability. In other nations, such as the United Kingdom, public-private partnerships (PPPs) are much more commonly found. In the United States there's more experimentation with PPPs at the state level.[21]

The principal motivation for more aggressively moving in this direction, however, goes well beyond the opportunity for private funding. Far more important is a factor often overlooked in the debate over PPPs: the *transformative* nature of value-based agreements. "No value, no pay" gets a contractor's attention because it is focused on *real* goal alignment, and *shared* risk. Indeed, specialists in these types of contracts point out that the approach alters the entire nature of the upfront discussion. The focus changes from specific actions and deliverables to *shared results*.

This change in focus can have an important effect on the buyer as well. To create a value-based contract you have to be very clear about what outcomes you want and what "value" the deliverables are intended to provide. For example, if an agency wants a new building, beyond the bricks and mortar what will provide "real value" to the agency and taxpayers? Is it energy efficiency? A worker-friendly environment? An attractive yet durable place to do business?

Value-based arrangements can be used for service purchases as well. In creating a shared-results tax collection system, for example, some government agencies have implemented arrangements that essentially use contractor funding to create an automated tax collection system, wherein the contractor's payments are based upon increased tax revenue recoveries and improved satisfaction from taxpayers.[22]

In the tax world this isn't as rare as one might guess. For example, some years back Wisconsin was having a terrible time collecting quarterly sales tax payments from small businesses. Compliance rates were so dismal that smart people in the Revenue Department knew the low level couldn't be attributed to sheer criminality alone. It had to be something else. They took a closer look at the incentive system for submitting those taxes and found it almost impossible to navigate. A redesigned performance-incentive collection process made receipts soar.[23]

Nobody understands this dynamic better than contractors; good ones will happily work for a share in the returns—and even provide some of the funding for the work if the incentive is worthwhile.

Before leaving the subject of value-based contracts, it should be emphasized that existing federal vehicles can be used to transform even pedestrian orders into value-based ones. For example, fixed-price award-fee arrangements can be configured into value-based contracts by inviting bidders to reduce the fixed-price component of the contract in return for enhanced payments for high performance. If the recovery on the fixed-price payment is only 25 percent of the actual value, for instance, and the remaining 75 percent is released upon acceptance of "value" as defined, it's a value-based arrangement!

Alignment with a contractor shouldn't end when the award is made. In many ways, it's just the beginning. The relationship must be maintained to ensure that you communicate as the project progresses and can make midstream adjustments to avoid drift in expectations.

Defining Value

It can be easy to confuse high cost with quality—but doing so is a mistake. *Quality* and *value* should be defined in terms of need. Sometimes you need quantities of low-cost labor to record data or deal with surge capacity; you want reliable help that matches your "value" proposition. In the commercial world, high-value and low-cost providers are renowned because of their responsiveness to their customers' need for low-priced, easily accessible merchandise or food (think K-Mart, McDonald's, or Sam's Club). Mercedes Benz and Victoria's Secret define value differently. What do you *really* need and how will you communicate that to the contractor?

Performance Work Statements

Rather than an old-fashioned statement of work to define the activities and deliverables sought, many agencies have moved to *performance work statements*, a more results-oriented vehicle that incorporates expectations in terms of outputs and outcomes. Such statements may include cost goals, though performance standards are more often the focus, such as how many times a call center phone will ring before being answered or how long a veteran must wait to receive medical care.

Note that these work statements define *quality*. It is simple enough to beef up staff during a short-term crunch, but if that temporary help isn't actually helping—that is, if they aren't giving accurate responses to ACA hotline calls, for instance—you're worse off. Some measure of *quantity* also should be considered. For example, defining the frequency and length of acceptable downtimes can be just as important as defining the proportion of correct replies.

Profiles in Contracting

Contractor responsiveness is critical to achieving positive results. This is why successful projects typically feature a strong working relationship between buyer and contractor. Asked to explain why she stayed with a particular contractor in a major procurement situation experiencing problems, then–Health and Human Services assistant secretary Janet Hale didn't miss a beat: "Every time I had a problem, Robert [the contractor's CEO] was there into the night working with me on the resolution."

Former Labor CFO Sam Mok lists "picking the right contractor that truly understands the customer's needs and priorities" as the top determinant of success.[24] Mok says he never actually had confidence the contractor would correct problems or complications during one of DOL's financial system difficulties; the contractor wanted to talk about specific contract terms, not about how to deal with the CFO's needs. "Contractors tend to focus on what they are good at," he notes, "not always on how best to solve your problem." No common understanding of value there.

Defining requirements makes a big difference. Charles Rossotti's use of internal teams to clearly define IRS's needs allowed the agency to be specific in seeking outside help. This was a very different approach than the broad requirements set forth in the agency's earlier, ill-fated modernization effort, or in the DOL financial management procurements. Contracts cannot ensure success if they fail to include a commonly understood definition of the requirements and value desired, if they are not based on a relationship of earned trust, and if they do not display a sincere dedication on the part of both sides to getting the job done together and well. In *The Responsible Contract Manager*, Steven Cohen and William Eimicke provide more detail on knowing when to contract and how to do it well, including approaches to addressing twenty common public-sector contracting problems. [25]

Considerations for Contractors and Consultants

Prospective contractors and consultants tend to be most concerned with buyers' *stated* needs—what's explicitly and formally cited in a solicitation. To be sure, it is important that a contractor sit down with the agency staffs to pinpoint what they say they need and what the work requires, rather than just reading and responding to an RFP. But there are almost always other needs government officials know of but haven't stated, either because they don't see these added needs as related to the scope of work or they are sensitive or controversial. These comprise a second category of needs: *unstated*. Perhaps I am uncomfortable telling you the secretary is only going to be on the job another four months, for example, and so getting something done in that timeframe is more important than getting a better result in a year.

The third and most challenging to respond to category of needs is the *unknown*: important requirements the buyer isn't aware of—yet. These can often lead to failure, even if the deliverables arrive on time. For example, a study considering how to eliminate some field offices might be technically competent using a workflow analysis. But closing field offices in the states or districts of particularly powerful legislators is often politically infeasible. The proposed solution can be analytically correct but unusable. Good deliverable; disappointing results.

A good contractor or consultant understands this "needs" dynamic—the interplay between *stated, unstated, and unknown needs*—and so should push buyers to ask themselves tough questions, given the potential for adding value. Often clients and vendors love a refreshing bit of probing. At minimum, urging an in-depth dialogue about needs will help a contractor or consultant stand out from the competition and increases the likelihood of a successful result.

Another way to stand out from the crowd is to make a "grand gesture"—fixing a problem or otherwise coming to the rescue without added charges, as a show of commitment. In the DOL case described above, a grand gesture might have been for the original contractor to go the extra mile to get the job done—without a dreaded "change-in-scope."

During a project to develop an executive dashboard at DOL, something I was involved in as a consultant many years ago, client expectations changed almost weekly without accompanying contract changes, something I failed to pick up on. The deliverable was disappointing to the client and he declined to pay for the work. Instead of protesting to the contract office, which might have won the battle (and the payment) but lost the longer-term relationship with DOL, we said, "Don't pay us. Let us redo this according to what you and we are now agreeing to—at our added cost." The goodwill that created won us other work, and the revised deliverable obtained full compensation. In the long run we retained a client (and friend) and the "investment" paid off well.

Key Takeaways

Clearly the federal acquisition and contracting system is more cumbersome than a commercial counterpart. Some of that is understandable; after all, we are spending taxpayer money. But examples of inefficiency and missed goals are plentiful. Following are a few suggestions for things that can be done to improve the likelihood of success in an acquisition program or specific contracting effort.

Create Your Offense

1. *Include and Involve Your Stakeholders.* Your acquisition strategy should involve multiple interactions with key users, managers, department executives, funders, and political interests. Don't forget the contractor community, which can offer insights based on their years of experience.

Market research and in-depth discussions with potential providers about their solutions and ideas are very helpful and provide the platform for learning who has the experience, capabilities, and products to meet your needs reliably, who can slash risk, and who can potentially save time and costs.

It's helpful to use such interactions to vet potential providers' approaches or define proofs of concept. This brings up new ideas and highlights the most innovative companies. For large acquisitions, consider using a specialized procurement advisor or company to conduct deep dives that compare supplier capabilities and help you identify the right procurement approach to balance risks and results. Make sure the discussions are based on drafts actually written for *this* procurement—not for "what we used the last time" or "what two other departments used." It's fine to *start* with models, but no two projects involve the same value tradeoffs.

Finally, differentiate between the "nice-to-haves" and the "must-haves." Doing so is essential to avoid buying more than you need, on the one hand, or encountering expensive changes in scope because you omitted something users must have, on the other.

2. *Use an Explicit Value Strategy.* Are you defining value in terms of outputs and outcomes that respond to user needs, or are you using good old-fashioned deliverables, like "complete pilot test by June 30"? Will value be a combination of quantitative and qualitative judgments, or are your requirements sufficiently precise to allow you to safely go with a low-bidder strategy?

Carefully assess who should make the ultimate decision on the tradeoffs between price and technical scores—including how each bidder will be ranked based upon ability, proposed solution, qualifications, quality of personnel, and risk, compared to price. This person, sometimes called the source selection official, ultimately decides whether to pay more for a better solution or to choose a lower-cost option that might save taxpayer money. There's no universally correct tradeoff formula; it depends on the "value choice" for your procurement, which is why you must be sure to designate a source selection official who understands the price-value program tradeoff desired by leadership.

Value-based contracts can help you align contractor performance with agreed-upon value. Whether you choose a *pay-for-performance* model, by which the contractor's payment is based upon goal achievement, or a *share-in-savings* model, by which the vendor is paid from an agreed-upon share of savings resulting from the project, a value-based arrangement can substantially improve value. Some GSA supply schedules now feature value-based billing, and some GWACs are being amended to include share-in-savings as well.[26]

Many agency contracting officers are unfamiliar with these models, however, so some education or training may be needed. The CFO can be a key leader and ally here, since these approaches can produce significant positive fiscal impacts.

3. *Build the Right Team with the Right Incentives.* For this, you need both an institutional strategy and a team-building approach. At the institutional level, you have to set the right tone at the top. Have you made it clear that meeting mission goals is *everyone's* shared responsibility, and that contracting, program, finance, legal, etc., *must* work together to provide the best result for the taxpayers?

My responsibilities at GAO included oversight of contracting personnel. Although I pushed them to work flexibly, I was also keenly aware of how it would look were GAO to cut contract corners or fail to adequately supervise procurements. "You have a tough job," I told them. "Your job is to help our divisions get their needs met and *also* to protect the organization from any impropriety. Be flexible and innovative wherever you can, using legal counsel to help support new approaches. I will provide top cover and rewards for those who can do that." One should never say, "No, you can't do that," without also following up with "but let me help you figure out a legitimate way to achieve the goals."

Aligning the goals and even job descriptions of contracting and program specialists is far more effective than leaving them in their respective silos. On individual procurements or acquisition programs, according to Beth McGrath, performance-based awards can include federal personnel. During House testimony McGrath has recommended the creation of a common incentive structure for program, procurement, and end-user personnel to foster teamwork and shared accountability.[27] Congressman Tom Davis, whose responsibility included oversight of federal acquisition when he served as chairman of the US House of Representatives Oversight and Government Reform Committee, agrees. Creating team incentives that are "tied to longer-term outputs and outcomes, not short-term cost avoidance—that's the best deal for the federal taxpayer," Davis notes.

4. *Cultivate and Support Innovative Customer Service.* Census deputy director Nancy Potok identifies this as one of the principal strategies supporting the bureau's mission:

> I look to the personnel of the acquisition shop to find the interesting and creative ways to help our Census managers and personnel succeed, including using all the vehicles that are out there in the federal space. Be knowledgeable, I tell them, particularly about learning the law and the regulations, but have an open mind to new ways of doing things. And build trusted advisor relationships with our customers.[28]

Specialized "centers of excellence" are one way to concentrate the energy of highly innovative personnel on challenges and solutions that can be used across an entire agency. Such centers also can support training and provide mentorship for high-priority acquisitions. (Chapter 8, on innovation, explores strategies for achieving this within the bureaucracy.)

Execute Effectively

1. *If Possible, Use an Existing Contract Vehicle*. This could be a GSA schedule, a GWAC, or a blanket-purchase agreement (BPA) that names multiple prequalified suppliers that can provide a range of services at negotiated rates. Time to decision is reduced dramatically and protests are generally limited with these preapproved contracts. In some cases decisions can be completed within weeks and/ or made with limited or no competition, making these especially useful for surge requirements or to satisfy short-term limited goals.

Specific contractors that you may want to consider—perhaps based upon prior experience—may not be on the preapproved list. *Ask* them. You can also access GSA schedules (and some GWACs) on GSA's website, including the list of contractors for each, and their rates.[29]

2. *Decide Which type of Contract to Use*. Weigh this carefully. *Cost-plus* contracts generally will be cheapest but will commit you to paying actual contractor costs plus a modest fee (generally 6 to 8 percent of the overall cost). Added fee incentives are usually too small or not sufficiently targeted to overcome performance or skill deficiencies in any but the largest programs. LH/TM contracts, which use different rates for specific labor categories and estimate the hours needed for various tasks, tend to be more expensive than cost-plus contracts because the rates are more market-based. These are generally best used to cover professional services because they offer access to higher-skilled talent (at a premium) without locking you into a rigid scope of work. The "unit" of delivery for LH/TM contracts is an hour worked.

If you know what you need and can clearly define desired quality and quantity, a *fixed price* contract is the way to go. This can be a wise choice for big projects, such as erecting a new building or bridge, or for small jobs, such as call-center support with predefined levels of response time, accuracy, and volume. The contract puts the onus on the contractor to get the work done at the agreed price and makes contractor selection more straightforward as well. The risk, of course, is that if your needs or specifications are not adequately defined in the contract, or if they change, you will encounter the dreaded "change in scope" that doggedly attends so many fixed-price contracts.

The point here is that each type of contract has its advantages and disadvantages, so it's important to determine which fits best with the desired level of flexibility and certainty.

3. *Use the Tools Built into the Rules.* Among the many available for assessing and motivating each competing contractor, four tools should almost always be part of your repertoire: oral presentations, final proposal revisions, incentive structure, and separate risk ratings.

Oral presentations. These don't cost much and are worth the minimal added time to get bidders (whether all or just the finalists) to talk to you face-to-face. Demand the *actual* delivery team, and use the opportunity to see whether they're culturally suited to your organization. For example, do they present their approach(es) in terms of *your* priorities and needs rather than their own? You can also test a contractor's problem-solving skills up close and personal. Hiring a contractor should be a full-contact sport.

Final proposal revisions (formerly known to insiders as *"best and final offers"*). Even if the lowest qualified bidder is quite desirable, it is generally wise to do a "best and final" solicitation, which in essence gives the contractor one more shot at improving bid specs or lowering costs. The one caveat: if you want to select the *current* low bidder and another's bid is close to the offered price, don't play around with a final proposal revision, just go ahead and award the contract.

Incentive structure. Of utmost importance is clarity on outcomes. Are you seeking customer responsiveness? A new technical ability? Is it cost that's most important? Some contract approaches, especially cost-plus-award-fee, cost-plus-incentive-fee, and fixed-price, can include incentives. But because these require a little extra work, many federal agencies and departments avoid using them. This is unfortunate, because only a small share of a contractor's total fee represents actual profit and you can use a relatively small increase in payment to get more of what you want, such as greater speed or accuracy at a call center.

Recently, some federal agencies have "bracketed" the price using an RFP with a preset range of payments, such as: "The agency plans to spend between $1.3 and 1.5 million." Releasing this kind of information provides contractors with a dramatic incentive to focus on performance in your desired price range. The key to bracketing is the need to have a pretty good idea of the likely cost of what you want so that you don't end up with a crazy lowball bid or a reckless actual overpayment.

Separate risk ratings. Many agencies have adopted a two-rating approach, which allows them to evaluate both the *quality* of the proposed solution or contractor and the *risk* each presents based upon the potential for failure. You must be able to balance these tradeoffs. One solution, for example, might fit the quality bill perfectly but might be more likely to encounter performance or cost problems. You should be able to compare this to another less-attractive or lower-quality solution that can be deployed with less risk of missing technical requirements or agreed timeframes. There's no magic formula for balancing these tradeoffs; it boils down to what best fits your need at the price and risk you can afford.

An additional tool to consider is *multiple award contracts*. If you have multiple related projects on the near horizon, it may make sense to recruit and prequalify a stable of contractors and then ask them to bid individually on separate tasks as needs arise. You can write the contract so tasks are awarded to prequalified contract holders without competition, based on availability and specialty; or have them compete among all prequalifieds to push up quality and drive down cost. Some flexibility to add vendors can be worthwhile, as new capabilities are needed or new contractors come to your attention.

4. *Use an "Iterative Build" approach.* Developing and maintaining long-term partnerships is important, but breaking deliverables into short-term achievements, with appropriate pivots and opt-out potential, keeps everyone on their toes and provides opportunities to adjust strategy and scope. McGrath notes that while at the DOD, one of her chief goals "was achieving initial operational capability at twelve to eighteen months, compared to the historical norm of hitting that milestone in four to five years." Lower initial functionality is okay because you can build upon that basic capability once it's established.

Play a Smart Defense

1. *Follow the Actual Laws and Rules—Not Misperceptions of Them.* When I was at the Social Security Administration's Office of Family Assistance, charged with administering the $14 billion cash welfare program, I encountered massive resistance to changing virtually any eligibility requirement, policy, or procedure. Perceptions of fairness and what flexibility could be granted to the states and localities that administer the program were often based upon historically accepted practices, not statutory requirements. It was essential to understand the actual written rule behind each embedded policy and, when necessary, the statute underpinning it. Many practices were seldom required by law, and most policies or

rules could be revised or reinterpreted using the flexibility legally granted to administrators.

Keep this in mind when you're looking for new or different approaches to procurement. Can the contracting officer and program manager share authority? Can you talk to the contractor directly to clarify or alter expectations? Can you ask for a short slide presentation and then go right to orals? Can you terminate a contract rapidly and go back to the list of bidders to pick a different one if things don't start out well? The ability to challenge long-standing procurement interpretations may require legal support to provide a careful review of prior GAO and court interpretations. But such challenges can pay off handsomely if the result is that you get the best value for taxpayers. Sometimes outside legal advice can provide an even broader view of the possibilities.

2. *Consider Using a Second Contractor for Technical or Performance Guidance or Monitoring.* A second contractor can be particularly useful when the technical judgments involved are beyond your team's knowledge, skills, or abilities. As noted above, Mitre Corp. provided the IRS with important technical support in managing its major contractor. During technology implementations, an independent verification and validation (IV&V) contractor can be useful, but you have to be careful to pick one with the right skills and take care not to lose agency visibility or control. Also, be ready for some discord: the verification contractor, after all, has an incentive to find problems the prime contractor doesn't see or won't acknowledge. Managed correctly, however, these disagreements can be extremely helpful in being able to see whether a program is meeting its goals.

3. *Head Off Problems Before They Occur.* Earlier I noted that IT failures are generally management failures. Similarly, mismanagement or nonmanagement of a contractor's performance can cause problems as well. Getting draft versions of deliverables in time to allow for substantive feedback is an important way to head off such problems. Demanding that schedule and quality milestones be met *before* further work proceeds is also smart.

4. *Squeak When You Need More Grease.* Don't be shy about reaching into the contractor's bureaucracy. Nothing will get the attention of a consultant more rapidly than a note from the boss saying the chief procurement officer at Agency X called to "ask for better help"; it may sting, but it can actually help in getting more or better resources. Remember that your contractor or consultant is competing within her own company for resources. If you are unable to make progress with your current team, it's probably time to go up the chain of command.

Of course, such intervention is a lot easier if the contractor and federal leadership teams have met early and often to cement their common vision of success. Either side can initiate such a "success summit," thereby facilitating joint problem resolution down the road. In our case study on the Decennial Census, Commerce Secretary Gutierrez's meeting with the Harris CEO demonstrated the wisdom and effectiveness of this type of early maneuver.

5. *Sometimes You Need to Let the Lawyers Talk*. Lawyer-to-lawyer conversations can be valuable if significant contract or performance disagreements arise, even during the procurement process. While I'm certainly not recommending bringing lawyers into management processes or even into early disputes as a first step, I've seen numerous problems worked out by attorneys "conferring" on a problem and determining the actions both sides could take to resolve it—and head off formal confrontation.

Even in competitive procurements, counsels know when and how they can talk without encountering anticompetitive practices or rules violations. Sometimes the answer may be "I can't talk to you about that," but your message nevertheless has been communicated to the other side. This wouldn't be part of the normal communication process, of course, and is best reserved for circumstances where you believe "wisdom" would prevail in interpreting rules or in resolving disagreements in ways that benefit both sides.

Conclusion

Ultimately the most important thing in working with contractors or consultants is to ensure that the signed contract's requirements are written to meet the objectives of the program. It is also important to create the right teams, including program, contract, and legal personnel, and with the contractor community. Make sure the type of contract or vehicle aligns the contractor's incentives and rewards with your goals. If possible, find a way to use a value-based contract so that the contractor shares in your success or failure. And don't forget to include your own personnel in this value-based reward and accountability structure. The federal sphere is perhaps the world's most difficult contracting environment. The stakes are high and the complications many. But experts in the field can provide the *how*, once you have defined *what* you want to accomplish.

Notes

1. Robert Andrews, in testimony to the House Subcommittee on Health, Employment, Labor, and Pensions (June 2011), http://www.gpo.gov/fdsys/pkg/CHRG-112hhrg66564/html/CHRG-112hhrg66564.htm.

2. Ibid.

3. David Perera, "Labor FCFMS Deployment Flawed, Says GAO," *FierceGovernmentIT* (March 2011); US Government Accountability Office, "Department of Labor: Further Management Improvements Needed to Address Information Technology and Financial Controls," Report No. GAO-11-157 (March 2011), http://www.gao .gov/assets/320/316654.pdf.

4. Sam Mok, in discussion with the author, June 2015.

5. Robert Andrews, in testimony to the House Subcommittee on Health, Employment, Labor, and Pensions (June 2011), http://www.gpo.gov/fdsys/pkg/CHRG -112hhrg66564/html/CHRG-112hhrg66564.htm.

6. US General Accounting Office, "Tax System Modernization: IRS' Challenge for the Twenty-First Century," Report No. GAO/IMTEC-90-13 (February 1990), 2, http://www.gao.gov/assets/220/212210.pdf.

7. "How We Transformed the IRS," interview with Charles Rossotti, Harvard Business School (March 2005), http://hbswk.hbs.edu/archive/4674.html.

8. Charles O. Rossotti, *Many Happy Returns: One Man's Quest to Turn Around the Most Unpopular Organization in America* (Cambridge: Harvard Business School Press, 2005), 289.

9. Timothy DiNapoli, "High-Risk Series: An Update," Government Accountability Office, Report No. GAO-15-290 (February 2015), 287,http://www.gao.gov/assets /670/668415.pdf.

10. Beth McGrath, in discussion with the author, May 2015; David Dortenzo, email message to the author, May 2015.

11. McGrath discussion; Beth McGrath, in discussion with Merv Leavitt, May 2015.

12. "Master Government List of Federally Funded R&D Centers," National Science Foundation, May 2014, http://www.nsf.gov/statistics/ffrdclist/; "Federally Funded Research and Development Centers (FFRDC)," Defense Acquisition University, March 2011, https://dap.dau.mil/acquipedia/Pages/ArticleDetails.aspx ?aid=5e3079b8-44f2-43df-a0e7-9f379e8c48ed.

13. Beth McGrath, "Federal CFO: Improving Savings and Outcomes in Acquisition Programs," *CFO Journal, From the Wall Street Journal*, December 2014, 2.

14. Frank Kendall, *Testimony before the Senate Committee on Armed Services*, April 30, 2014, 6, http://www.armed-services.senate.gov/imo/media/doc/Kendall_04-30 -14.pdf.

15. William Welsh, "LPTA Contracts Stifle Government Innovation," *InformationWeek: Government* (October 2013), http://www.informationweek.com /government/leadership/lpta-contracts-stifle-government-innovation/d/d-id /1112071.

16. Kimberly McCabe, currently president and CEO of Value Storm Growth Partners, in discussions with the author, January 2015.

17. US General Services Administration, Department of Defense, and National Aeronautics and Space Administration, "Federal Acquisition Regulations Part 15— Contracting by Negotiation, Subpart 15.2- Solicitation and Receipt of Proposals

and Information," March 2005, https://www.acquisition.gov/sites/default/files /current/far/html/Subpart%2015_2.html.

18. Ibid.

19. Daniel Gordon, "'Myth Busting': Addressing Misconceptions to Improve Communication with Industry during the Acquisition Process," memo in *Office of Federal Procurement Policy (OFPP)* (February 2011).

20. US Office of Federal Procurement Policy, Office of Management and Budget, and Executive Office of the President, "A Guide to Best Practices for Performance-Based Service Contracting," October 1998, https://www.whitehouse.gov/sites /default/files/omb/procurement/pbsa/guide_pbsc.html.

21 Jessica Digiambattista Peters, "Maximizing State Benefits from Public-Private Partnerships," California's Legislature Nonpartisan Fiscal Advisor, Legislative Analyst's Office, November 2012, http://www.lao.ca.gov/reports/2012/trns /partnerships/P3_110712.aspx; Jitinder Kohli, in discussion with the author, August 2014.

22. Accenture, "District of Columbia Office of Tax and Revenue Wins National Award for Outstanding Technology Application Developed with Assistance from Accenture" (May 2002), http://newsroom.accenture.com/article_display.cfm ?article_id=3897.

23. Wisconsin Department of Revenue, "Managing for Performance Conference," *Governing Magazine* (2002).

24. Mok discussion.

25. Steven Cohen and William Eimicke, *The Responsible Contract Manager; Protecting the Public Interest in an Outsourced World* (Washington: Georgetown University Press, 2008), 91–103, 125–43.

26. US Office of Personnel Management, "Training and Management Assistance Program" (June 2015), https://www.opm.gov/services-for-agencies/training-and -management-assistance-program/.

27. Beth McGrath, "Defense Acquisition Reform: Where Do We Go from Here? A Compendium of Views by Leading Experts," *US Senate, Permanent Subcommittee on Investigations, Committee on Homeland Security and Government Affairs*, October 2014, 124.

28. Nancy Potok, in discussion with the author, November 2014.

29. US General Services Administration, "GSA eLibrary," April 2015, www.gsa.gov /elibrary.

CHAPTER 7

Risk-Based Decision Making

On January 28, 1986, Americans were horrified as they watched the space shuttle *Challenger* explode within 73 seconds after launch, killing all on board and eventually raising profound questions about NASA's process for decision making. The cause was the failure of a rubber O-ring, due to the unusually cold temperatures at the Florida launch site that day. Although the recognition that space exploration carries risks was certainly not new to NASA's programs, three years of design and decision-making reforms followed before any shuttles were allowed to fly again.[1] Yet on February 1, 2003, another disaster occurred. The shuttle *Columbia* disintegrated, this time upon reentry, due to damage to its heat shields caused by foam pieces being dislodged at launch.[2]

In both cases, the tragedies had causes that NASA had *already* identified and studied. NASA had recovered singed and burnt O-rings many times before the 1986 *Challenger* launch, and it also knew the rings became more brittle in colder temperatures. Dislodged foam pieces had been noted as a risk long before *Columbia's* last flight. Yet NASA had been regarded as one of the top risk-management enterprises in the federal government and a learning organization.[3] What happened? Are there lessons *everyone* can learn from these events?

Much has been written about enterprise risk management (ERM), with examples from NASA and other federal organizations having high-risk, high-visibility missions. Risk is inherent in the private sector, too, though more commonly in economic rather than life-threatening terms. Risk is everywhere, and handling it is a key determinant of success—and indeed of survival.

The literature on risk management tends to focus on organizational principles and frameworks. I here offer a more proactive perspective on risk: serving the public well *requires* that we understand risks of all sorts and that we take intelligent risks. Informed *risk-based decision making* is essential to achieving success in today's rapidly changing world. If we forsake the sorts of innovations that involve some inherent risk, stakeholders' constantly rising expectations will cause government satisfaction ratings to slide downward. So providing best-value results to taxpayers requires a balance between the upside value of new and better services and the downside potential for disasters that can result from a failure to identify, measure, handle, and communicate the risks many choices bring with them.

The federal HealthCare.gov website launched as part of the Affordable Care Act provides an example of the need for this balance. There are low-tech, low-risk techniques for educating and registering enrollees, such as paper-based manuals and mail-in registration forms. These clunky processes work, but they will almost certainly yield lower customer satisfaction scores and higher costs than an efficient, easy-to-use online system—unless, of course, the system *isn't* efficient, easy to use, or crashes constantly.

Making the right decisions in risky settings requires careful consideration of the probability of success versus the unpleasantness of failure, both personal and political. Effective leaders learn to make "risk-intelligent" decisions in their strategies and planning, and they learn to monitor and respond constantly to changes in the risk profile.

It's Personal

A critical but often overlooked component of risk management is the role of *personal* risk in decision making. This can be particularly challenging for federal managers and leaders, for whom there is frequently little incentive to take risks. Considering the current political and media mentality, which is compounded by oversight organizations reporting on any mistake and an absence of risk-friendly incentives within the civil service system, why *would* any federal employee take a risk?[4] Add to the mix the always recurring budget pressures, and balancing risk in the federal environment becomes a real challenge.

"It's not a choice federal officials have," says Todd Grams, a former senior official at the OMB, IRS, and the Department of Veterans Affairs. According to Grams, who is currently president of the Association for Federal Enterprise Risk Management (AFERM):

> organizations, even federal organizations, create value by taking informed risks—and lose value by failing to manage risks. Assuring that knowledge of the right risks gets to the right people at the right time is key. For federal enterprises, doing this wisely can provide three benefits: it reduces problems and crises, so leaders can focus on mission and strategies, protects agencies' reputations, and better informs budget decisions.[5]

This chapter explores risk in federal decision making, at both organizational and personal levels, including types of risk (some rewarded, some not), sources (like information gaps and human biases), and impacts. I offer strategies and techniques for recognizing and managing risk, from GAO and other expert organizations, with the goal of being able to *optimize*—not eliminate—smart risk-taking on behalf of taxpayers. The discussion concludes with suggestions for spotting and communicating threats and establishing an independent risk officer to help battle complacency.

Types of Risk

Risk can be defined as the threat of *harm, loss,* or *diminished opportunity* to achieve goals.[6] These include rewarded risks and unrewarded risks; high-impact strategic risks and limited tactical or program risks; and inherent risks and residual risks. They can originate from everyday imperfections in human or mechanical performance, from ignorance or error, or from environmental changes or human bias. They can affect financial, operational, and technological success, not to mention reputation.[7] Some risks are unique to the public sector.

If you want to *increase* value by taking appropriate risk, and not *lose* value by failing to manage risk, you must begin with a clear understanding of the various types of risks.

Rewarded risk can be thought of as a voluntary risk, or one that promises great value if handled well.[8] Developing a new digital app that helps vacationers book National Park Service campsites, for instance, might be more risky than requiring paper forms a month in advance. But booking by app is much more efficient and in keeping with current user expectations, and would almost certainly drive up customer satisfaction levels (and, perhaps, appropriations). The electronic data generated, moreover, would be valuable for agency planning. This "rewarded risk" provides a chance of success that is high enough to outweigh potential implementation problems or new or unknown risks that the improved approach might bring. At the IRS, for example, providing electronic access to prior-year tax returns (a benefit to taxpayers) created this kind of new risk because it enabled criminals to access and use the information to file fraudulent tax returns.[9]

Unfortunately, not all risks are voluntary or come with the chance of added value. Every program faces certain **unrewarded risks.** These undesirable outcomes are inevitable because of the many things that can (and do) go wrong in all endeavors, whether that is erroneous payments, ethics scandals, floods, epidemics, or criminal activities such as cyber attacks.[10] In such cases there is no benefit to be sought; the focus is on reducing or avoiding the unrewarded risk and deciding how much you can accept. For example, if an agency wants to dramatically reduce erroneous payments (an unrewarded risk) but also expects the budget cost and inconvenience to compliant customers to be too high to offset all the potential savings, a zero error rate usually isn't worthwhile. Some entities' risk management capabilities are focused solely on minimizing unrewarded risk. In my view, this is *always* playing defense and results in missed opportunities to improve services by taking prudent, rewarded risks.

Some risks can affect an agency or program profoundly; these are by definition **strategic risks**, and they must be considered regardless of likelihood.[11] Sometimes your action plan for such risk is an early warning sign or "risk-sensing" system that is designed to allow you to anticipate and head off, or prepare for, negative events. Computer weather models indicate that New Orleans will suffer at least three major hurricanes each century, but they don't tell us when. The probability of a hurricane in any given year is not great. But the city's vulnerability proved so high during Katrina that a serious risk-mitigation strategy seems essential.[12]

Military and national security programs provide the most visible examples of strategic risk. Risks that threaten our lives and our everyday way of living are so compelling that a request for an extra carrier group or squadron of fighters can be hard to reject. The Energy Department's protection of nuclear stockpiles and NIH's handling of deadly microbes represent similar strategic risks. You don't compute your optimum "risk appetite" in cases such as these; they must be mitigated regardless of probability.[13]

Sources of Risk

Anything unforeseen creates risk. That's why **information gaps** are perhaps the most common source of risk.[14] In the federal setting, imperfect or inaccurate information on stakeholder needs and customer expectations can be particularly serious.

Two examples illustrate the potential consequences of entering situations with information gaps. In early 2001 while working at Arthur Andersen I was engaged in a review of the FBI's handling of some high-profile cases, including confrontations at Ruby Ridge, Idaho, and Waco, Texas, that raised questions about federal protocols for use of deadly force with groups of citizens. In a 2002 briefing to newly appointed FBI director Robert Mueller and Attorney General

John Ashcroft, the team was prepared to address issues such as deployment protocols and hostage negotiation. Ashcroft, however, opened by asking what we had learned that could help make the FBI more effective against events such as the 9/11 attacks that had more recently occurred. Our customer's entire focus had shifted in the middle of our work, and all of it had to be recast in light of the new environment and the AG's revised expectations.

Sometimes minor personal ignorance can trip you up. On my first visit to HEW secretary Joseph Califano's inner office, I sat in the only chair left open, a rocking chair. I noticed raised eyebrows all around, but just a smile from Califano as he launched into the agenda. I thought nothing of it. Upon exiting, a colleague informed me I had occupied the "Kennedy rocker" gifted to Califano by President John F. Kennedy—where *nobody* sits. I survived due to Califano's tolerance, but I also learned that information about a client's "territory" is just as important as understanding the client's priorities, and it represents a continuing risk for any program (indeed, any career).

In the federal service, **resource gaps** are virtually inevitable, considering ongoing political and budgetary pressures, and they constitute a second major source of risk. Sometimes this means fewer or less-skilled staff members than planned, or budgets sized to "best case" assumptions rather than the real world;[15] when expectations are not adjusted accordingly, risk of program failures increases.

The third major source of risk is a **changing operating environment**. Remember the admonition that "objects in the mirror are closer than they appear"; that's the way external change tends to come upon us, i.e., more rapidly that we expect. An example from the private sector is Blockbuster Video, which had nine thousand shops and sixty thousand employees in 2004. By 2010 Blockbuster had been virtually destroyed by its failure to respond effectively to the rise of e-commerce, grocery store kiosks, streaming video, and web-based client services.[16]

This changing environment problem is relevant for federal services as well, whether related to social security payments, agricultural subsidies, food stamps, or housing subsidies. The lesson is that you need to scan the horizon constantly to stay ahead of environmental changes. This could mean a sudden change in committee chairs or other more gradual changes, such as increased use of health care and veterans services created by an aging population, higher wounded soldier survival rates, or changing demand for Head Start programs and food stamps. Failure to "stay tuned" to your environment can be ruinous.

A fourth source of risk is **human bias,** or the flaws inherent in how the brain processes information, especially when asked to look at something as ambiguous and complex as the future. These pervade every analysis and decision in ways far more profound than is generally recognized. According to a recent Deloitte report entitled "Disruption," behavioral economics has "shed light on just how hard-wired we humans are for some key cognitive biases," regardless of how smart or successful we are.[17]

The Deloitte report describes four types of human bias. Each has profound impact on public sector risk assessment. *Overconfidence bias* leads us to trust what we already believe, making us unable to realize the limitations of our own knowledge. This is sometimes present on both sides of environmental debates. *Availability bias* encourages us to inflate the importance of things learned most recently and thus most easily remembered, giving us a distorted view of what's most important. This is sometimes at play when media coverage of short-term events overwhelms longer-term strategies. *Confirmation bias* causes us to pay more attention to information that aligns with our preconceived notions while ignoring contradictory evidence. This is frequently visible in political budget battles. *Optimism bias* fools us into thinking that bad things aren't likely to happen and that our plans will work out fine. This bias was clearly visible in the NASA shuttle cases.[18]

Impacts of Risk

Regardless of the kind or cause, it is important to understand the impacts of risk, particularly in the public sector. We care about these impacts, of course, because they have the potential to expose federal assets to loss or abuse, to disrupt agency operations, or to compromise important public objectives.[19] It might be a deliberate effort to steal or expose personal or national security data or free consumer access to Apple Maps Internet service undermining map sales at the US Geological Survey.[20] Risk can involve **operating vulnerabilities** resulting in customer-service failures or **financial vulnerabilities** resulting in overruns or erroneous payments. In addition to present effects, risk can undermine **future ability and effectiveness**, a subtler but equally threatening impact.

For example, the disruptive power of social media and crowdsourcing has become a significant risk to our nation's intelligence and defense capabilities. In modern-day "asymmetric warfare," far weaker opponents such as terrorist groups are using global social media as a new front for enabling communications and striking fear.

But mass access to rapid communications can also be a positive. Today we can push out early warnings about flooding or missing children directly to the phone in the consumer's pocket or AppleWatch™ wearable device. Agencies using these types of social media tools can achieve efficiency gains as well.

Finally, consider **reputational risk**, which, while more visible in the private sector, can have significant effects in the world of government as well.[21] Ask former Transportation Security Administrator Jon Pistole, who tasked an entire team to change the image of the TSA organization that the traveling public deals with every day.[22] Even agencies tasked with tax collection want and need to be viewed in a positive way.

Managing reputational risk can be critical in the political process. In the 2015 tax season, for example, the IRS suffered a $346 million loss of appropriations due to a combination of the political fallout from the Affordable Care Act and the reputational impact of accusations concerning the targeting of "tax-exempt" nonprofits with a particular political point of view.[23]

Inherent Risk vs. Residual Risk

Inherent risk refers to the level and kind of risk that exists *before* it is addressed—the risk an agency, program, or initiative encounters absent any action to mitigate it. **Residual risk**, also known as "vulnerability" or "exposure," is the risk that remains *after* action has been taken to mitigate the inherent risk.[24] (See the discussion later in the chapter about how to identify and mitigate inherent risks in a way that reduces exposure to residual risk.)

Considering and Managing Risk

If you feel overwhelmed by this plethora of risk categories and considerations, you understand the situation perfectly. Some managers perceive their jobs as avoiding or eliminating risk. That's an oversimplification and a prescription for failure. To succeed you have to understand which risks are *inherent* to your program, organization, or initiative, and you must adopt the right strategies to deal with them. What rewarded risks should you take to enhance customer service? Which resource shortfalls create unacceptably high levels of risk? Are there any environmental or stakeholder changes likely to affect your time lines, and how can you capitalize on those changes to advance your goals? Fortunately, some existing frameworks for considering risk can help guide you.

Recalling the **Four Dimensions of Success**, remember that achieving organizational goals requires identifying threats and making decisions based, at least in part, on the best balance between potential risk and reward. *Enterprise risk management* (ERM) is the term for organization-wide programs for identifying, tracking, and responding to key risks.[25] *Risk-based decision-making* is a term for using that information to make decisions about the program or issue at hand. Both are essential.

ERM has been around in the private sector for decades. Many federal entities have more recently developed increased interest in the practice of ERM, especially after witnessing crises at fellow agencies such as OPM, IRS, VA, and the Secret Service. They are also experiencing pressures to explicitly address risk driven by reduced budgets, OMB directives, congressional oversight, and a host of publicly visible security and safety concerns. What is an agency to do?

At the federal level, OMB Budget Circular A-11 was amended in 2014 to put agencies on notice that they are responsible for identifying, assessing, and managing risks, which are described broadly as all threats to successfully achieving mission. A new section on enterprise risk management describes the benefits of a comprehensive framework and encourages agencies to develop plans. But it leaves the planning to them, including decisions on the details of implementation.[26]

The goal is to incorporate what OMB calls "foresight" in assessing risks and challenges—by focusing on and anticipating new threats.[27] In a meeting at the National Academy of Public Administration in February 2015, OMB officials highlighted ten risk management good practices (see Figure 7.1) and predicted that new guidance under development (now expected by mid-2016) will establish a more formal federal ERM structure that is tied to each department's internal control requirements and strategic planning. This will make ERM a major driver of budget and mission success.

While you can build a risk management system from scratch, adopting an existing and already-proved-successful framework offers major advantages in efficiency, credibility, and effectiveness. One noteworthy private-sector model with reasonable applicability to some large federal entities (such as the US Mint, the Government Printing Office, or major federal military and veterans healthcare facilities) is the Enterprise Risk Management Integrated Framework developed by the Committee of Sponsoring Organizations (COSO), a consortium of respected private entities. Another potential model is the Risk Management Principles and Guidelines (ISO 31000) from the International Organization for Standardization (ISO). You can easily learn more about these on the COSO and ISO websites. Both may provide useful benchmarks for your own risk management efforts.[28]

A third framework—which is important due to its credibility and oversight

Survey of Emerging Practices

1. The CRO or equivalent role should be an objective role.

2. Make better use of data analytics.

3. Quantify the impact of past risk reward.

4. Establish a culture of risk reward.

5. Senior management buy-in is essential.

6. ERM and A-123 should coexist but not as stand-alone activities.

7. Identify/leverage a formal governing body.

8. Simultaneously engage performance, strategic, risk management, and budget activities.

9. Document risk decisions and the rationale for managing risk.

10. Implement a Risk Management Framework and phased-in ERM implementation approach.

Figure 7.1 Survey of Emerging Practices

Source: David Mader, "Perspectives on Risk Management in the Federal Government," presentation at National Academy of Public Administration, February 20, 2015, 8, http://aferm.org/articles/ERM%20for%20Civilian%20Agencies%20FY%202015%20Strategy%20Overview%20-%20%20Feb%20202015-1.pdf.

power—is contained in a GAO report on enterprise risk management for homeland security efforts. The GAO framework can be adapted for more general application:

- identify strategic goals and objectives, the actions needed to achieve them and constraints to be overcome;
- identify key potential risks and devise countermeasures;
- assess these countermeasures based on expert input and cost-benefit analysis;
- decide how to deploy resources based on alternatives evaluation and management criteria; and
- implement, monitor, and revise based on effectiveness and evolving risks.[29]

Individual Risk-Based Decision Making

An ERM framework, of course, will not itself manage the risks you might encounter. Any framework will only be as strong as the information it contains and the participants who use it. Making the right decision about a promising rewarded risk, developing a mitigation strategy, crafting defensive countermeasures to unforeseen threats: these all require *individual* risk-based decision-making skills. In the shuttle events, for instance, while there had been extensive ERM planning, it is essential to understand what information on risks was readily available at the points of decision and to whom. Did those in charge pay attention?

Realistic Targets and Alternatives

It is important to define realistic (read: modest) expectations at the beginning of any project because later judgments on success will compare outcomes to those early promises. Figure 7.2 illustrates this relationship and the value of resisting the tendency to overpromise so later you are not called upon to explain shortfalls against optimistic targets.

Setting modest goals, of course, can be especially challenging in the public sector. While private sector entities often use risk assessment to decide *whether* to undertake a project, governments sometimes become solution providers of last resort—as with flood or pension plan insurance, or similar services too risky for private enterprise. Political issues far outside a program can paralyze a manager's ability to get funding; and fighting for more funding or answering detractors can pressure managers to drive *up* expectations for outcomes. All this comes with little benefit in the civil service system for sticking one's head out or suffering career-ending penalties for bad results.

Having an explicit risk-based decision-making assessment plan and mitigation alternatives ready is all the more important in this environment. Identifying the possible risks and opting for outcomes that are important to the most valued stakeholders can help.

The earlier examples highlight fairly stark contrasts due to questionable assessments of risk. Deploying more people for early direct ACA registration and lowering expectations for the initial web-based exchange might have mitigated the risk inherent in the initial rollout delay, although the level of political opposition did create a disincentive to announcing lowered expectations.[30] The Census

$$\text{SUCCESS} = \frac{\text{perceived outcome}}{\text{recalled expectation}}$$

Figure 7.2 Understanding the Success Ratio

Bureau, by contrast, recognized the risk represented by its adoption of handheld devices and actually retreated to its previous paper-intensive system. The impact on the bureau was still significant, of course, in reputation, added processing costs, and loss of the "wow" factor it had anticipated from the handhelds. But these impacts were relatively minor compared to a failed census.

Consider the Worst Case

Risk assessment requires managers to consider a variety of possible outputs and the chances of attaining them, and to compare those to the possible downsides of each. This requires a realistic look at worst-case scenarios.

Years ago I was involved in a project called "Igloo White" (since declassified) that was aimed at disrupting the flow of enemy troops and vehicles along the Ho Chi Minh Trail and across the demilitarized zone in Vietnam. As part of the program the navy decided to reconfigure sonobuoys, originally built to detect submarines, for air deployment over land. Unfortunately, navy designers accustomed to sea operations didn't ponder "worst-case" considerations they'd face on land. Enough of the sonobuoys were dropped to do great good, but enemy personnel found buoys too easily and could avoid them or, worse, trick them. Insufficient attention had been paid to the downside risks, which eventually were mitigated somewhat, at least, using tools such as motion detection or tamper/destruct triggers.

It's the balance between best- and worst-case possibilities that allows you to vector in on the optimal choice. In doing so it's critical to put high-impact risks in a category all their own. Risks that can entirely destroy a project—or a career—usually aren't worth it, no matter how low the probability of a bad outcome.

The cacophony of players and goals makes the federal environment uniquely challenging. But it actually gives power to the leader who defines most clearly what can be done and is able to frame the risk-reward choice in terms of realistically available resources, timeframes, and political will. A risk-based decision-making tool of some sort can help you counter the seductiveness of attractive options (what one Washington veteran calls "shiny objects") that sometimes have dangerous consequences. Such a tool can also highlight the wisdom of an "80 percent" solution.

Of course, the safer compromise may not always prevail. Clay Johnson, director of presidential personnel and OMB deputy director for management under President George W. Bush, describes how adamantly President Bush defended his desire to set aggressive goals for his second term, even considering how "risky" it could be in a famously contentious Washington environment. Bush reportedly said that anyone claiming to achieve all their goals was probably lying anyway, so it was better to work toward concrete outcomes, making corrections as needed, even if total "success" was never achieved.[31]

Getting to "Optimal"

So what sort of risk-reward relationship should define the realistic and therefore "optimal" goal for a project or program? For each possible choice, decision makers must consider three things: the upside "best-case" result and the inherent risk of not achieving it; the consequences of failure and failure's impact on stakeholders; and the steps needed either to reduce the risk to acceptable levels or to pivot toward safer alternatives when necessary.

Of course, we all give some thought to risk when deciding how to proceed on a project. But a hard-nosed discussion about the consequences of failure often gets lost in the push for action and progress. You may hear "then bring in enough resources to make it happen!," or "I know you'll find a way," or even "I don't believe that, I think you're trying to scare us." These reveal confirmation bias and optimism bias: the tendency to discount information that contradicts beliefs and to think that bad things are simply unlikely to happen.

Add to these the ancient difficulty of speaking truth to power. In both space shuttle disasters, executives and scientists participated in multiple meetings specifically to determine levels of risk, potential remedies, and possible consequences. Yet decision makers declined to delay the *Challenger* launch despite record-low temperatures. Considering the relatively acceptable "downside" of a delayed launch, prudence would suggest waiting for a warmer day. In the case of the *Columbia*, rigid organizational and bureaucratic lines of authority kept NASA from acquiring and acting on vital information concerning wing damage, as an analysis following Allison's *Essence of Decision* would predict.[32]

Risk is a dynamic variable that changes continuously over the course of the project because it can be altered by test results, personnel performance, and technology successes or failures. In the federal sphere, add budget cuts or sequesters, leadership changes on the Hill or in the bureaucracy, and evolving customer expectations to the list of variables. Whose job is it to enable agencies to make the right risk-based decisions and adjust their goals and actions to each new reality?

The court jester was probably the earliest risk manager; it was his job to tell the king what others would not, for fear of losing their heads. Fortunately, chief risk officer roles now exist within major agencies like the Transportation Security Administration and the Internal Revenue Service. These officials can candidly speak with protection from beheading (or the federal bureaucratic equivalent, transfer to the proverbial office in the middle of nowhere).

Treasury's Financial Crimes Enforcement Network (FinCEN), which fights money laundering and other financial crimes, provides a positive example of risk management across multiple sectors and the ability to pivot when realities change.[33] The increasing sophistication and diversity of cybercriminals spurred FinCEN to upgrade its analytics and, in effect, move to a multisector strategy by providing data access to four hundred federal, state, and local law enforcement, intelligence, and security organizations. This involved adapting 170 million records covering eleven years to different data and security capabilities across governments and law enforcement entities nationwide; a risky upgrade, to be sure. Many problems with data quality and security arose. Furthermore, OMB moved the project deadline up by eighteen months and cut its budget from $140 to $120 million.[34]

Despite all the obstacles in its way, "FinCEN Query" went live in September 2012 and won a 2013 *Government Computer News* project award.[35] Constant attention to stakeholder needs across sectors and the ability to pivot when resource and timeframe changes were made successfully addressed the risks and carried the day.

Key Takeaways

In the world of risk, what can you do to capitalize on rewarded risk and defend against unrewarded?

Create Your Offense

1. *Create an Enterprise-Wide Risk Management Program*. Risk-intelligent agencies create a structure to ensure that risks are identified and managed effectively across the enterprise.

The structure should be a center for leadership, preferably with a risk management officer, that establishes: clear risk-related policies, procedures, and governance; risk-based decision-making guidance, such as who is authorized to make what sort of decisions; and periodic review. Using the GAO guidelines presented earlier or a variant of the ISO 31000 or COSO standards can assist in accomplishing this. GAO's focus is specifically federal, while ISO 31000 has a more international governmental audience and the COSO standards focus more specifically on adequacy of internal controls.

Your ERM program must support decision making based on adequate information, including risk appetites and tolerances. For example, what level of risk to pilots' lives is acceptable for aircraft-carrier night deployments in rough seas? What amount of customer-service degradation will the Mine Safety Administration accept before going to Congress for more resources? Who will be empowered to argue against popularly held positions to ensure objective decisions in sensitive situations?

2. *Establish a Risk-Based Decision-Making Framework.* To ensure consistency in critical judgments, your ERM program should establish a risk-based decision-making protocol.

There's no federal template for this, although OMB is expected to provide further guidance by mid-2016, likely in the form of ERM requirements, a suggested "playbook" or "how to" for federal ERM.

In any such framework, six key steps need to be considered, as illustrated in Box 7.1. This isn't a magical "six-step program." Rather, it's a starting point for weighing choices and tradeoffs. The steps have to be adapted to the environment and to the specific issues at hand.

3. *Find Ways to Reward Intelligent Risk-Taking.* The risk-reward profile in the federal civil service system clearly makes it more difficult to reward risk-taking.

Despite this, leaders such as Association for Federal Enterprise Risk Management president Todd Grams report being recognized and rewarded for taking intelligent risks. It's up to individual managers and executives to encourage personnel to take reasonable risks and to provide cover when things don't go well. "Incubators" that include groups of potential risk-takers—sometimes called "solutions teams"—is one way to support creative risk-taking. Most important, smart leaders remember to take responsibility for failures and attribute success to others. And they *never* shoot the messenger—or behead the court jester.

Execute Effectively

1. *Attend to Your Most Important Stakeholders.* Try to give your stakeholders at least some of what each of them wants, paying particular attention to those who matter most to funding, progress, and perceptions of success or failure. When you propose risk-reward tradeoffs, be sure to highlight what can be good, or bad,

---

★ **Box 7.1** Sample Risk-Based Decision-Making Framework

---

1. **Define a range of acceptable outcomes.** What are the optimal and the minimally acceptable outcomes for the major decision(s) at hand?
2. **Identify potential options and the risk inherent in each.** What's the full range of possible actions that can be taken, and the probability of success for each? Can the inherent risk be quantified?
3. **Create mitigation strategies and define residual risks.** What steps, resources, or processes can mitigate the inherent risks of each option, and what residual risk remains for each?
4. **Identify the worst case for each option.** What are the worst consequences that might result from each option, once the defined mitigation strategies are implemented?
5. **Define decision-making standards.** Considering the risks and likely results of each possible choice, what quantitative and qualitative standards should be used to choose the best, most "risk-intelligent" option? Which stakeholders should weigh in on these standards?
6. **Designate a decision maker.** Who will make the decision, after weighing the various opportunities and risks?

---

for each major stakeholder—including the avoidance of problems that might hurt their constituents or their bosses.

In 1992 House Energy committee chairman Mike Synar challenged spending by the Energy Department's Orphan Isotope Production Program, which used tax dollars to manufacture radioactive isotopes for commercial uses such as health-care diagnostics, airport runway markers, and smoke detectors. Synar, a then-six-term Democratic congressman from Oklahoma, questioned whether Uncle Sam should be using national laboratories to compete with private isotope producers.[36]

Faced with this risk to their program, DOE executives developed risk profiles for how this could affect their most important isotope users, such as (per our examples) sick children, recreational flyers, and homeowners. Highlighting the risks inherent in leaving production of these isotopes to the market, DOE mobilized allies in Congress and within the industry to alert Synar to the "downside" of interrupting the isotope supply. Synar concluded, after hearing testimony from multiple consultants and stakeholders, that the risk to the supply of needed isotopes was too great to justify eliminating the program, particularly in view of the relatively small cost of using DOE labs to make them.[37]

2. *Create a Chief Risk Officer (CRO)*. Although OMB does not (yet) require it, it is nevertheless wise to have a CRO at the executive level—someone who understands ERM requirements, tools, techniques, and tactics, who knows how to spot and evaluate risk, and who can provide independent advice on whether or not to proceed with a risky action.

3. *Clearly Communicate Risks and Tradeoffs*. It's wise to ensure that everybody of importance—your superiors, in particular—understands the risk and tradeoffs involved in any decision. This shares ownership of those risks and avoids unpleasant surprises. If possible, you should communicate this as publicly as possible in order to "frame" the common perception of your choice as well.

Admittedly, you can't always share risks and tradeoffs with the public, especially if it's politically sensitive, a subject of internal decision making, or related to national security. In addition, as noted in earlier chapters, programs are often burdened with conflicting stakeholders or goals. In such cases, key stakeholders should be brought in and briefed. Never assume that people have a broad understanding of the reasons for certain tradeoffs. Make sure the tradeoffs are visible to all and communicate them most clearly to those who could be your most severe critics, in front of witnesses, if possible. It's your best protection if things go south.

Play a Smart Defense

Contractors, consultants, and federal leaders all know that nothing ever goes *exactly* as planned or hoped. That's why you must build in "contingencies" to cover realistic risks. Your best defense is clarity on what might go wrong and what you will do if it does.

1. *Be Ready for Failure*. Included in the sample framework for risk-based decision making in Box 7.1 is explicit recognition of things that could go wrong and the development of mitigation strategies for each. But it's also important to have a defensive plan if these strategies fail to head off a bad result, as some inevitably will, or when a new or unforeseen problem arises.

Mitigation strategies can reduce exposure to risk, but they are no substitute for having an action plan if they fail. What is your fallback plan if body armor designed to protect soldiers against IEDs (improvised explosive devices) fails its acceptance test at the Aberdeen Proving Grounds? A defensive strategy should include *defined pivots to other solutions*.

The total collapse of Blockbuster in an incredibly short time provides an example of an enterprise's failure to do this: the company was ill-equipped to respond to the threats it faced and had provided for limited flexibility to handle them.[38] The 2010 Census example provides a successful contrast: testing of the handheld devices was conducted early enough to allow the bureau to pivot to a paper-based solution, which they kept in reserve for just such a possibility.

2. *Listen to the "Tech Talk."* In many complex projects, the "techies" know and understand the potential difficulties and risks. Usually they share them with those of us who are less technically adept. But too often lay managers gloss over this "fine print," only to later discover that the scope is different or the project costs twice as much or implementation takes twice as long because details weren't well understood at the outset.

Construction, infrastructure, and major IT projects frequently encounter this problem. A project begun without leadership clarity on risks and responsibilities may continue until it's too late to adjust easily. Construction management specialists, for example, report that many building cost overruns and scope changes result from sloppy initial contracts.[39] The devil's in the details, and sometimes the players will intentionally obscure those details for commercial advantage or simply to "get the ball rolling." Take the time and care (and maybe hire a specialist) to make sure you and your key oversight stakeholders fully understand the major risks and tradeoffs from the beginning.

3. *Create Learning and Memory Tools.* Don't get complacent. Nine singed primary O-rings were recovered from twenty-three shuttle launches before the *Challenger* exploded.[40] Don't get lulled to sleep by seeing multiple risky events work out well. Careful analysis is required to determine if this is a case of "past is prologue" or "eventually the odds will even out."

In *Organizational Learning at NASA*, Julianne G. Mahler explores NASA's ability to learn from the *Challenger* and to understand why that did not prevent the *Columbia*. Among her recommendations is that organizations invest in "memory" retention and retrieval tools so lessons learned are readily retrievable for new generations and challenges.[41]

4. *Recognize Threats and "Surprises" Early.* The Army War College calls our world *VUCA*: volatile, uncertain, complex, and ambiguous.[42] In this world, conditions change fast and in ways hard to foresee and even harder to plan for. So you have to work at spotting changing expectations and new technologies while they're still years away from affecting your program. You need the added time to get ready, so that you can in turn make the best use of your talent, time, and resources to adapt. Spotting change early, whether internally or externally, is a critical defensive tool.

It's not just a challenge for government, of course. "Smart companies," according to *Disruption*, "will set up internal 'red teams' to play the role of corporate adversaries and task them with identifying small changes in the market that could kill the company in the future." What's on your horizon that the Army War College's VUCA metaphor predicts? I guarantee something's there. You're just not seeing it yet.

5. *Confront Your Biases, and Theirs.* No person or organization is immune to cognitive or institutional bias. Once you admit to yours, you can step outside yourself to observe more clearly, and adjust. To do this well you need others in the room who will challenge assumptions and the status quo. As a leader I welcome these new perspectives and the value they can provide in countering my own inherent biases. Berkshire Hathaway chairman Warren Buffet famously challenged his own biases by inviting one of his most vocal critics to participate in the company's annual meeting.[43] (Of course, that's also a helpful way to keep track of what your opponents think!)

Federal agencies are frequently challenged by human biases relating to the programs and populations they serve. Oklahoma Senator James Inhofe, a leader on environmental issues, has long declared global warming a hoax (and brought a snowball into the Senate Chamber to prove it). It's safe to say that the senator and Environmental Protection Administration (EPA) leaders would each attribute the other's views to confirmation bias. Citing confirmation bias in particular, *National Geographic*'s March 2015 cover story documented the difficulties of dealing with populations whose biases drive beliefs regarding climate change, vaccinations, and genetically modified food, all of which create important challenges for EPA, the CDC, and the Department of Agriculture.[44]

Conclusion: A World of Risk

Risk is everywhere—and essential to human progress. It has become central to federal management challenges in recent years largely because the pace of change is escalating exponentially while resources, to say the least, are not. Today most executives recognize the importance of using an effective enterprise risk management capability and program, and the federal government includes increasing numbers of ERM officials.[45] At the local and program levels it is important to employ risk-based decision making, using an adequate assessment of options and their downsides to make balanced and risk-intelligent choices. Optimal ini tial choices and a flexible response to changing patterns of risk and reward can help us serve the taxpayer better.

Notes

1. Elizabeth Howell, "*Columbia* Disaster: What Happened, What NASA Learned," Space.com (February 1, 2013), http://www.space.com/19436-columbia-disaster .html.
2. Michelle La Vone, "The Space Shuttle *Challenger* Disaster," Spacesafetymagazine .com (2014), http://www.spacesafetymagazine.com/space-disasters/challenger -disaster/, accessed April 6, 2016.
3. *Columbia* Accident Investigation Board, "*Columbia* Accident Investigation Board Releases Final Report," vol. 1, National Aeronautics and Space Administration (Washington, DC: Government Printing Office, 2003), 195, http://spaceflight .nasa.gov/shuttle/archives/sts-107/investigation/CAIB_medres_full.pdf.
4. Tom Davis, in discussion with the author, October 2014.
5. Todd Grams, in discussion with the author, September 2014.
6. Deloitte Development, LLC, "Nine Principles of a Risk Intelligent Framework for Risk Management —A Briefing for Federal Executives" (2012), 4, http://www2 .deloitte.com/content/dam/Deloitte/global/Documents/Governance-Risk -Compliance/dttl-grc-puttingriskinthecomfortzone.pdf.
7. Ibid.
8. Deloitte Development, LLC, "The Risk Intelligent Enterprise: ERM Done Right" (2013), 9, https://www2.deloitte.com/content/dam/Deloitte/global/Documents /Governance-Risk-Compliance/dttl-grc-riskintelligent-erm-doneright.pdf.
9. Chris Smith, "IRS Hack Bigger in Scope Than Initially Believed, Up to $50M Stolen in Fraudulent Refunds," BGR.com, August 18, 2015, http://bgr.com/2015/08 /18/irs-hack-fraudulent-tax-returns/.
10. Deloitte, "Risk Intelligent Enterprise," 9.
11. Deloitte Development LLC, "Deloitte on Disruption" (2014), 11–12, https://www2 .deloitte.com/content/dam/Deloitte/us/Documents/risk/us-risk-deloitte-on -disruption-interior-101714.pdf.
12. Deloitte, "Risk Intelligent Enterprise," 6.
13. Deloitte, "Disruption," 12.
14. Deloitte, "Risk Intelligent Enterprise," 5.
15. Ibid., 4.
16. Todd Davis and John Higgins, "A Blockbuster Failure: How an Outdated Business Model Destroyed a Giant," Chapter 11 Bankruptcy Case Studies, Trace .tennessee.edu (Spring,2013), accessed April 6, 2016, http://trace.tennessee.edu /cgi/viewcontent.cgi?article=1010&context=utk_studlawbankruptcy; Deloitte, "Disruption," 4–5.

17. Deloitte, "Disruption," 16.
18. Ibid., 15–18.
19. Deloitte, "Risk Intelligent Enterprise," 13.
20. "Managing Success in the Federal Government, Even in an Era of Poison Politics" is an independent publication and has not been authorized, sponsored, or otherwise approved by Apple Inc.
21. Ibid., 6.
22. Chris Schmidt, "How TAS Changed Its Public Reputation, Enhanced Security, and Improved Employee Morale," Catalyst.com, January 9, 2015, http://catalystdc .com/2015/01/how-tsa-changed-its-public-reputation-enhanced-security-and -improved-employee-morale/
23. Kent Hoover, "If You Like Tax Cheats, You'll Love IRS Budget Cuts," *The Business Journals* (2015), http://www.bizjournals.com/bizjournals/washingtonbureau /2015/02/if-you-like-tax-cheats-youll-love-irs-budget-cuts.html?page=all; Josh Hicks, "IRS Shutdown Possible Amid Budget Cuts, Agency Chief Says," *Washington Post*, January 16, 2015, http://www.washingtonpost.com/blogs/federal-eye /wp/2015/01/16/irs-shutdown-possible-amid-budget-cuts-agency-chief-says/; *Written Testimony of Commissioner Koskinen before the House Ways and Means Committee's Subcommittee on Oversight on the 2015 Tax Filing Season*, IRS.com, last modified April 22, 2015, http://www.irs.gov/uac/Written-Testimony-of-IRS -Commissioner-Koskinen-before-the-House-Ways-and-Means-Committee.
24. Deloitte, "The Risk Intelligent Enterprise," 6.
25. Ibid., 4.
26. "OMB Circular No. A-11 (2014)," sections 270.24 to 270.29, July 26, 2013, https:// www.whitehouse.gov/sites/default/files/omb/assets/a11_current_year/s270.pdf.
27. David Mader, "Perspectives on Risk Management in the Federal Government," presentation at National Academy of Public Administration, February 20, 2015, 4, http://aferm.org/articles/ERM%20for%20Civilian%20Agencies%20FY %202015%20Strategy%20Overview%20-%20%20Feb%202020155-1.pdf.
28. For more information, visit http://www.coso.org/ and http://www.iso.org/iso /home.html.
29. Margaret Wrightson and Stephen Caldwell, "Risk Management: Further Refinements Needed to Assess Risks and Prioritize Protective Measures at Ports and Other Critical Infrastructure," US Government Accountability Office, Report No. GAO-06-91 (December 2005), 23–29, 99–109.
30. Wade Horn, in discussion with the author, January 2015.
31. Clay Johnson, in discussion with the author, December 2014.
32. *Columbia* Accident Investigation Board, Board Releases Final Report," 199–202.
33. For more information visit http://www.fincen.gov/.
34. Brian Lorenze, in discussion with the author, April 2015.
35. "Fifteen IT Projects Win 2013 GCN Awards," *Government Computing News*, August 13, 2013, http://gcn.com/articles/2013/08/09/gcn-award-winners -announced.aspx.

36. J. Rojas-Burke, "Congressional Subcommittee Scrutinizes Looming US Radioisotope Supply Crisis," *Journal of Nuclear Medicine* 33, no. 10 (1992): ub16N–34N.

37. Ibid.

38. Deloitte, "Disruption," 3–5.

39. Peter Fewings, *Construction Project Management: An Integrated Approach* (New York: Routledge, 2013), 256–81.

40. Coire Maranzano and Roman Krzysztofowicz, "Bayesian Re-Analysis of the Challenger O-Ring Data," University of Virginia, June 2005, 9, http://faculty.virginia.edu/rk/Bayesian%20Re-analysis%20of%20the%20Challenger%20O-ring%20Data.pdf.

41. Julianne G. Mahler, *Organizational Learning at NASA: The Challenger and Columbia Accidents* (Washington, DC: Georgetown University Press, 2009), 203–9.

42. Deloitte, "Disruption," 7–9.

43. Ibid., 24.

44. Joel Achenbach, "Why Do Many Reasonable People Doubt Science?" *National Geographic*, March 2015, http://ngm.nationalgeographic.com/2015/03/science-doubters/achenbach-text.

45. Karen Hardy, "Managing Risk in Government: An Introduction to Enterprise Risk Management," IBM Center for the Business of Government, 2010, https://www.rims.org/resources/ERM/Documents/Risk%20in%20Government.pdf.

CHAPTER 8

The Wide Wonderful World of Innovation

In the early 1990s the state of Maine had managed to earn two distinctions that to even the most casual observer of government were perplexing: on the one hand, it led the nation in per capita workplace illnesses and injuries; on the other, it was one of the most heavily policed states in the nation when it came to workplace safety. The US Department of Labor's Occupational Safety and Health Administration's (OSHA) Maine office was generously fining and penalizing Maine businesses, but doing so just seemed to make matters worse.[1]

The twin distinctions inspired the New England regional OSHA office to take a closer look at the cause of this phenomenon. What they learned—and how they responded—would not only lead to a revolution in workplace safety enforcement strategies in Maine, but also to inspire other regulatory agencies in different policy areas to completely reconsider their basic enforcement models as well.

Look at the Data

It is certainly discouraging to learn that, like many federal regulatory agencies at the time, OSHA was a land of "outputs" and not "outcomes." What got you a reputation at OSHA as a "tough enforcer" wasn't the relative safety of the workforce or workplaces under your oversight; it was the number of fines and citations that you levied on businesses, regardless of the overall effect of all that enforcement activity on actual workplace safety.[2] Anyone familiar with the incentives for police officers to give traffic citations near the end of the month understands the dynamic. Not only did aggressive enforcement in Maine have negligible impact on worker safety, it had a perverse effect: it created a vast gulf of hostility between OSHA and the business community, which exacerbated the entire unhealthy dynamic.

In the mid-1990s that dynamic caught the attention of Joe Dear, a serial public sector innovator and recent Bill Clinton appointee to be the top federal OSHA administrator. Dear was known as a data-savvy, straight-shooting problem solver who brought to every job an insatiable curiosity about how to improve the performance of the organization he ran. Dear tragically died of cancer at age sixty-two, but not before winning two Innovations in American Government awards, one as director of the Washington State Workers' Compensation Administration in 1992 and the other as the head of OSHA in 1995.[3]

Dear was especially good at gathering folks around a table to work a problem with him: identifying the internal innovators, and then giving them the political cover they needed to try out new ways of doing business. He found his innovator in Bill Freeman, head of the Maine OSHA office, a longtime regulator with a reputation as a tough enforcer.

Tough as Freeman might be, though, he realized something was fundamentally askew in his state. So when asked by Dear to consider a new enforcement approach, Freeman was game. Working with other regional staffs, Freeman came up with an audacious plan: focus on the two hundred *most dangerous* businesses in the state and see if OSHA could do something to make a dent in their actual safety records.[4] In essence, he aimed to shift from monitoring inputs and some outputs to achieving important outcomes.

In designing this new approach Freeman still had two concerns. He surmised that if he were to discontinue random statewide inspections of *all* Maine businesses, working in Maine would become *even more* dangerous. Equally worrisome was the fact that he didn't have the resources needed to focus on the two hundred offenders. That was the lightbulb moment: What if OSHA flipped its enforcement model, and put the incentive for safety on the businesses themselves, instead of on the traditional "inspect and penalize" approach that had served them so poorly?

The concept was simple but bold: businesses on Maine's Top 200 list would be given a choice: either deal with OSHA in the traditional way—which meant inspections, penalties, and fines—or partner with OSHA to come up with business-generated workplace safety plans, a less OSHA staff–intensive (but arguably riskier) approach to regulation. The concept became known as "choose your OSHA."

Not all labor advocates were thrilled with this new do-it-yourself approach to workforce safety and a handful of businesses did try to take advantage (in a negative way) of the new more self-directed regime. But overwhelmingly the businesses elected the "choose your OSHA" route, partnering with Freeman's team on voluntarily analyzing hazards and risks in the workplace and on fixing them themselves. Nobody could argue with the results. Within a couple of years the businesses had invested tens of millions of dollars in worker and workplace safety, with more than two-thirds of the participating businesses documenting workplace injury and illness rates that dropped by one-third or more.[5] The idea eventually spread to other OSHA field offices.[6]

This chapter offers insights on finding and supporting innovative solutions in a government fraught with barriers. It identifies conditions essential to spawning bold new approaches and the building blocks needed to institutionalize them. Examples from the John F. Kennedy School of Government's Innovations in American Government (IAG) Awards program, as well as the GSA's own Challenge.gov competitions, illustrate that effective innovations can be simple, appealing, and apolitical, plus they can provide rapidly visible results. The chapter concludes with suggestions that include using intergenerational teams, finding and protecting disruptors, and creating incubators.

Anatomy of Innovation

The Maine Top 200 is a classic example of how innovation occurs, even in the public sector. *First* there is some precipitating controversial and tough problem that requires radical new thinking and new strategies. *Second* is a leader with an open mind and an eye for people with good ideas who is willing to take risks and provide "top cover." *Third* is a staffer or leader who is unhappy with the status quo and who is able to spot a big problem developing, sometimes even before others do, or is willing to raise her hand when a challenge is presented. (Virtually every paper or book on innovation tells us that to spot innovators we should look for "restless" staff who are "dissatisfied with the status quo" and are looking to take on solving problems.[7]) *Fourth*, and important, the solution can be proved out in field tests. And *fifth*, once proved, the solution can be implemented across a single or multiple institutions and endure the test of time. Indeed, the new OSHA approach quickly migrated to other regulatory agencies, including the EPA.

What Is Innovation?

There are many ways to define innovation. For the purposes of this chapter, let's use the Kennedy School Innovation program definition: innovation is any significant new way of doing business that substantially improves performance and results and that is replicable and scalable.[8]

Increasingly, innovative or new ways of doing business involve technology, but that is certainly not a requirement. Many innovations can result from simply finding a different, smarter way of doing something. In fact, among innovation junkies, IT overhauls are sometimes considered the natural evolution and application of today's technologies to an existing task, rather than pure innovation. Nowadays, for example, renewing your auto registration online is no longer innovative.

Debates over definitions notwithstanding, the actual formal study of innovation in the public sector arguably began when the Ford Foundation teamed up with the Kennedy School to launch the innovation awards in the late 1980s.[9] At first open only to state and local governments, the program was swamped with applications from the very start. Some of those early entries included an application from a group of electronically interconnected libraries in Vermont. The Vermont program won, with what turned out to be, in essence, the first civilian use of what would become the Internet. It was also a harbinger of the wave of public sector innovations that arrived with rapidly improving and expanding IT.

A scan of federal Innovations in American Government award winners since 1995 (when the program was expanded to include federal applicants) runs the gamut of noteworthy trailblazers.[10] In the late 1990s the IRS won for enabling taxpayers to file their taxes online, making the whole process simpler and faster for tech-savvy taxpayers—which is now a routine practice. Other federal awards involved banning the use of chlorofluorocarbons by military facilities in order to protect the ozone layer, devising creative ways to shut down "sweatshops," building anticipatory disaster response systems, and speeding up recalls of dangerous commercial products.

Thus "innovation" comes in all shapes and sizes and from every organizational layer. As this book emphasizes in every chapter, it's often quite simply (in concept, if not execution) about finding and motivating people with the right skills who know how to build relationships and how to groom and maneuver those relationships to get things done. This basic approach applies to innovation in spades. Nevertheless, in the federal realm, as the following sections demonstrate, it's still not easy to get bureaucracies to change how they do business.

Barriers to Innovation

For all the reasons enumerated in the introduction to the book—from a fractious, fragmented Congress to confounding bureaucracies and a rule for every eventuality—the federal government is not a place that exactly encourages people to stick their necks out to do things in a significantly different fashion. As former chairman of the US House of Representatives' Oversight and Government Reform Committee, Tom Davis likes to point out, the people who created our government were not looking for expansive central empowerment. In fact, they were looking for ways to "keep the government in control." Take, for example, one of the more fundamental pillars of the constitutional structure they gave us, the Electoral College. It is an eighteenth-century construct designed to ensure that an entrenched elite maintains ultimate control over the levers of federal power rather than trusting that control to the unpredictable masses. A system originally and fundamentally designed to protect powerful landholders is not going to easily encourage and reward mavericks.[11]

The federal government provides limited incentive for those thinking about testing some new way of doing the public's business to take the leap. "It's the whole risk and failure thing," says Carmen Medina, coauthor of *Rebels at Work: A Handbook for Leading Change from Within*.[12] Medina, who spent more than thirty years at the CIA, ultimately as deputy director for intelligence and director of the Center for the Study of Intelligence, notes, "If I take a risk and succeed in the private sector I get kudos (and perhaps more remunerative acknowledgment). If I fail, it's part and parcel of commerce. If I take a risk in the public sector and succeed, there's no reward. And failure is a killer."[13]

Another frequent barrier, frankly, is the layer of career bureaucracy that has "always done it that way." As discussed in "Create Your Offense" below, mixing longer-term and new staffs is a way to short circuit this syndrome.

Silos are another innovation killer. More and more, innovative organizations are coming to realize that organizational cross-pollination is an effective way to encourage fresh thinking. Looking outside your own organization for good ideas can reap real benefits.

How to break the cycle of "stuck" is the critical question in the federal realm. What can leaders do to spot problems that are ripe for innovative efforts, find the right talent to assign fixing them, and provide the institutional encouragement and cover that will allow good ideas to percolate up, be field tested, and rolled out system-wide?

Key Building Blocks of Innovation

There is no shortage of literature on innovation; over a dozen sources are identified in the endnotes to this chapter. In looking through the literature and in interviews with leading practitioners, however, some essential building blocks for innovation sift out.[14]

Identify an Important Problem

Finding an important problem ripe for innovation ought to be, for government leaders and managers, the least difficult step in innovating. In essence, problem solving is at the heart of what the federal government does, whether that is in housing the homeless, defending the homeland, protecting the environment, helping the unemployed find jobs, keeping our national transportation system humming, helping injured veterans regain their health, regulating financial markets, ensuring food safety, or looking for a cure for Alzheimers. There is no shortage of program and policy areas crying out for new approaches aimed at more effective or efficient outcomes.

There is a difference, though, between household-variety problem solving and real innovation. In Kennedy School innovation terms, the main distinction is that many ideas that have percolated up for new approaches might be "praiseworthy" but not "prize worthy." This distinction, of course, may be in the eye of the beholder. But to be ripe for innovation there needs to be a widespread and fairly universal level of frustration with how some program or policy is or isn't working so that it rises to the level where you want to marshal your top talent to focus on fixing it. The pain point should be high, whether that is stress or confusion among internal staffs, dissatisfaction among outside stakeholders, or visible political or public concern.[15]

The need for visible pain creates a dilemma when "visionaries" see a big problem coming that's not yet evident to everyone else. In these situations, as in the Y2K example discussed in chapter 1, it is usually hard to support the case for action. So high levels of leadership attention would generally be required to communicate broadly the value of early attention, as John Koskinen did regarding Y2K. Picking the right moment is equally important. HEW assistant secretary Bill Morrill, who was highlighted as a "consigliere" in chapter 5, said "some problems just need to age a bit."

Identify Your Innovators

It's all well and good to have framed a problem, and perhaps even thought through some solutions to it. The real key is to find and support innovators—even incentivizing the search, to the extent you can—with whom you can collaborate on refining and rolling out a new idea.

Here it's important to recognize your own abilities and limitations. Some leaders are brilliant unilateral problem solvers. Some are better at spotting great ideas and building teams around them. As a manager and leader my approach was always to bring a diverse group of thinkers together to brainstorm, to press them to build on one another's best thinking, then to converge on the best idea and get the team to adopt it.

How do you identify the people in your organization who aren't satisfied with the status quo *and* are capable of successfully pushing boundaries? In *"Understanding Innovation: What Inspires It? What Makes It Successful?,"* Jonathan Walters describes people who are simply constitutionally predisposed to questioning the status quo, who chafe at the normal boundaries, and for whom the phrase "we've always done it that way" is like waving a red cape at a bull. Carmen Medina's book is devoted to this subset of public employee innovators who pop up at every level of government in every imaginable policy area.[16]

A 2011 joint report published by the Partnership for Public Service and the Hay Group highlights the key attributes to look for in innovators. True innovators are resilient, visionary, and able to navigate in challenging organizational environments; they know how to leverage networks; and they are well versed in the fine arts of persuasion and team building.[17]

One of the most interesting federal Innovations in American Government Award–winning programs, for example, was the US Forest Service's "Collaborative Stewardship Program," which was aimed at reducing long-standing tensions between groups involved with federal logging permits. Years of "cold warfare" between and among Native populations, developers, loggers, and environmentalists had led to a situation where every proposed logging permit set off open hostilities, mostly including lengthy and expensive lawsuits but sometimes vandalism as well.[18]

It was a lone ranger—literally, a man named Crockett Dumas, who visited everyone on horseback—who stepped up to try out a new way of doing business, starting with simply convincing people to talk. In the end the Forest Service was able to forge a fascinating coalition of previously warring factions into an amalgam of interests that together created forestry plans everyone could live with, largely because all felt "heard" in the development of the plans. It revolutionized the Forest Service's relationship with stakeholders out west.

Incubate, Nurture, and Protect

Once you've identified your innovators you must wrap them in a subculture, or protected sub-environment, system, or mechanism in which smart, creative individuals can work their magic while being protected from a very tough, arguably anti-innovation federal-government-wide environment. This includes protecting and rewarding them. In *Implementing Innovation*, Toddi A. Steelman concludes that certain organizational structure and culture factors, like incentives and problem-solving strategies, provide a critical framework to actually implementing (or hindering) effective innovation.[19]

Box 8.1 lays out Sandford Borins's list of organizational characteristics needed to nurture and support innovation, ranging from actually investing in it (by creating a skunkworks or similar incubator) to encouraging diversity of interdisciplinary teams that bring together a wide variety of expertise (e.g., technical skill, philosophies).

Another respected commentator, Jonathan Walters, who for twenty years covered the Innovations in American Government Awards for *Governing* magazine, argues that six drivers are needed to inspire and spawn innovative solutions; these are presented in Box 8.2.

The term *incubate* covers a lot of ground. Sometimes creating the right environment originates at the very top, as when Vice President Al Gore launched the National Partnership for Reinventing Government in 1993, a top-to-bottom look at ways to make the federal government more efficient and effective.

In fact, when one considers the dozens of Innovations in American Govern-

---

★ **Box 8.1** Seven Characteristics of Innovative Public Sector Organizations

Sandford Borins, professor of strategic management at the University of Toronto–Scarborough and a much-published author on innovation in the public sector, offers these seven characteristics of innovative organizations. As you read them, ask yourself what the federal government's (and your agency's) disposition is with respect to each, and what you can do about it:

1. They support innovation from the top.
2. They reward individuals who push change.
3. They specifically dedicate resources to innovation.
4. They harbor a workforce with diverse perspectives.
5. They encourage learning from the outside.
6. They make innovation everyone's responsibility.
7. They exhibit an inclination to experiment and evaluate.

Source: Sandford Borins, "The Challenge of Innovating in Government," Innovation series, IBM Center for the Business of Government, 2nd ed. (2006), 28–32, http://www.businessofgovernment.org/sites/default/files/BorinsInnovatingInGov.pdf.

★ **Box 8.2** Six Drivers of Innovation

---

1. Frustration with the status quo. Innovation is brought to you by people who are profoundly impatient with doing things the same old way.
2. Responding to a crisis. It's one of the most common forces behind significant change.
3. Focusing on prevention. One of the things that government does least well but which has the potential for the greatest payoff.
4. Emphasizing results. Clear, measurable goals and a solid set of results metrics are a powerful way to focus people on smarter ways of doing business.
5. Adapting technology. Government has been a perennially "late adopter," but that seems to be changing.
6. Doing the right thing. Too many programs are spending too much money for bad results. It's not just bad public policy, it is, arguably, downright immoral.

Source: Jonathan Walters, "Understanding Innovation: What Inspires It? What Makes It Successful?," New Ways to Manage series, The PricewaterhouseCoopers Endowment for the Business of Government (December 2011), 11–24, http://unpan1.un.org/intradoc/groups/public/documents /un/unpan011090.pdf.

---

ment award winners since the program's inception, a pattern appears. There is usually some maverick, or group of mavericks, operating quite autonomously and more or less in secret (real risk takers, in other words), or there's an industrious, creative person or team with explicit permission and "top cover" from enlightened and bold higher-ups who begins to experiment with more effective ways to get jobs done. The pattern often includes precursor initiatives at state and local levels, frequently cited as the nation's principal laboratories of democracy and incubators of change, or at field locations that must adapt to local needs, as illustrated in the Maine OSHA case.[20]

One of the more celebrated examples of the latter phenomenon comes from the United Kingdom. Known as the Behavioural Insights Team (or BIT), the group was a small "skunkworks" tucked away in the UK cabinet office and charged with finding ways to improve the effectiveness of government programs and policies. The team gained traction in 2010 under Prime Minister David Cameron, who took office evincing a keen interest in both "nonregulatory solutions to policy problems" and in spending public money more efficiently.[21]

The BIT was set up as something of a policy research lab to scientifically test multiple approaches to specific public policy problems on a limited, controlled basis through "randomized controlled trials" (RCTs). By comparing the results of various trial approaches—whether those were efforts to boost tax compliance or move people from welfare to work—policymakers could hone in on the most effective practices before full-scale program and policy rollouts were initiated. More recently, this approach has begun to take root in the United States, as evidenced by OMB's 2014 guidance that encourages expanded use of behavioral insights in the federal government.[22]

In addition to encouraging internal incubation of new ideas, the federal government is now turning to user communities for help in figuring out how to improve. In fact, the 2013 federal winner of the IAG award was the GSA's Challenge .gov, a "one-stop shop where entrepreneurs and citizen solvers can find public-sector prize competitions." This is an innovation aimed at encouraging innovation, and it is available to federal managers and leaders to launch their own innovation projects![23]

GSA claims that since 2010 federal agencies have used the site to post more than three hundred competitions that engaged more than forty-two thousand citizens in diffuse problem-solving efforts. Some successful examples are:

- Robocall challenge: In October 2012 the Federal Trade Commission (FTC) announced the Robocall Challenge, which awarded a $50,000 prize for the individual or group that could create the best technical proposal to help consumers block "robocalls" from computers. "Nomorobo," one of the winning proposals, allows incoming calls to be routed to a second telephone line that identifies and then hangs up on a robocall before it rings twice to users. Its inventor emphasizes that he never would have worked on the robocall problem were it not for the FTC's challenge. In 2015 FTC again used a crowdsourcing competition, with prizes, to upgrade tools to catch the robocallers themselves.[24]
- My Air, My Health challenge: With $160,000 in prizes offered jointly by EPA and HHS, the My Air, My Health challenge was a multidisciplinary call to innovators to create a personal, portable, near-real-time, location-specific system to monitor and report air pollutants and potentially related health events. Judges unanimously awarded a $100,000 prize to a team that designed a Conscious Clothing prototype, which could cost users as little as $20.[25]

Nurture and protect. Numerous experts point out that innovators need protection, or the aforementioned "high cover." When the US Air Force decided to phase out the use of chlorofluorocarbons as a key cleaning agent—another Innovations in American Government award-winning program—it set up what it describes as a "safe" site where alternative cleaning agents could be tested. "Technological dead ends were quietly abandoned; successes were phased in," writes John D. Donahue in his 2010 book, *Making Washington Work: Tales of Innovation in the Federal Government.*

Robert Reich was a master of this, as evidenced by the three innovation awards that the Department of Labor won while he served as the agency's secretary. Harvard public administration professor Donahue describes Reich's attitude toward innovation while at DOL as "emphatically and explicitly supportive of innovation." Indeed, Donahue has a whole chapter on DOL titled "The Unaccustomed Inventiveness of the Labor Department," which describes how Reich and his top team worked with career staffs and within the DOL bureaucracy to incubate, nurture, and protect "a sharply disproportionate share of innovation awards semifinalists, finalists and (especially) winners."[26]

Test

Innovation is only innovation if it works, so testing a proposition is critical. One of the more celebrated examples of this came with the sweep of "scared straight" programs that arrived in the United States in the 1990s and that were touted as a significant breakthrough in crime prevention. The programs involved shepherding at-risk youth into maximum security prisons to be confronted by inmates who, presumably, would sufficiently scare them about the consequences of a life of crime so that the visiting youth would "straighten out."

Scared straight seemed, intuitively, like a good idea. With initially reported "success rates" as high as 94 percent, the results seemed great. There was international attention, and other countries, including the United Kingdom, eagerly adopted scared straight–like programs.

However, a group of more skeptical (and rigorous) social scientists decided to do a controlled test of the program. They compared a control group—kids in similar circumstances with similar backgrounds who didn't experience scared straight—with kids who did. The findings were alarming: youths who went through a scared straight program were actually *more* likely to offend (or reoffend) than those who did not.

According to a report on scared straight by the United Kingdom's Behavioral Insights Team, "[T]he cost associated with the programme (largely related to the

increase in reoffending rates) were over 30 times higher than the benefits, meaning that 'Scared Straight' programmes cost the taxpayer a significant amount
of money and actively increased crime."[27] The takeaway message is, of course,
to test first. Using regional, state, or local locations interested in being the "hot
bed" for a new idea is usually a popular thing to do and capitalizes on our diverse multisector federalist system. Randomized controlled trials can meet
the need as well, an approach the Obama administration expanded at federal
levels.[28]

Institutionalize

The other key measure of "success" in the innovation world is to know whether or
not the improvement endures the test of time, which in the public sector typically
means through a significant political transition or into a new administration. According to the Walters report, six key characteristics are present in innovations
likely to be successful over the long run (not to be confused with *key drivers* that
prompt innovation, shown in Box 8.2):

First, keep it simple in concept. The goal of the Maine 200 program was to
reduce workplace accidents and injuries.

Second, make it easy to execute. Clear steps for implementation are crucial.
When Crockett Dumas climbed on his horse in New Mexico, the goal was simply
to open up lines of communication.

Third, shoot for quick and visible results (after testing, of course). When the IRS
flipped the switch on its online tax return filing system, a host of early adopters
were quickly hooked, which meant no going back.

Fourth, be frugal. This is especially true today, but a review of dozens of federal
IAG award winners is a testament to ingenuity more than any mega-investment
could have produced. In that regard, Maine 200 was a real home run since its
design was shaped specifically by scarce resources.

Fifth, make your innovation appealing. Innovative ideas have to connect with
people at a basic level. President Bill Clinton's landmark effort to "end welfare as
we know it" had a ring of basic fairness to it that appealed to people across the
political spectrum.

Sixth, keep it apolitical. One big killer of great new ideas is a change in administration. If an idea is based on a more efficient way to do the public's business,
rather than on an administration's policy agenda, you are less likely to wind up
in anybody's political crosshairs.[29]

Going Viral

If you manage all the key drivers and your innovation program survives and thrives, you may actually reap a bonus—great ideas sometimes go viral. Probably the archetype for this is "Compstat," which won a 1996 IAG award. Compstat was a revolutionary data-driven approach to policing, adopted by New York City police commissioner Bill Bratton, that used crime statistics and police performance information to improve law-enforcement effectiveness.[30]

While it was catching on in police departments around the country, Compstat also expanded rapidly in scope. The concept was broadened at the municipal level by the city of Baltimore in the form of "Citistat," to evaluate and improve the performance of a variety of municipal agencies, not just law enforcement. And when mayor Martin O'Malley, the father of Citistat, was elected governor of Maryland, he launched "Statestat," a similar cross-program and policy assessment of government performance.[31]

The federal government launched its own version of "stat" using the Government Performance and Results Act of 1993 (GPRA). There are three basic requirements under GRPA , which created the beginning of a strategic evaluation framework for federal entities. First, agencies must develop five-year strategic plans and make them available to the public; second, agencies must document annual performance plans that set out annual goals; and third, agencies must report annually to Congress on how they are doing in meeting those goals.[32] The GPRA Modernization Act of 2010 further strengthened this by requiring data driven progress reviews with results tied to the powerful budget process. While the noble goal of data-informed federal programming and budgeting continues to be a work in progress in the nation's capital, the institutionalization of GPRA by statute has helped assure that the drive toward a more data driven approach to governance will survive changes in administration and will continue to be a focus of each new administration.

Why Bother?

None of the issues mentioned so far address the basic reality of what motivates innovation and why the federal government's default position is inevitably risk averse. "In government, the same kinds of pressures to innovate don't exist as they do in the private sector," says Carmen Medina. "There is a commercial imperative in the private sector that just doesn't exist in the public sector."[33]

This is correct: the federal government certainly is not subject to exactly the same kind of pressure. But other students of public sector innovation see an emerging imperative that may disrupt that old dynamic: "You have increasing expectations from citizens," says Shrupti Shah, who leads Deloitte's public sector innovation arm, GovLab, and who brings extensive experience in the public sector. "These days—as technology has begun to infuse itself into every imaginable area of private sector commerce, from buying groceries to booking airline tickets—citizens are used to taking control when it comes to what they want and when they want it. They're now used to being able to order an Uber car in seconds." Government, by contrast, too often forces people to queue up on the phone or take a place in line in some office or wait weeks or months for a mail-based transaction to finally come through.

Long lines and face-to-face transactions aren't something that citizen customers are accepting well today. A recent survey from the American Customer Satisfaction Index (ACSI) shows that Americans aren't very happy when it comes to the services the federal government is delivering, with satisfaction ratings hitting their lowest levels since the index launched in 1994 and in 2015 falling for the third consecutive year.[34] The survey, a national cross-industry, cross-sector benchmark of customer satisfaction in the United States and the United Kingdom, was started by researchers at the University of Michigan in conjunction with the American Society for Quality and the CFI Group, all of whom were interested in gauging (and presumably improving, through comparison) the quality of services in both the public and private sectors.

To innovation experts like Shah, the reason for the continuing drop in satisfaction is no surprise: "Increasingly, in many aspects of government service delivery, there's pressure on budgets and the need to do more with less. But now we're getting to the stage where we're cutting to the bone while expectations continue to increase, and we cannot maintain customer service levels without finding different, better, and cheaper ways of achieving the same ends." The ACSI noted small gains in areas such as customer service and information quality, but government continued to score far below every private economic sector in overall user satisfaction.

Rising citizen expectations is the most potent reason for successful managers and leaders to innovate. But there is another reason, according to Medina, and it's generational: new generations of workers aren't interested in maintaining the status quo. If the best and brightest are to be attracted, somehow, to government work, they must believe they will be able to make some improvements, argues Medina.

A third reason we need to bother working toward innovation is that today's federal managers and leaders face a basic resource question: how to maintain acceptable quantities and quality of service in a severely budget-constrained world. The answer must include innovative process changes (and now-common technologies) to help take up the slack wherever possible, shifting more of what used to be face-to-face transactions to more efficient customer control as well as involving users to actually help solve the pressing problems facing federal agencies and operations. One of the most fundamental responsibilities as federal managers and leaders is to encourage staff to experiment with bold solutions to these current-day challenges and protect them in the process.

Key Takeaways

The discussion of the whys and hows of innovation has stressed the importance of being careful not to imply that there are rote steps to innovative approaches. But there are some basic strategies and tools that can improve your odds of successfully innovating.

Create Your Offense

1. *Identify Your Best and Brightest Innovators and Give Them Cover.* There is a whole new generation of employees, both those already working in government and others waiting in the wings, who are utterly impatient with the outmoded everyone-in-a-cubicle-with-a set-job-description-and-defined-responsibilities style of working. This generation wants to be involved and feel like they can make a difference. Your job as a federal manager and leader is to give the innovators and trailblazers the space and support to figure out how to deliver programs and services in the most efficient, effective ways.

Dr. Michael Gelles, a psychiatrist involved in high-level defense intelligence work, argues that longtime federal leaders and managers can, in fact, enhance their own careers and career longevity by surrounding themselves with new generation workers for whom innovating is just part of their day-to-day functional DNA.[35] Seasoned leaders have to bring needed risk-management strategies to the combination in order for it to work.

2. *Create New Competencies.* When you look at the core competencies listed for the Senior Executive Service, limited attention is paid to being creative, innovative, bold, or forward thinking.[36] Look for those qualities in recruits anyway, and

incorporate them into specific job descriptions for key positions in your department or agency.

3. *Mix It Up*. There's mounting evidence that by grouping together people with very different backgrounds and strengths the result tends to be a more powerful synergy aimed at innovation; this is certainly preferred over staffs in silos that are handed separate problems to solve.[37]

4. *Mix It Up II*. Move people around in your organization. You will be more likely to spark some energy around new ways of doing business, argues Shrupti Shah. Stodgy bureaucracies occur when order and stability make every cog in the wheel act according to habit and comfort.

5. *Create an Innovation "Calendar."* Ask yourself if you are setting aside time to focus on innovation, says Carmen Medina. "Your calendar should reflect that as a priority," she says.

6. *Create an Innovation "Portfolio."* Choose the most vexing problems in your organization and start focusing on fixing those, argues Medina. Not every problem merits an innovation investment and not everything you try is going to work, she says, but your internal action agenda should certainly reflect key issues facing your agency.

7. *Channel Conflict*. A group that sits around agreeing about everything isn't going to successfully buck the status quo. As a leader, it's your job to create eclectic mixes of staff working on problems and then guide the inevitable conflicts in the positive directions that will lead to breakthrough ideas.

Execute Effectively

1. *Mix Up Experienced and New*. Experienced and new thinking often come in different packages. Studies on innovation strongly suggest that teaming younger workers with more experienced personnel often creates a potent mix of knowledge and entrepreneurship. Studies also suggest that communication and collaboration are the most common conditions underpinning innovation; very few great ideas come as an "Aha" moment courtesy of a single brilliant individual.[38]

Consider pushing the right newer staff up on the organizational chart, perhaps with mentors assigned to curtail risk. Michael Gelles regularly points out that innovation is "only an older generation problem, not a new generation problem." He suggests that by placing younger workers in strategic positions they will solve the workforce dynamics problems around innovation, if we just let them.

Gelles also argues that we should become less tolerant of some "traditional" supervisors who are too attached to outdated views of structure and authority. Retooling or reassigning them out of positions that need highly innovative thinking, when done properly, "will automatically make government entities more focused on new solutions." Of course process, performance, and equity questions must be considered when taking Gelles's advice. But working toward setting up mixed teams and putting some new folks in charge of some innovative changes is a goal worth pursuing.

2. *Share Information.* This one sounds simple, but in no sphere is the phrase "knowledge is power" more widely held (and practiced) than the federal government. Historically you amass power and hierarchical dominance by holding information close to the vest. Consider J. Edgar Hoover. (Of course, then also consider the negative impact on his organization over time.) In today's world, information sharing can be power. As leaders, creating a successful program of information sharing can define the agenda, profoundly influence stakeholders, build a network, and empower truly innovative people.

3. *Look Outside for Good Ideas.* Among incumbents, the natural tendency is to continue doing past activities and approaches. Often you have to bring in outside people and perspectives to come up with smarter, better ways to do the public's business. In addition to simply keeping an eye on the literature for good ideas outside your agency, reach out to comparable federal entities with similar problems, to state and local officials, and even to other countries' agencies with similar missions. Essentially, GSA's Challenge.gov is all about doing just that by providing an open portal to collect suggestions from motivated outsiders.

4. *Create an Idea Incubator,* or "skunkworks," as they are often called, to bring together a small mix of diverse and creative staffers, cut them loose, and give them cover. The key to a successful incubator, argues OMB's Clay Johnson, is to "set goals and a time frame—both short and long term—for progress, like with everything else, and then be honest about whether you're making progress toward your goals or not."[39] Always remember that a large proportion of potential "breakthrough" new ideas fail. The key is to take the few "winners" and drive those successes out into the broader organization.

5. *Use the Theory of Diffusion of Innovation.* Tim Young, former deputy administrator at OMB's Office of eGovernment and now director of Deloitte Consulting LLP's Federal Digital Services, describes another tactic managers and leaders should employ to spawn organization-wide adoption of innovative ideas. He uses Everett Rogers's bell curve, reproduced as Figure 8.1, to differentiate between categories of employees based on their openness to adopting innovative changes.

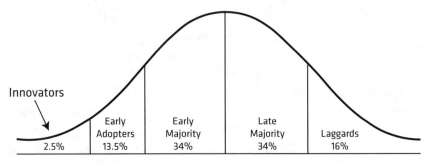

Adopter Catergorization on the Basis of Innovation

Figure 8.1 Diffusion of Innovation Curve
Reprinted with the permission of Free Press, a Division of Simon & Schuster, Inc., from
Diffusion of Innovations, Fifth Edition, by Everett M. Rogers. Copyright © 1995, 2003
by Everett M. Rogers. Copyright © 1962, 1971, 1983, by Free Press, a Division of Simon &
Schuster, Inc. All rights reserved.

First, says Young, identify the small proportion of innovators in your organization (at the far left of the curve) and provide them with the basic permission
and cover already discussed. Once there's a solution framed, avoid the temptation
to try to launch it agency-wide. Connect it first to the "early adopters" in your
agency, those who may not necessarily be generating ideas but who are eager to
try new things out. Following that, continue moving to the right on the curve;
early majority acceptance is possible next.[40]

The personality traits and characteristics of each adopter category are detailed
in Rogers's book, *Diffusion of Innovation,* so I won't describe them here. But you
should use different timeframes, messages, and communication patterns as you
move from left to right on the curve. In the early stages it's wise to stay away
from the late majority and the laggards, who are often the power structure of the
organization, says Young. Once they see success they are more likely to jump on
the bandwagon, too.[41]

6. *Find Other Disruptors.* During Carmen Medina's long experience as a fed, she
has continually run into and networked with others like her who were restless
and wanted to find new ways of doing the public's business. These can be very
informal networks (all the better, to stay below the radar). She offers one caution,
though: be careful in deciding who you choose to invest in. There are people interested in positive, productive change who have the capability, internal respect,
and stature to move an initiative but there also are some who are just plain "off
the wall," in Medina's words. "Find people who are creative but who know how to
be successful in the organization as well."[42]

Play a Smart Defense

1. *Avoid the "Doom Loop,"* says Tim Young. In Young's experience, even the brightest and most creative people eventually get stale if they stay in one place. They tend to come up with a number of great ideas and then they can lose enthusiasm after being too long in the same environment. The key is keep moving those creative and energetic staffs around so they can bring their energy and talent to new areas of program and policy.

2. *Forget a Thousand Points of Light.* David Cheplick, of Veterans Affairs, argued this at the 2014 Potomac Forum summit on tech innovation.[43] "It doesn't generate innovation because the ideas don't touch each other," says Cheplick. That slows things down and compounds the problem of how you build on one thing to get to another.

3. *Don't Get Too Big.* Nick Lemboros, at the Defense Advanced Research Projects Agency (DARPA), says there is a critical mass above which the interpersonal dynamics of innovation just aren't going to click. DARPA is kept intentionally small to ensure prolific cross-pollination and communication, both of which are essential to ensure mission cohesion. If you get too big all the imperatives of bureaucracy start to accumulate: calcification, caution, and the need for self-preservation.[44]

4. *Stay under the Radar.* It's not a bad idea—unless you're in some agency or office whose job it is specifically to churn out innovative ideas—to keep a low profile, at least until leadership signs on to a change. Bureaucracies have a habit of turning on perceived troublemakers or those who challenge the status quo.

Keep your head down and funnel your ideas through conduits of change that don't attract a lot of attention. Sometimes it's wise to make good ideas appear to be someone else's—like someone with the power to implement.

Conclusion

Innovation doesn't just "happen," especially in the federal environment. Innovation requires constant nurturing and careful protection by leaders who recognize that finding and implementing new ways of doing things is essential in today's era of lower budgets and higher expectations.

To do this well, managers and leaders have to pay attention to spotting the innovators and enabling them to work on the toughest problems, testing and perfecting their ideas and sponsoring adoption across the enterprise. Plenty of innovative successes turn up through competitions and websites; the job now is to increase the rate at which leaders find and deploy them. Constantly increasing taxpayer expectations demand it.

Notes

1. John D. Donahue, ed., *Making Washington Work: Tales of Innovation in the Federal Government* (Washington, DC: Brookings Institution Press, 2010), 122–26; Jonathan Walters, "Understanding Innovation: What Inspires It? What Makes It Successful?," New Ways to Manage series, Price Waterhouse Coopers Endowment for the Business of Government (December 2011), 18, http://unpan1.un.org/intradoc/groups/public/documents/un/unpan011090.pdf.
2. Donahue, *Making Washington Work*, 116–125; Walters, "Understanding Innovation," 31, 36.
3. Walters, "Understanding Innovation," 36.
4. Donahue, *Making Washington Work*, 114–27.
5. Ibid.
6. Joseph Dear, "Memorandum for Regional Administrators National Office Directors Design Team—Core Elements for Maine 200-type Programs," Occupational Safety and Health Administration Archive, January 25, 1996, https://www.osha.gov/pls/oshaweb/owadisp.show_document?p_table=interpretations&p_id=22053.
7. Ash Center for Democratic Governance and Innovation, "Innovations in Government," 33, http://ash.harvard.edu/innovations-government, accessed April 7, 2016; Walters, "Understanding Innovation," 12; Jing Zhou and Jennifer M. George, "When Job Dissatisfaction Leads to Creativity: Encouraging the Expression of Voice," *Academy of Management Journal* 44, no. 4 (2001): 682–96.
8. Ash Center for Democratic Governance and Innovation, "Award Selection Criteria," Kennedy School of Government, Harvard University (2008), http://www.innovations.harvard.edu/sites/default/files/1642461.pdf.
9. Walters, "Understanding Innovation."
10. Donahue, *Making Washington Work*, 114–27; Ash Center for Democratic Governance and Innovation, "Celebrating Twenty Years of Government Innovation: Twentieth Anniversary Survey Report of the Innovations in American Government Award Winners," https://www.innovations.harvard.edu/sites/default/files/1642461.pdf, last accessed June 7, 2015.
11. Tom Davis, in discussion with the author, October 21, 2014.
12. Lois Kelly, Carmen Medina, and Debra Cameron, *Rebels at Work: A Handbook for Leading Change from Within* (Sebastopol, CA: O'Reilly Media, 2014).
13. Carmen Medina, in discussion with the author, January 21, 2015.
14. Ibid; Shrupti Shah, in discussion with the author, January 21, 2015.
15. Medina discussion.
16. Kelly, Medina, and Cameron, *Rebels at Work*.

17. Thanks especially to Sally Jaggar for her insights. Judy England-Joseph et al., "Leading Innovation in Government," Partnership for Public Service and Hay Group, 3–4, http://www.haygroup.com/downloads/us/leading_innovation_in _government_-_a_study_with_the_partnership_for_public_service_and_hay _group.pdf.

18. Donahue, *Making Washington Work*, 128–43.

19. Toddi A. Steelman, *Implementing Innovation: Fostering Enduring Change in Environmental and Natural Resource Governance* (Washington, DC: Georgetown University Press, 2010), 196–97.

20. Donahue, *Making Washington Work*, xi.

21. Jonathan Walters, "How Britain's Getting Public Policy Down to a Science," *Governing*, May 2014, http://www.governing.com/topics/mgmt/gov-getting-public -policy-down-to-science.html.

22. Sylvia Burrell et al., memo to The Heads of Departments and Agencies, dated July 26, 2013, "Subject: Next Steps in the Evidence and Innovation Agenda," Executive Office of the President, Office of Management and Budget, Memo No. M-13-17, https://www.whitehouse.gov/sites/default/files/omb/memoranda/2013 /m-13-17.pdf.

23. "Introduction to Challenge.gov," Challenge.gov, last accessed June 3, 2015, https://www.challenge.gov/about/.

24. "Robocall Contest: Robocalls: Humanity Strikes Back," Federal Trade Commission, FR Doc. 2015–05439, 80 Fed. Reg. 45 (March 9, 2015), https:// www.ftc.gov/system/files/documents/federal_register_notices/2015/03 /150309robocall2rulesfrn.pdf.

25. US National Institute of Environmental Health Sciences, "My Air, My Health Challenge," last updated February 12, 2014, accessed April 7, 2016 http://www .niehs.nih.gov/funding/challenges/myair_myhealth/index.cfm.

26. Sandford Borins, ed., *Innovations in Government: Research, Recognition, and Replication* (Washington, DC: Brookings Institution Press, 2009), 93, 109–11.

27. Walters, "How Britain's," 2014.

28. Tom Kalil, "Funding What Works: The Importance of Low-Cost Randomized Controlled Trials," whitehouse.gov, July 9, 2014, https://www.whitehouse.gov/blog /2014/07/09/maximizing-impact-social-spending-using-evidence-based-policy -and-low-cost-randomize.

29. Walters, "Understanding Innovation," 25–32.

30. Police Executive Research Forum, "Compstat: Its Origins, Evolution, and Future in Law Enforcement Agencies," Bureau of Justice Assistance, United States Department of Justice (2013), http://www.policeforum.org/assets/docs/Free_Online _Documents/Compstat/compstat%20-%20its%20origins%20evolution%20and %20future%20in%20law%20enforcement%20agencies%202013.pdf.

31. Chad Vander Veen, "Governor Martin O'Malley Uses StateStat to Transform Maryland," *Government Technology*, August 4, 2009, http://www.govtech.com /featured/102492329.html.

32. US Office of Personnel Management, "GPRA: Performance Management and Performance Measurement," last accessed June 3, 2015, http://www.opm.gov/WIKI /training/Performance-Management/Print.aspx.

33. Medina discussion; Shah discussion.

34. American Customer Satisfaction Index, "ASCI Federal Government Report 2015," January 26, 2016, https://www.theacsi.org/news-and-resources/customer -satisfaction-reports/reports-2015/acsi-federal-government-report-2015.

35. Mike Gelles, in discussion with the author, October 28, 2014.

36. US Office of Personnel Management, "Guide to Senior Executive Service Qualifications," June 2010, https://www.opm.gov/policy-data-oversight/senior -executive-service/reference-materials/guidetosesquals_2010.pdf.

37. Jonathan Walters, "Twenty Years of Highlighting Excellence in Government," *Innovations in Government: Research, Recognition, and Replication* (Washington, DC: Brookings Institution Press, 2008), 13–28.

38. Gelles discussion; Kate Bruges, "Wisdom Just Got Hot," Speech at IPA Talent Adaptation conference London, October 7, 2014; Mark Dodgson, "Technological Collaboration and Innovation," *The Handbook of Industrial Innovation* (Cheltenham, UK: Edward Elgar, 1994): 285–92.

39. Clay Johnson, in discussion with the author, December 2014.

40. Everett M. Rogers, *Diffusion of Innovations*, 5th ed. (New York: Simon & Schuster, 2003), 281–99.

41. Tim Young, in discussion with the author, January 15, 2015.

42. Medina discussion.

43. David Cheplick, "Management of Government Technology Annual Summit—Driving Government Innovation: Process and Technology to Achieve Success," Presentation at Potomac Forum Executive Breakfast, Washington, DC, November 13, 2014.

44. Nick Lemberos, Presentation at Potomac Forum Executive Breakfast, Washington, DC, November 13, 2014.

CHAPTER 9

Tips for Living with Oversight Organizations

When I first arrived at GAO in 1982, it was hardly by choice. Having worked nine years in federal agencies, I was planning to leave government in order to test whether I could help improve government performance from the outside. An opportunity at Arthur Andersen Business Consulting was the ideal career step and I had accepted an offer to go there from the Social Security Administration.

Then came the call. Charles Bowsher, Andersen's managing partner for government services, said he was being named the next Comptroller General of the United States, leader of the GAO, and he wanted me to join him rather than start at Andersen in ten days. "Thanks, Chuck," I recall saying, "but I really want to go private for a while, even if under a new managing partner." I remember his reply as though it was yesterday: "You don't understand, Ira. I hired you. I won't be there anymore. You don't have a job at Andersen. [long pause] How about joining me at GAO?" I joined GAO in early 1982, about four months after Bowsher was confirmed as the sixth Comptroller General of the United States.

As the "dean" of revered oversight organizations, GAO has much to be proud of. It annually releases hundreds of reviews on federal effectiveness, efficiency, and compliance and is viewed as independent and highly credible. But in 1982 there were concerns about GAO and Bowsher had accumulated a list of them.

Funded and defended by Congress, committees nevertheless expressed privately that reports took too long to complete and sometimes did not "adequately" reflect what the requesting committee wanted in the conclusions. Agencies, for their part, sometimes felt that the conclusions drawn were out of proportion to the work of overall programs or sometimes a bit naïve, and even that reports sometimes did not fully recognize fixes that had already been made.[1]

Bowsher himself wanted to shift GAO's work to more sophisticated, in-depth program effectiveness on major issues (a move begun by his predecessor, Elmer Staats) and leave compliance and lesser issues to the inspectors general. Bowsher also wanted to enjoy a different relationship with executive agencies, one that was focused more on convincing and helping them improve.[2]

Using a task force of embedded GAO leaders, we hammered out a "reform the reformer" agenda that created new GAO reporting standards and approaches, such as shorter reports, clearer evidence, and more practical recommendations. To sustain the reforms we created an Office of Quality Assurance to support the development of new skills—such as creating a cadre of new-generation "evaluators" to augment traditional "auditors"—and to review high-profile reports before their release.[3] Additionally, to assert our independence from the sometimes-political congressional agendas, we added to our mission statement the idea that GAO works for the American people, not just for Congress.[4]

Anybody who reaches higher levels of government management and leadership—whether through career move or by appointment—is inevitably going to interact with one oversight organization or another. Although the functions and methods of these agencies differ, they all present some common challenges to those in government who are trying to get big jobs done. Handled right, however, these overseers can be valuable partners and force-multipliers (defined in chapter 1) and help smart leaders achieve program goals and improve performance.

This chapter explains how to do just that. Five oversight entities and categories are examined: GAO, the inspectors general, congressional committees and staffs, the Office of Management and Budget, and department-level management and controller organizations (like CFOs or assistant secretaries for management). First is a look at some issues and challenges common to working with them all; following that is a discussion of each entity's strengths and vulnerabilities; and then, some suggested strategies—and defenses—to help get value from working with these groups and from co-opting their efforts to your goals. One associate sums it up: "Play ball. Play nice. Play smart."

Shooting the Survivors

Bluntly stated, instead of being viewed as "partners" in improvement, auditors and evaluators are too often viewed as the force entering the battlefield after the fight to shoot the survivors. In nine years at GAO I experienced mostly cooperative relationships. In the two-plus decades since, I have learned that many federal operators who profess to accept or welcome oversight do so more because they simply need to be diplomatic and "take" it, rather than because they willingly accept the criticism.

Numerous friction points, of course, make that hard to avoid. How well does the oversight reflect an appreciation of the total mission challenges of your operation, not just the topic under current review? Is the scrutiny focused on something important to your overall mission? What criteria are being used to evaluate performance, and what knowledge and experience do the specific reviewers bring to the assignment? On the receiving end, how uncomfortable (or perhaps defensive) are you when true weaknesses are displayed for public viewing?

Census deputy director Nancy Potok notes that unlike in the private sector, where senior personnel generally oversee programs run by junior staffs, sometimes it's the opposite with federal oversight entities: the most experienced personnel run the agencies, while junior personnel—many of whom have limited operating experience—work in oversight. This can result in reviews that are driven by a second-guessing mentality and sometimes leads to a situation where information provided by the agency itself is used to point out shortcomings that the agency brought to oversight's attention.[5]

Potok's suggestion for getting the best out of the relationship is to dedicate in-house staffs to work with oversight organizations so they can constructively handle documentation of budgets, programs, and performance, and can support recommendations that will improve performance. Having staffs that understand the needs of oversight organizations can greatly increase an agency's responsiveness and transparency.

Progress and Problems

Oversight incentives are typically aligned in a way that encourages staff members to find something to fix, which leads to reports with familiar titles such as "Progress Has Been Made but Much Remains to Be Done." Still, many oversight leaders, like Chuck Bowsher, are able to focus on boosting management effectiveness, so from the receiving side of the coin the key is to capitalize on and reward effectiveness gains. After all, there are many valuable insights that can be adopted to improve performance.

Having spent time on both sides of oversight altercations—as scrutinizer and as the scrutinized—I learned that fighting with or openly challenging an oversight organization's findings may feel good in the short run but is often counterproductive in the long run. There are smarter and tactically more sound ways to function.

Play Ball, Play Nice, Play Smart

Of course, fighting oversight or bristling at criticism may be an honest reaction, but smart leaders need to avoid doing it. A better strategy is to take a more positive and proactive approach. If you develop collaborative strategies for working constructively with oversight entities, educating them to your real-world program management challenges and constraints, and are open to their suggestions, you'll find you can actually leverage their oversight to your advantage—and the taxpayers'. Federal veterans like Todd Grams and Tom Davis urge early and frequent involvement and sharing of information and problems with oversight entities so as to craft the information to your benefit and avoid surprising the Hill or OMB staff with bad news that they might have helped you avoid or manage.[6]

In working with the Labor Department's CFO on a new financial management system a few years back, I discovered that a key member of OMB's eGovernment staff wanted to be more directly involved. Although some department leaders were cool to the idea, as a contractor I was able to cooperate—with the client's agreement—with the OMB staffer in the process, which actually proved to be very helpful; he had some good suggestions on implementation. Although it may have been an unorthodox alliance of contractor, client, and OMB, it actually worked a whole lot better than if OMB had come in after the fact. My position as a contractor also gave the CFO some desirable distance from OMB, which helped the interactions.

Another response to avoid, when oversight entities come calling, is what I call a "We got this" mentality. There is a tendency to attempt to contain emerging problems without reaching out for or accepting help. Agency leaders sometimes feel that they can get everything under control without involving oversight entities, whether internal or external. In my experience this is seldom a successful strategy. Getting (all of) the "story" out quickly hastens your ability to focus time and effort on finding solutions—and on finding the added resources needed for the fix (discussed later in the chapter).

Five Oversight Entities: A Primer

Government Accountability Office

The Government Accountability Office (GAO), housed in the legislative branch, is charged with reporting on efficiency and performance across all federal government agencies and departments. Established in 1921 as the General Accounting Office, the agency was created to manage financial transactions and payments. When the quantity of World War II transactions overwhelmed it and the job of paying the bills was transferred to the Treasury Department and other executive branch agencies, the work of GAO changed to conducting federal audits and reviews.[7]

In recent decades GAO has transformed itself again and now focuses more on broader issues of government effectiveness and major federal issues while leaving most individual integrity reviews and audits to presidentially appointed departmental inspectors general. GAO does retain the responsibility to perform the annual audit of the consolidated financial statements of the US Government as well as other duties such as ruling on federal procurement protests.[8]

GAO is run by the comptroller general, who enjoys a fifteen-year term, removable only by impeachment.[9] Although GAO's span is as broad as the federal government and its conclusions and recommendations are clearly accorded great credibility, GAO's actual authority over executive branch entities is quite limited, constitutionally, because it resides in the legislative. In 2014 over 95 percent of GAO's resources were spent on reports either mandated by Congress or specifically requested by congressional committees (or committee ranking minority leaders) on topics of interest to the Congress or individual committees.[10]

The credibility of its work and the fact that Congress and the media accord great deference to its recommendations give GAO its influence and power, which means any target of a GAO inquiry needs to take the exercise seriously—and even try to influence a report's outcomes.

Four Opportunities to Influence a GAO Report Outcome

There are four opportunities for influencing the outcome of a GAO report:

- during the creation of the initial scope
- while interacting with the evaluators as they do their work
- when responding to the draft before it is finalized
- during congressional discussions or testimony after the report is issued.

GAO's policies actually encourage active agency participation in reviews, and a smart leader will find ways to build a relationship with the GAO staff doing the reviews. (See further discussion under **Key Takeaways**.) GAO is organized principally by program area, so generally every program, agency, or department has a GAO director with long-term oversight responsibility for it. While directors must be appropriately independent in their judgments, their standing as GAO leaders is enhanced if they can influence programs to make improvements. That also opens up room for subtle persuasion or negotiation, which is why embracing them rather than stonewalling is your best bet.

Not surprisingly, congressional requests often come with a negative spin, but GAO itself is committed to balance, which means there are opportunities to provide agency perspectives in most reviews. Indeed, in most cases GAO policy requires that a draft must be submitted to the agency for review, which gives the opportunity to respond before the report is finalized. If the agency takes action on a problem, GAO will include that information in the report and give credit for improvement, which is clearly a smart way to position your agency for more positive hearings once Congress receives the report.

Know the High Risk List

Publishing the High Risk List has been an effective mechanism for GAO to highlight the most important vulnerabilities, problems, or inadequacies the government faces. Begun in 1990 and generally issued to coincide with each new Congress, the list focuses attention on programs and agencies most vulnerable to fraud, waste, abuse, or mismanagement, or that are most in need of transformation.[11] The 2015 list contains thirty-two areas called out for special attention, ranging from government-wide property management to funding the national transportation infrastructure to more specific items, like mitigating gaps in weather satellite data.

The High Risk List is a "living" document; for example, Veterans Affairs health care and IT acquisitions and operations were added in 2015. Progress in successfully addressing oversight of medical products and in managing DOD contracts was documented as well.[12] Savvy agencies and departments use inclusion on the High Risk List to their advantage. According to Census deputy director Nancy Potok, being on the list gives you an opening to discuss with OMB and with Congress the impact of resources on performance.[13]

At an informal level, GAO is also a great source of talent for other oversight entities, most notably the inspectors general, and for C-suite talent, particularly CFOs of departments and agencies. These are great career moves for GAO personnel and it provides agencies with a source of major insight, talent, and content knowledge that come with political and relationship benefits as well.

Inspectors General

Sometimes characterized as the "junkyard dogs" of oversight, federal inspectors general (IGs) have responsibilities somewhat similar to GAO's, but the IGs reside in the executive branch and their duties are specific to particular departments or agencies. They focus more on combatting waste, fraud, and abuse, and through their audits and investigations into compliance and efficiency they address actual program effectiveness.[14]

The IGs for cabinet departments and major agencies are appointed by the president and confirmed by the Senate, and by statute they report jointly to both the agency head and Congress. They can be fired by the president—as with other presidential appointees—but notice must be provided to the Senate and the House as a way to protect their independence. Special agents of IGs have law enforcement authority and are able to carry guns, make arrests, and execute warrants so they can investigate more aggressively than GAO, which is somewhat limited by its legislative-branch status. As a group, the IGs make up the Council of the Inspectors General on Integrity and Efficiency, which is led by the OMB Deputy Director for Management, an institution that attempts to address IG standards, skills needed, and cross-agency issues within a structure whereby each IG has an independent role.

The ability to work constructively with your IG depends heavily on two things: how independent he or she wishes to be from the department or agency and how far the IG wants to go in actually working *together* to correct problems. There is great variability. Many IGs view their role as finding out what is going wrong while refraining from helping in the repair. Others view their role as working with the secretary or management on program improvement.

When Norman Mineta headed the Transportation Department, and Kenneth Mead became his IG, they developed a close working relationship. A former GAO lawyer and deputy director of quality assurance, Mead brought an activist attitude to the IG job: "You have a special position to help programs work better, not just report what's wrong," Mead says.

> Cabinet officers like Norm Mineta can't really trust they're getting all the information from bureaucrats and agency heads, so you help them know the facts and choices they have. That gives the program heads motivation to get help from the IG in solving problems. And, because of the dual reporting to the Hill, I could help them get the best solutions with committee chairs as well.[15]

When problems arose with federal transit grants, for example, Mead was able to reason through politically difficult discussions with key senators to help them realize that funding a pet project before it was really ready would likely end in disaster for all—including the senator.

The use of IG criminal investigation authorities to find broader program improvements was another motivator for Mead, and one that illustrates how agency officials can (properly) use IGs to their benefit. Noting repeated criminal investigations of truckers with duplicate books that reflected bogus driving times (the amount of daily driving time allowed), Mead flipped the recurring criminal investigations to an "evaluation" approach and made recommendations on which rules should be changed to eliminate the abuse entirely.[16]

Congressional Oversight

Wielding the power it has to write legislation and control the purse, Congress expresses its desires through statutes, appropriations, and ongoing oversight of programs. A complex quilt of legislative and oversight committees and reports have emerged to both write legislation and express Congress's view on how each dollar can and cannot be spent, as well as on how to interpret the often broad policies and authorities in statute. These include conference committee reports, which can be thousand-page documents explaining what the House and Senate "meant" when they included this or that clause or Title in a bill; appropriations language accompanying funding, which can explain how they want the appropriation to be spent; or committee reports from the specific authorizing committee (such as the House Energy Committee) on what they intended when they penned the wording.

Committee reports are not binding and appropriations language only covers the year in which the funding is provided, but you will ignore them at your peril. They are an expression of the most important desires of the members and staffs that write the authorizations and fund the programs. Some horse trading is often possible, especially if you have built a relationship with key members or staffs. Outright ignoring of congressional directives can prompt a summons (albeit an informal one) from the staff director or chairman, an unpleasant hearing or public attack, and ultimately loss of funding for the program, or even for you personally.

Fifty committees serve the US Senate and the US House of Representatives, which divide their work among over one hundred subcommittees, including investigations staffs.[17] Getting to know the key staff leaders and members who are involved in your program and policy area should be a high priority for any executive branch manager or leader who wants to succeed.

Tom Davis, who chaired the House Government Oversight Committee from 2003 to 2007, has some advice when it comes to congressional oversight:

> You have to bring them in on issues before those issues get hot. Congressmen legislate anecdotally, in the absence of good information, so the more you can prepare them for bad news and provide background on how you are fixing it the better. Recognize they can't always agree with you publicly, usually because of district politics, but you can build a relationship of personal trust that can carry you through. The people you sometimes see hauled up before the committees, such as the "Fast and Furious" Justice Department people a few years ago, often are the ones who didn't keep the members informed. Use intermediaries to make those contacts if individual congressmen or their staff won't meet with you, or if the administration doesn't allow you to meet directly.[18]

Office of Management and Budget

Housed within the Executive Office of the President, OMB has typically enjoyed a great level of respect, both for the caliber of its career professional staff and the institutional role it plays in executing the president's programs across government. Initially called the Bureau of the Budget, in 1970 a management arm was added, headed by a deputy director for management. Budget examiners make recommendations to the deputy director about how program budgets should grow, drop, or do something in between, depending on broad planning guidelines for each fiscal year. Part of this whole process is the internal hearings, during which OMB staffs will "discuss" with you what your needs are and where efficiencies and reductions might be realized.

My budget examiner for the $14 billion Aid to Families with Dependent Children program at Social Security was a brilliant guy who used the hearing to achieve two goals: test whether my requests had good basis in fact and policy and show me that he knew more than I did about the program. I quickly learned that I could accomplish both goals by assuring him that he *was* smarter but also pushing back when I knew I was right. It's a practice I recommend.

The management side of OMB ("the M-side" to insiders) provides guidance and writes rules, on issues from federal financial management, to regulatory reform, to electronic governance and technology—all issues of importance in the proper management of departments and agencies.

Some presidents run their administrations using strong OMB involvement, while others work more closely with the cabinet and agency heads. In either case, OMB should be considered an oversight organization because policy positions, budget testimony, procurement, and management principles are set and enforced by OMB. It also is the institutional home for the OMB controller (federal CFO) and the OMB CIO.

The Office of Management and Budget differs from other oversight entities because its published management letters, rules, and circulars are binding. Many are not written that way, however, and present themselves more as advice and guidance, sometimes giving agency personnel choices when needed. It's wise to make yourself familiar with the specific language of the circulars and policies that cover your areas of responsibility.

Councils of government-wide management, such as the Chief Financial Officers Council or the Council of the Inspectors General on Integrity and Efficiency, are managed from the management office as well. Federal-wide strategic and performance management is also housed "on the M side," although with different levels of power and control, depending upon the administration.

OMB is different in another way: it sometimes takes a leadership role in running major initiatives administration-wide. The creation of the Y2K initiative, led by OMB, had a calming, confidence-building effect across government and commercial entities because of the way the office went about empowering federal and commercial entities to define, set the scope of, and mitigate the risk.[19] Implementation of the 2009 American Recovery and Reinvestment Act, under the leadership of Vice President Joe Biden, also demonstrated OMB's potential role in high-profile, high-stakes executive initiatives: the office distributed almost $816 billion dollars in infrastructure and economy-boosting jobs between February 2009 and December 2013.[20] In both cases the OMB's leadership was welcome and effective.

All OMB alumni interviewed for this book strongly advise making friends at OMB to provide timely, factual information (no surprises) and build the kind of relationships that can carry through budget or policy differences or other trials or tribulations. Opinions differ on how much and how often to share that information. OMB alums urge maximum sharing: "Bring them into the tent," advises Janet Hale.[21] "Overshare, keep them informed, and bring them along in your thinking so that OMB staff will do the same for you," advises Todd Grams. "Earn their trust so you will be invited into the room when the decision making occurs," he adds.[22] Others are more cautious about information-sharing with both OMB and department-level leadership, opting to reserve contact for major issues. (This last approach, of course, also reduces potential oversight on more minor things.)

Department Oversight

A surprising number of cabinet-level departments were actually created as consolidations of agencies with much older pedigrees. The Census Bureau and the Patent and Trademark Office, for example, preceded the Department of Commerce. More recently, the Coast Guard and Secret Service were folded into the newly created Department of Homeland Security to facilitate law-enforcement sharing and coordination.

To staff and leaders at the agency level, the departments often feel and operate like oversight entities. CFOs, CIOs, chief procurement officers, chief human capital officers, chief information security officers, chief data officers, and the like all have been established to help departments accomplish their goals. The most effective leaders in those roles define their jobs as helping agencies operate efficiently and effectively. They also act as regulators and rule-makers, which, while often necessary, is sometimes viewed by agency leaders as oversight of questionable value, as the next example illustrates.

I arrived as policy director for the Aid to Families with Dependent Children program shortly after it had been moved from the Social and Rehabilitation Service to the Social Security Administration. It took two years to align AFDC rules and processes with those required in our new SSA home, some of which were really not relevant to the AFDC population. Not too long after, the program was moved into a newly created Administration on Children and Family, whereupon the process of conforming management approaches began anew.

Key Takeaways

First and foremost, do not fight the concept and reality of oversight. Participate in the process and display a positive attitude, focusing on where agreements exist and where your agenda can be supported. The numerous places in the process where you can do this strategically, both during implementation and when you are forced to play defense are described below. Remember: play ball, play nice, and play smart.

Create Your Offense

1. *Adopt and Express a Positive Approach on the Value of Oversight.* Tactically speaking, it is not smart to take critical findings personally. As OMB's Mark Reger notes, "they are not the enemy."[23] You will be in a much better position to influence their views and their reporting if you accept findings gracefully and positively than if you get into an argument over them. Janet Hale's advice to "bring them into the tent" is also worth heeding.[24] If you cooperate—and even embrace—outside review, the likelihood that your side of the story will be heard will be improved, not to mention potentially getting the benefit of added insights, early warnings on problems, and ideas on how to fix them.

Building **personal relationships** *with all five oversight entities, at both leadership and operating levels*, is an essential part of this positive approach. Get your deputy secretary together with the comptroller general or committee chair for an annual lunch, and do the same yourself at comparable levels. Sharing as much as you can often leads to reciprocal sharing. If you have a program or agency in the crosshairs of the IG or on GAO's High Risk List, or if Congress is pursuing you, discuss your plans to get off the hot seat, including soliciting your overseer's reactions and suggestions. Show them you're serious about improving.

2. *Adopt and Co-Opt the Agenda.* According to Ken Mead, the smartest agency heads often asked him what his office was looking at in their programs and what specific concerns had been expressed by the Hill; he always responded positively. In short order the IG or committee staffer can tell you, "Here are the problems we see and what we're hearing from others," i.e., the things it would take you a year to discover or would never get at all.[25] Use these conversations to contribute to, steer, or even add to the planned oversight program. Sometimes it makes sense to "call in friendly fire" to target problems or vulnerabilities that need an independent set of eyes and judgments to highlight. This gives you the benefit of the added insights and suggestions and also is a great way to build the relationship and gain credibility that you actually care about improving performance. When problems are found, oversight organizations can be powerful allies in helping get them fixed.

3. *Job Swap with an Oversight Agency.* Consider rotating staffs on a temporary—or even permanent—basis from your agency to an oversight entity and vice versa, suggests Reger.[26] It helps oversight staff learn to appreciate how hard it really is to get the needed outcomes, while your staffs get training on how oversight people think and work, including teaching their new colleagues what the real management challenges are.

Execute Effectively

1. *Agree to as Much as You Can.* Accept the maximum number of findings as a matter of overall practice. Numbers matter, and it's worthwhile, when reporting to your oversight committees or the media, to be able to say, "We accepted seven out of the nine recommendations" before you explain why two were not reasonable or helpful. This also makes the review team look good, which helps soften their stance on the remaining issues.

2. *Create a Unit to Handle Oversight Relationships and Communications.* This unit's job would be to establish positive relationships with oversight entities and to establish thoughtful, credible positions on findings and proposed changes recommended by them. Hire a respected oversight alum to lead the unit and adequately resource the function so that line leadership is spared the distracting and draining impact of constantly responding to findings. Managed well, such a unit can better assure both continuously positive relationships and less internal turmoil.

3. *Master the Art of Testifying.* Although generally initiated by committee request, it is imperative to have a strategy when you're called to testify. Cultivating friends on the committee helps, as does having staffs working with committee staffs to frame the issues and perhaps even develop some questions you'd like to be asked. In the case of an IG or GAO report, you should expect to be preceded by the senior evaluator who did the report and asked about your compliance with it.

Since a request by the chairman or ranking minority leader was probably the impetus for the report, you can surmise that they will generally not be sympathetic to your position. It's good to have your own friendly member on the dais to intercede in ways you cannot from the witness table. Your "friend" can help during the question-and-answer period, providing you with opportunities to speak openly even if OMB or department leadership didn't allow it in your formal statement. Testifying offers an opportunity to respond to GAO or the IG and to make your case, beyond whatever is put in their report. Remember to lead with the items you agree to and accept.

4. *Understand the Politics.* Regardless of the issue, it helps to recognize something that political veterans like Tom Davis regularly note: it is never entirely about the program or policies under review or subject to testimony. Indeed, as Kenneth Ashworth notes in his book, *How to Survive Public Service*, congressmen or senators are often playing to their constituents rather than actually talking to you, whether those constituents are voters back home or certain interest

groups.[27] It's most important to learn what is behind the review or request to testify and to not become personally defensive or engage in heated debate with an elected official.

Be smart; maintain a positive demeanor, and welcome oversight that can make your program better for the taxpayers. I still have the marks on the outside of my knee from Comptroller General Bowsher's taps, under the witness table, reminding me that I needn't reply to every challenge from the chairman. Mostly they just want the comments on the record.[28]

Play a Smart Defense

Program people will reflexively get defensive, but as a leader you have a choice. If the critiques are accurate, take the high road and agree wholeheartedly. Actively engaging in trying to fix problems not only makes you look better, it gives you some measure of input and control. Use the pivot points in oversight reviews identified earlier to provide opportunities for constructive intervention. If you do this well you can sometimes channel the oversight to advance your program goals and serve as agents of change.

1. *Be a Constructive Player at Each Opportunity.* Ask for a friendly preview or kickoff conference, which almost always is available for IG, GAO, or Hill reviews. Use that interaction to get clarity on the goals of the review and who initiated the request. Ask for copies of the requesting letters so you can collect all the appropriate information. If it is a self-initiated review, find out the reason for its launch. You should also use the kickoff conference to scope out timeframes, including when a draft will be available for review. Most important, use the discussion to help target the review on areas helpful to your program whenever possible, whether that is to support activity you wish to spur or to highlight areas in need of more funding.

At the kickoff, and in the period following, it is important to understand and test the criteria the oversight organization will use in the review—that is: What will they use to measure your performance in order to determine if it has been acceptable? Are they comparing you to a much more adequately resourced organization? If you can affect that selection you are likely to get a more fair evaluation than against criteria based upon user expectations that are independent of real-world constraints. For example, prior to the 2015 filing season, IRS commissioner John Koskinen routinely and publicly highlighted the congressional reductions to the IRS budget after 2010 in order to assure that service levels were not viewed without that highly relevant fact. Be sure you understand what criteria your overseer is using, but do so in a constructive way.

2. *Make Constructive Changes ASAP.* If you institute changes as the review unfolds—finding and fixing problems in tandem with the evaluators—you will get credit for that action in the final report and can carry that positive position into the hearing. It is beneficial to do this before the draft is sent to you for review to assure that it recognizes your progress. The evaluators simultaneously benefit because they can claim to have been instrumental in the improvements and get some credit for any savings.

3. *Use the Oversight to Request Resources.* Resources being tight, you can be certain that some things cannot be done without getting added funding, finding efficiencies, or "trading off" against other programs. Be clear about the tradeoffs that will be required, absent additional resources; if the problem is big enough, use it to strengthen your argument for added funding, as Nancy Potok noted earlier. When I was at GAO, some reports on the inadequacies of foreign military sales prompted defensive reactions from stakeholders in some affected buyer countries. One "played smarter," accepting most findings as valid and pointing out how increased levels of funding would be needed to fix the problems identified by GAO.

4. *Right Problem, Right Answer?* Even if the problem is subject to debate, focus especially on the recommendations because they may be desirable anyway. Make alternative suggestions for recommended actions when it may benefit your program. You can adopt alternatives even if GAO doesn't. Since GAO reports are advisory to the executive branch and the Hill, alternative action plans can be accepted by Congress as adequate actions.

5. *"I Disagree."* Occasionally you simply cannot agree with overview findings, perhaps as a matter of administration policy or funding priorities or there's a professional difference of opinion on what services are highest priority. Disagreement with a small proportion of recommendations should be expected. If disagreement looms larger, you may put your leadership or oversight staffs in a defensive spot, so you can bargain for a compromise. The trick, really, is to give everyone some wiggle room. If the disagreement is purely an error, invite them to fix it quietly. If it's a professional difference, just leave the recommendation challenged and unimplemented.

6. *Finally, Develop a Thick Skin.* As a high-level federal manager or leader you're always going to be the subject of criticism from some quarter. Don't let that par-

alyze you. Work to get the positive word out about all the good work you—and those charged with oversight—do for the taxpayers.

Conclusion

Right or wrong, you really don't want to fight with oversight entities because most of the time you will lose. Whenever possible it's best to work with them, co-opt their work to your advantage, and try to stay one step ahead. Comptroller General Bowsher summed up the importance of keeping a positive attitude about oversight: "Remember these oversight functions are important to Congress and you have to tell them you feel that way. Especially with appropriations, I always made sure I assigned my best people to work with them. Even if you disagree with your IG or the others, you're still more credible if you agree on some things."[29]

Play ball. Play nice. Play smart.

Notes

1. US General Accounting Office, "Excellence through the Eighties: Report of the Comptroller General's Task Force on GAO Reports" (1982), http://www.gao.gov /assets/590/586020.pdf.
2. Charles A. Bowsher, in discussion with the author, October 2014.
3. GAO, "Excellence through the Eighties."
4. US Government Accountability Office, "GAO: Working for Good Government Since 1921," accessed May 21, 2015, http://www.gao.gov/about/history/articles /working-for-good-government/06-gaohistory_1966-1981.html.
5. Nancy Potok, in discussion with the author, November 2014.
6. Todd Grams, in discussion with the author, November 2014; Tom Davis, in discussion with the author, October 2014.
7. US Government Accountability Office, "History," GAO, accessed May 20, 2015, http://www.gao.gov/about/history/.
8. Government Accountability Office, "GAO: Working for Good Government since 1921" and "About GAO," accessed June 1, 2015, http://www.gao.gov/about/index .html.
9. Comptroller General and Deputy Comptroller General, US *Code* 31 § 703.
10. US Government Accountability Office, *Testimony before the Subcommittee on Legislative Branch, Committee on Appropriations, US Senate, Fiscal Year 2016 Budget Request*, 114th Cong., Report No. GAO-15-417T (March 2015), 14, http://www.gao .gov/assets/670/668946.pdf.
11. US Government Accountability Office, "High Risk List," accessed May 14, 2015, http://www.gao.gov/highrisk/overview.

12. Ibid.

13. Lauren Larson, "Agencies on GAO's High Risk List Find the Bright Side," Federal News Radio, May 13, 2015, accessed May 14, 2015, http://www.federalnewsradio .com/440/3856968/Agencies-on-GAOs-High-Risk-List-find-the-bright-side.

14. Council of the Inspectors General on Integrity and Efficiency, "Who Are the IGs?" accessed May 20, 2015, https://www.ignet.gov/.

15. Kenneth Mead, in discussion with the author, April 2015.

16. Ibid.

17. "Committees," United States Senate website, accessed May 21, 2015, http://www .senate.gov/committees/committees_home.htm; "Committees," United States House of Representatives website, accessed May 21, 2015, http://www.house.gov /committees/.

18. Tom Davis discussion.

19. Jerry Lohfink, in discussion with the author, February 2015; President's Council on Year 2000 Conversation, "The Journey to Y2K: Final Report" (March 29, 2000), 23–26, https://www.gwu.edu/~y2k/keyreports.html.

20. Edward DeSeve, in discussion with author, March 2015; G. Edward DeSeve, "Managing Recovery: An Insider's View," IBM Center for the Business of Government (2011), 16, 18, 27, http://www.businessofgovernment.org/sites/default/files /Managing%20Recovery.pdf.

21. Janet Hale, in discussion with the author, May 2015.

22. Todd Grams discussion.

23. Mark Reger, in discussion with the author, September 2014.

24. Janet Hale discussion.

25. Kenneth Mead discussion.

26. Mark Reger discussion.

27. Kenneth Ashworth, *Caught between the Dog and the Fireplug, or How to Survive Public Service* (Washington, DC: Georgetown University Press, 2001), 126–27.

28. Charles Bowsher discussion.

29. Ibid.

CHAPTER 10

Tips for Political Appointees Managing Civil Servants

In early 1992, as a newly minted consultant at Arthur Andersen, I took my new colleagues to a luncheon featuring the CFO of the Department of Housing and Urban Development, whose background was entirely from the private sector, like theirs, wherein he laid out publicly his achievements and aspirations for his tenure in the George H. W. Bush Administration. With the presidential election just nine months away, attendees hoped to hear big achievements and an ambitious transformation agenda for the next four years.

They were not disappointed. The presidential appointee's agenda was nothing less than total transformation of HUD business management, including finance, technology, program management, service delivery, org. chart—the whole ball of wax. Like so many appointees before him, he noted he would rely heavily on lessons learned during his private-sector career.

My consultant colleagues, neither of whom had any government experience, were wowed. Finally, here's a person with vision and guts who recognizes the value of bringing private-sector experience to government. Finally, here's someone who understands that things have to change.

My takeaway was more about what the speech lacked: any understanding of the limits of the HUD and CFO environments. It is a world of limited authority, rough-and-tumble Hill politics, embedded bureaucratic interests, and a crazy quilt of personnel and procurement rules, all closely monitored by a gaggle of housing interest groups for whom, in many cases, the status quo was working just fine, thanks.

As a newly "privatized" former civil servant, his tone somewhat irked me, too, as did my colleagues' comments: heavy with innuendo that, finally, a person of great capability, vision, and passion had arrived to singularly fix HUD's problems in an eighteen-month swirl of action that made no mention of the career staffs there. As we returned to our K Street (where else?) office, I whispered, "I give him 'til the election and he's gone." I was wrong. In October, a month before the election, the president nominated a new CFO at HUD.

A little later in my tenure as a private-sector consultant to the federal government, I attended a conference of commercial and federal CFOs, keynoted by Gen. Colin Powell. In addition to addressing issues of overall policy and global defense, General Powell discussed his views on leadership. Commonly accepted as one of the most highly respected leaders of our time—both in uniform, as a general and chairman of the Joint Chiefs of Staff, and also in civilian service, as secretary of state—Powell's speech focused on what he called "followership." It was a new term to me. Without followers, you can't be a leader, he noted. So the key to leadership is to focus on meeting the needs of those you hope will follow you . . . both those in uniform and civilians.[1]

I found the difference in the two speeches to be profound and telling. The HUD speech was all about the speaker versus (implicitly) the people responsible for screwing up the department in the first place and then not fixing it. I had no trouble predicting how *that* story would end.

Powell's speech, by contrast, was ultimately about "us"; it was grounded in the recognition that in order to achieve your goals—whether as a commanding general or a presidential appointee—the successful leader must understand the rules of the playing field (or battlefield) and meet the needs of those who will go into battle with and for that leader. It is on their knowledge and motivation that success will depend.[2] Simply commanding "Take that hill!" or "Left face!" or even "Jump!" doesn't cut it. This is key because even while he was in the military—just like in the civilian world—Powell knew he couldn't handpick most of his soldiers, noncoms, nor lower- and mid-level officers either; he had to get the ones he inherited to follow him over the hill.

The Twin Challenges of Complexity and Time Frame

The federal realm is as complex as it gets, and the political cycle demands notable progress before the next mid-term and results by the next presidential election. The more complex the environment and more rapidly we need to show results, the more important it is for leaders to motivate followers who are willing to share their knowledge of the terrain and their deep understanding of the terms of the game in order to help achieve their leaders' goals. Leaders who arrive with simplistic notions like, "We're going to run government like I ran my business," will quickly find out just how unruly and frustrating this particular business can be.

The federal environment is so challenging for inexperienced leaders parachuting in that Ed DeSeve, a longtime and widely respected government leader who did "hard time" as chief financial officer at HUD, as controller and deputy director for management at OMB, and as assistant to Vice President Joe Biden, was motivated to produce an entire *Presidential Appointee's Handbook*.[3] The handbook is focused on explaining to new appointees the basics of being effective and is a must-read for all appointees, especially first-timers, since your success is closely aligned with learning quickly the landscape, the key stakeholders, and the levers and leverage needed to achieve goals. I will not repeat its multiple wisdoms here, but some key points are noted in the following pages.

This chapter, addressed directly to political appointees, is focused on helping you get the best from career civil servant personnel in this challenging environment. You simply cannot be effective in the short time you have to meet your commitment to the president without teaming with career staffs. You must understand how to motivate the existing bureaucracy and rapidly master the needs of inherited stakeholders, capitalizing on the patriotism and territorial knowledge of career leaders and respecting their valid role in keeping government operating as administrations come and go. The chapter concludes with strategies for securing career support for the president's program by establishing a framework and walking career leaders through the goals, while showcasing and protecting top performers along the way.

Policy Alignment and Execution

Making a speech—as the HUD CFO did in our opening vignette—may be fine for signaling a new policy or noble intent, but it has little to do with effective implementation. (Conversely, if the focus is too much on you and too little on "the team," it can have the effect of "ticking off" a bunch of career staff you really would rather have on your side.) No, appointees don't really inherit a bully pulpit—although the situation can become that, to some extent. But they do inherit a centuries-old, powerfully entrenched status quo of existing statutes, regulations, budget attachments, congressional oversight committees (each invested in a specific aspect of status quo), and a seemingly endless list of "stakeholders," all of whom claim a legitimate right to be at the table when it comes to discussions and action on program or policy changes. It's a lot to get your arms around in a short period of time.

"The career staff are dedicated to public service and know what needs to be done better than anyone else," says former HEW assistant secretary Henry J. Aaron. "If you don't use them, you're tying your hands behind your back." Medicare was implemented so fast and well because the administrators and career leaders charged with making it work in the real world, led by HEW secretary Wilbur Cohen and Social Security commissioner Bob Ball, were brought "in the room" when the laws were drafted. "Not so in the Affordable Care Act design," says Aaron, noting that the White House largely chose to let the Hill write the legislation.[4]

Where to Start

As a beginning, it's useful to revisit the **Four Dimensions of Success;** see Figure 1.1 in chapter 1. Virtually every element must be rapidly addressed in order to have impact within the two-, four-, and eight-year windows so important to administrations. To make a difference requires that appointees must attend to all four dimensions, including defining clear priority goal outcomes to achieve; what is needed in the resources tool kit to achieve those outcomes; how to identify and define desired stakeholder impacts at the three levels outlined; and, of course, the timeframes needed to get all this important work done (e.g., short-term—before the next congressional election; mid-term—over the lifetime of the administration; and longer-term—to have a positive, lasting impact well after this administration is gone).

There are two key steps to accomplishing this. First you must define the new personnel or modified activities that will get you where you want to go, along with a way to measure and monitor their progress and effects. In assuring Native American tribal access to housing support as required under the Low Income Energy Assistance legislation, for example, SSA needed to find and use federal career specialists in tribal governance and finance in both the Bureau of Indian Affairs and the Indian Health Service. Fortunately, the career staffs in those agencies knew their constituents well and could tell us which approaches would work best.

In addition, you need an established mechanism for reporting results to key stakeholders, including the public, when appropriate. We adapted existing monthly reports, already in use to track federal welfare grants to states, to report on Indian tribal grants, which gave us a quick way to get Indian grants out before the cold winter of 1981.[5]

Your effectiveness in getting the president's program implemented relates directly to how much you learn quickly about the *internal government levers* available for executing change. Janet Hale, a presidential appointee in the Bush 43 administration, notes that some appointees remain outward focused, presumably because it's the sexier window for government outsiders. "But if you're going to drive the agenda, you need to know what levers you have, what the regulations actually require, and what will happen if you change them. Time on the job really helps, as well. As a federal employee, I found what every other fed—appointed or career—has found: the longer you're on the job the better you get at understanding the nuts and bolts."[6]

If this sounds daunting, it is. Fortunately, you have a built-in cadre of experts who can help you: your upper-level career managers who have been at the task for years (and often decades) and who have the knowledge and the savvy to help you work through and around all those embedded policies, procedures, and interest groups.

Career civil servants, contrary to so many stereotypes, have more in common with newly appointed leaders than they get credit for. One after the other appointed leader, including all interviewed for this book, will tell you they inherited a career staff with much the same patriotic motivation as many presidential appointees: to faithfully execute the laws and serve the president and the country. In her *Public Administration Review* article "Are Large Public Organizations Manageable?," former HHS secretary Donna Shalala emphasizes that the relationship between career staffs and appointees is reciprocal, and that many potential mistakes and failures can be avoided by recognizing the needs and using the experience of career civil servants.[7]

Tapping "Execucrats"

Research bears out this idea. In *Unsung Heroes* author Norma M. Riccucci describes the success of six representative federal "execucrats" who made a difference. Coining the term "execucrats" to refer to senior career executive bureaucrats without the negatives some attach to the term, Riccucci chronicles major achievements in global diplomacy, public health, environmental policy, and criminal investigations by these six career professionals to illustrate a broader conclusion: there is much similarity between successful *career* leaders and successful *appointed* leaders.[8] Execucrats make the most difference when they know and understand their environments, demonstrate management and leadership skills, and, ironically, have finely tuned political skills.[9]

Unfortunately, most of us career folks are not the superstar execucrats of *Unsung Heroes*. Indeed, the Riccucci six were selected precisely because they had done extraordinary things. The characteristics that were built into career service when it was created by the Pendleton Act in 1883—longevity, protection from political and patronage pressures—created a management challenge because it also means there's little incentive to take risk and virtually no reward for doing so. "So you have to give them cover and incentivize them," says Tom Davis, former chairman of the House's Oversight and Government Reform Committee. "Get the best advice from them and use them."[10]

When entering a land dominated by knowledgeable career staffs with a strong command of the rules, mores, and history of the successes and failures, and who can identify the power brokers and budget sources, it is always wise to first do a lot of listening and observing. Happily, you will find almost all staff dedicated, proud, and eager to help you succeed. Before you launch any significant initiative, establish the most important common bond: we both are here to serve the president and the people, and we will do it together. Then start asking the key program questions that will allow your top appointed team to move forward in partnership with the career staffs.

Different leaders with whom I have worked have managed this interface differently. President Nixon's HEW secretary, Caspar Weinberger, was a master when it came to working with career staffs. Contrary to his nickname "Cap the Knife" (based on his OMB budget-cutting days), he was kind and considerate and he appreciated his career staff's support and said so. In return, people sincerely wanted to help him achieve agency goals. Over forty years later I still remember every word of the following handwritten notation on the monthly legislative status report I had produced for him as a GS-9: "*ira you do a good job on this. cw.*"

As a former University of Alabama president, David Mathews, Gerald Ford's secretary of HEW, focused on involving career personnel in "thinking sessions" in which David would pull out the markers and white board and lead us through enlivening discussions on how to best fashion social and welfare services so they served the country to maximum effect. They were positive exercises in bringing in career staffs and making us feel part of the administration's top team.

Joseph Califano, who succeeded Weinberger when President Carter was elected in 1976, was almost the direct opposite of both. He had faith in data and was impatient with internal relationship-building. Career staffs learned that Califano's heart was in his formidable health agenda (no small positive) and his department-wide "management by objective" (MBO) initiative. A master *external* coalition builder, he left it to surrogates to befriend and motivate career leaders.

Bill Morrill, an assistant secretary at HEW during the Nixon-Ford administration, adopted a "consigliere" role by working with career staffs on the data-driven policy reforms he and the administration wanted. Morrill's focus on data—rather than on ideology—to drive change was unique; it made him a favorite of career staffers and drew some brilliant appointees and career execucrats to work for him. It also paved the way for decades of empowered assistant secretaries for planning and evaluation across the government to cut data-driven paths for policy and evaluation.

However their personal approaches differed, Weinberger, Mathews, and Morrill exhibited a common tactic: develop a commonality of purpose with the career staffs in order to tap insights and expertise in support of the president's agenda. First they listened, and along the way everyone bonded. Califano, who was more intensely focused on policy than on relationships, was ultimately fired by the president in 1979.

I Want To Be "On the Team"

Anyone who has been on a playground when team sides were being picked, or on the sidelines of a dance when partners were chosen, understands how powerful the desire is to be "on the team." So, too, do career civil servants want to be valued parts of a leadership team. Certainly many career staffers come with some suspicion or fear of a new administration, along with personal biases about what should get done and how. But these biases generally work themselves out if the career staffs are approached with respect and understanding. Playing to the desire to be part of the team is key to success.

Once you've started to establish rapport with the career staff, once you've shown them that you respect their positions and their experience, it's time to begin discussing the policies and desires of the administration. Career staffs don't have to agree with everything you want to get done—some won't and it's not their job to anyway. If you communicate respectfully and provide the underlying rationales for policy and program initiatives, you'll be surprised at how quickly most people come around to help and how freely they will share key insights about the last time this or that was attempted or to provide ideas about a better way to achieve the goals. For more on the importance of creating "conditional cooperation" with civil servants, interested readers should see Hugh Heclo's *A Government of Strangers: Executive Politics in Washington*. Although written in 1977, many of its points remain quite relevant today.[11]

Certainly there will be situations in which personnel will have to be moved or reassigned, but it is wise to start with the premise that everyone is on the team together and all are invited to work hard to support the administration's goals. Simply stating a new policy or preaching massive reform, as our HUD CFO friend did in the opening example, is just a very bad way to start.

Career Motivations and Hot Spots

The average tenure of a presidential appointee in a single position is eighteen to twenty-four months.[12] Many political appointees switch out even if the administration is reinstalled for a second term. By contrast, while horizontal career paths are becoming more common, the usual pattern is for career civil servants to be in agencies for at least twenty and often more than thirty years.[13] Our current system was set up to assure professionalism and continuity from administration to administration. But this also leads to certain unintended consequences:

Been there, tried that. It is a major frustration to see new leadership teams, one after the other, come in with "newer" new ideas. Remember, career staffs have seen just about everything "new" under the sun. That is, of course, not a valid reason to abandon a good idea or suggested initiative. But it's wise, tactically, not to sweep in and assume you were the first one to think of a particular idea. In fact, there are very few really new ideas, so you would be wise to borrow one of the tools from Tracy Haugen's toolkit: an analysis of why things didn't work the last time.[14] The key is to listen, learn a little history, and solicit suggestions about how to achieve the administration's goals given that history. There is a good chance that such perspectives will actually help you refine and improve action plans and the likelihood of success.

Shared goals, different timeframes. Even though they may have experienced numerous changes in administration during their careers, civil service staffers still might view timeframes differently than you do; "short-term" for them may seem "long-term" to you. A good technique for recognizing and capitalizing on this potential mismatch is to create six-month "pivot" points and break important longer-term goals into sprints aimed at "benchmark" achievements that are valuable to the administration in the short run. Another technique, identified by George W. Bush appointee Sam Mok, is to include power brokers among the career leaders in your effort to identify something every single day to help the administration look good. Share the credit with the careerists.[15]

Belief that precedent is binding. With career longevity it's inevitable that career personnel absorb the interpretations and practices of generations of leaders (and lawyers), and become guided by such "precedent." This may manifest itself in career staffs sincerely believing that certain policies and practices are fixed and not open to interpretation. Recognize this as a blind spot and usually not an intentional effort to be obstructionist. The best way around the problem is simply to ask about the basis for such precedent and then walk doggedly through possible alternatives.

At SSA, when I took over as policy director for the federal cash welfare program, the Carter administration expressed interest in cracking down on able-bodied welfare recipients and those violating income reporting requirements. In taking over the post, I replaced a delightfully devout woman who would use biblical quotes to support her vision (and formulation) of federal welfare policy, including "thou shalt not bestow upon the children the sins of the father" to support retaining aid to families where parents (and thus their children) would be subjected to reduced benefits.

Faced with a staff who thought policies were carved in stone (maybe literally), I carefully and repeatedly discussed with them the legislation, court interpretations, and the basis for the rules in concert with career staff and attorneys to illustrate to the career staff that the regulations could indeed be changed to allow for the reduction of support for certain families who were earning above the threshold or turning down work. Under "Playing Defense" below, I expand a bit more on approaches that work in "challenging precedents."

Taking criticism for past failures. Civil servants need to be held accountable, of course, like we all do. Performance and results matter. But it's important for you as an appointee to separate program results from whatever control a given career staffer might have had over that program. Remember, too, that whoever was in your seat prior to the current administration may have had very different priorities and goals than you do—and, indeed, perhaps different from the career staffs too.

Ask for help and advice. Nothing brings a career staffer solidly onto the team more than asking for their opinions and advice. Even the most hardened civil servant will soften up when asked what he or she thinks or recommends. The beauty of this, of course, is that whether there is policy alignment or not, listening—and understanding history—definitely improves both the likelihood of adopting a successful strategy and building the support of career staff who will be key to its success.

Lifestyle considerations. Many civil servants have made a choice to trade off more aggressive career paths for one that offers a bit more predictability and stability, with positions that allow more time with family and pursuing outside interests. This reflects the more modest performance/reward tradeoffs of the civil service program and should be respected. Indeed, many of us claim to desire a lifestyle that provides more time for family and community.

This is not to say that career staffs won't step up during surges and other times of special need. Most will and will do so willingly; just ask citizens for whom the Federal Emergency Management Agency (FEMA) proved to be a lifeline when they were hit by flooding in the Midwest,[16] or those whose homes and families are saved by thousands of Forest Service firefighters who risk (and sometimes lose) their lives fighting fires in virtually every state west of the Mississippi River.[17]

Career staffs include plenty of "Type A's" dedicated to serving the public while advancing their careers at the same time. While it's true that many head for the doors promptly at quitting time, if you've built a solid team the career staffs will be there when you need them.

Key Takeaways

With limited time and a lot to get done, what can you do to maximize your use of career personnel?

Create Your Offense

1. *Walk Through the Administration's Commitments and Objectives.* Taking the time to explain to career staff the administration's goals and objectives—making the case for why you (and the president) feel they are the right way to go—and providing them with the opportunity to be involved in shaping initiatives are probably the best strategies for bringing career staffs into your corner.

2. *Be Explicit in Addressing Four Success Factors.* Harvard Business School professor John Kotter identifies eight factors underpinning successful change. I have distilled and adapted them into four that are particularly critical to an appointee's ability to get buy-in:

- Communicate the vision to the career staff, and talk with them about it.
- Create a coalition with career staff and interest groups. Take the time, it is worth it.

- Define short-term, midrange, and longer-term goals that address two-, four-, and eight-year horizons. Create an urgency around inputs for the shortest timeframe (such as the needed funding, staffing, and program changes); outputs for the midrange four-year horizon (e.g., new services to food stamp recipients or veterans); and outcome changes in the eight-year horizon and beyond (e.g., improvement in children's nutrition or integrated state government service delivery). Note that the latter includes longer-term goals that career staffs can take pride in even after the administration is long gone.
- Graft initiatives onto the agency culture so as to avoid "tissue rejection" with the arrival of a new administration. The types of initiatives that will survive at HUD, for example, will be dramatically different from what will stick at the State Department or Treasury.[18]

3. Challenge Precedent. This can sometimes be done by simply going back and asking for the source documents—statutes, rules, formal interpretations—and tracing the source of the current policy or practice. At GAO I learned time after time that what was characterized as "immutable" often ended up actually being an interpretation and therefore quite mutable. There is a hierarchy, though: adopted practices can be altered by directives; formal interpretations can be revised based upon new leadership policies or changed social conditions; and regulations can be amended or altered given due process, and these occur every day. More difficult to change are statutes. But very often the statute is imprecise and can be open for interpretation or altered significantly by language contained in the annual program appropriation bill (one of the most powerful arrows in your quiver for getting rapid change). Sometimes it helps to bring in outside legal advice when you're wrestling with questions of interpretation, regulation, law, or procedure.

4. Befriend the C-Suite, especially the chief financial officer and the assistant secretary for administration and management. While the CIO can also be an important ally, whoever controls the budget and appropriations process holds the key to having an impact on program and organizational effectiveness, according to Mary Corrado, a career CFO at both the National Reconnaissance Office and the Central Intelligence Agency. Pointing to the role she played in helping agency directors and appointed staffs control programs and obtain support for appropriations from the Hill, based upon her impartial efficiency and effectiveness roles as CFO, Corrado states there's really no substitute for having a smart, independent "management geek" on your side.[19]

Sam Mok's view about which individuals to befriend is broader. Mok recommends explicit "manage-up" and "manage-down" strategies. In "managing down," new appointees should find the personnel who are influencers and who run the organization. "At Labor I learned, sometimes too late, that the Administrative Officers' Council was key to getting any back-office changes done, like new financial management processes." They really ran the place, says Mok, and so giving them attention should have been a higher priority for implementing his desired new financial system.[20]

Interestingly, in managing up and across (see the explanation in chapter 2) Mok uses a highly selective strategy: find the few people you know well and manage to their needs, whether it's the deputy secretary or secretary, for example; and among colleagues, pay attention to those with the power and influence you need. There are personal risks and team consequences to such a selective approach, of course, which Mok readily accepts.

Finally, use your influence within the administration to avoid career bashing, the periodic political blood sport of blaming bad government results on derogatory stereotypes like "poorly performing" or "lazy" government employees. In Bill Morrill's words, "If a CEO were to regularly take to the news media to denounce his employees, he would be considered a little crazy."[21]

Execute Effectively

1. *Adopt a Visible Framework for Goals, Activities, and Results.* Preferably do this at two levels, one focused on inputs and outputs at the granular level and the other on outcomes that the general population (and the media) can understand. Often the former is called a "balanced scorecard," which can be used to measure and report progress and resourcing in an integrated, sensible way. Initiated in the private sector, balanced scorecards expand traditional financial measures to include other important metrics. Ed DeSeve proposes a straightforward adaptation for the public sector that tracks desired *results*, needed *enablers, customer impact,* and *public acceptance.*[22]

Unfortunately, balanced scorecards can get unwieldy for public and media consumption. Among the most successful tools for reporting progress are the now-familiar red/yellow/green ratings at agency and cabinet levels. So powerful is the "I got to green" signal that cabinet-level officials in the George W. Bush administration reportedly used it on numerous occasions in cabinet meetings to highlight progress on the president's agenda. That's an impact you and your career staffs can identify with and take pride in.

Play a Smart Defense

1. *Showcase and Protect Career Personnel.* Many political appointees attribute their success in large part to befriending and protecting career personnel who supported their programs and policies. Others have repeated the general adage that "successes are attributed to staff while shortcomings are all mine." When you can, include career staffs at press events or White House meetings. Acknowledge their contributions publicly whenever you get the chance. Remember Donna Shalala's Lesson Six: stand up and fight for the people who work for you. It doesn't have to be a big production, but recognition and protection win real loyalty, live on long after your tenure is over, and help solidify private and public accountability for continued success of the initiatives into the future.[23]

2. *Beware the Praise Trap.* Some career staffs welcome an appointee with enormous praise as *the first truly talented person* in the job. "Be suspicious of the worshipful sycophant," advises Wade Horn. What you need is "honest advice, not gushing praise" that feeds a false sense of self-importance. Horn cautions to remember that the next appointee in the position may well be met with *the same* welcome.[24]

3. *Use 'Em or Move 'Em.* You have little time and you must form your team, including career leaders who get on board. Most will do so, if you frame a motivating vision and define ethical actions. For the few who cannot get on board, whether for reasons of policy or competence, making a change early can be important. Remember that a primary goal for setting up the career SES was to enable and encourage movement to other SES jobs across the government. Though career personnel are protected for the first 120 days following the arrival of a new agency head (or newly appointed immediate supervisor), changes after that can be wins for both you and the SESer.[25] After all, it is no fun working for someone you disagree with, even if the short-term change can be personally challenging.

4. *Manage Up.* Presidential appointees, says Janet Hale, can spend inordinate amounts of time responding to overreactions from OMB or the White House based upon inexperience in the Washington fishbowl. These often result from challenges posed by the media, GAO, an IG, or the Hill. Hale's solution is to get advance word to leaders before they overreact, along with your action plan(s).

Avoid trying to control or fix the problem before alerting leadership. Bad news gets worse through surprise.

Conclusion

All appointees interviewed for this discussion repeated the admonition that effectiveness as an appointee depends on bonding with the career personnel you inherit or hire. How inclusive or selective that bond is to be is a matter of personal style. Most recommend selling the career leaders on your goals and listening to their advice. After all, they know where the skeletons are buried. Whatever approaches you choose, remember Henry Aaron's admonition: "Respect the career. They know it better than anyone. If you don't use that, you're tying your own hands."[26]

Notes

1. Colin Powell, 15th Annual CFO Vision Conference, Deloitte Development LLC, Washington, DC, September 2011.
2. Ibid.
3. G. Edward DeSeve, *The Presidential Appointee's Handbook* (Washington, DC: Brookings Institution Press, 2008).
4. Henry Aaron, in discussion with the author, December 9, 2014.
5. Libby Perl, "LIHEAP: Program and Funding," Congressional Research Service, July 18, 2013, 1, http://neada.org/wp-content/uploads/2013/08 /CRSLIHEAPProgramRL318651.pdf.
6. Janet Hale, in discussion with the author, May 7, 2015.
7. Donna E. Shalala, "Are Large Public Organizations Manageable?" *Public Administration Review* 58 (July-August 1998): 286.
8. Norma M. Riccucci, *Unsung Heroes: Federal Execucrats Making a Difference* (Washington, DC: Georgetown University Press, 1995), 227.
9. Ibid., 13.
10. Tom Davis, in discussion with the author, October 21, 2014.
11. Hugh Heclo, *A Government of Strangers: Executive Politics in Washington* (Washington, DC: Brookings Institution Press, 1977).
12. Jeff Neal, "Are New Political Appointees Ready to Govern?," ChiefHRO.com, August 5, 2013, http://chiefhro.com/tag/political-appointee/.
13. Cary Elliot, "A CBO Study: Characteristics and Pay of Federal Civilian Employees," Congressional Budget Office (March 2007), 25, http://www.cbo.gov/sites/default /files/03-15-federal_personnel.pdf.
14. Tracy Haugen, in discussion with the author, May 26, 2015.

15. Samuel Mok, in discussion with the author, June 2015.
16. Associated Press, "Victims of Midwest Flooding Praise FEMA," *USA Today*, June 23, 2008, http://usatoday30.usatoday.com/weather/floods/2008-06-23 -fema_N.htm.
17. Sarah Kliff, "Uninsured and Fighting Blazes: Welcome to the Life of a Federal Firefighter," *Washington Post*, June 27, 2012, http://www.washingtonpost.com /blogs/wonkblog/wp/2012/06/27/uninsured-and-fighting-blazes-welcome-to -the-life-of-a-federal-firefighter/.
18. John Kotter, *Leading Change* (Boston, MA: Harvard Business School Press, 1996); DeSeve, *Presidential Appointee's Handbook*, 10.
19. Mary Corrado, in discussion with the author, March 2015.
20. Samuel Mok discussion.
21. William Morrill, *A Journey through Governance: A Public Servant's Experience under Six Presidents* (New York: Cosimo, 2013), 159.
22. DeSeve, *Presidential Appointee's Handbook*, 10; Jonathan Walters, "The Buzz Over Balance," *Governing the States and Localities*, May 2000, http://www.governing .com/topics/mgmt/Buzz-Over-Balance.html.
23. Hale discussion.
24. Wade Horn, in discussion with the author, January 16, 2015.
25. Office of Personnel Management, "Guide to the Senior Executive Service," April 2014, http://www.opm.gov/policy-data-oversight/senior-executive-service /reference-materials/guidesesservices.pdf.
26. Aaron discussion.

CHAPTER 11

Tips for Civil Servants "Managing" Political Appointees

In July of 1881, just four months after he was inaugurated as the 20th president of the United States, James A. Garfield was shot while boarding a train in Washington, DC. He died less than three months later, just the second US president to be assassinated.[1] Sixteen years earlier, in 1865, Abraham Lincoln had been cut down by John Wilkes Booth, a Confederate sympathizer and supporter of slavery who feared that Lincoln was "determined to overthrow the Constitution and to destroy his beloved south."[2]

Charles Guiteau's motivation for killing Garfield was a bit more mundane than Booth's. An unsuccessful lawyer, evangelist, and insurance salesman, Guiteau killed Garfield over a job: a patronage position in the diplomatic corps Guiteau felt the president owed him to repay a debt for Guiteau's political support.

Until that point, patronage was the method the federal government used to recruit professional talent, based on the constitution's vesting of all executive power in the president. Guiteau's action was catalytic in ending that system as a common practice. In January of 1883, fewer than eighteen months after Guiteau was hanged for the murder, the Pendleton Civil Service Reform Act put in place a career civil service, with most jobs based on merit rather than patronage.[3]

The Pendleton Act did not, of course, eliminate federal patronage altogether, nor did its sponsors intend it to do so. Thousands of presidential appointee positions continue to exist today. Critical to the success of all administrations, these appointees are selected because of their support for the policies the president desires to implement and the promises the president has made to get elected—and sometimes to reward high-spending political donors as well. The highest-level presidential appointees (cabinet and agency leaders, typically) are subject to Senate confirmation, fulfilling that chamber's constitutionally required role of "advice and consent" to keep a check on the executive's patronage practices.

As in any successful commercial enterprise, it's critical that the president assemble an executive team that will reliably support the goals and commitments made to shareholders—in this case, the electorate—by the chief executive. More "junior" political appointees, typically named by cabinet officers and administration officials under Schedule C of federal employment rules, also exist.[4]

The interactions between the roughly eight thousand political appointees placed in positions across the executive branch of the federal government and the career employees already at work there are challenging for both. Nevertheless, there is no apparent record of any deadly violence since Guiteau took to the gun in 1881. This chapter is devoted to providing advice for those career staffers who want their relationship with political appointees to be one from which both sides, and the taxpayers, can get the most benefit. Included is a review of the essential roles appointees play in bringing new direction that reflect the will of the electorate, and the challenges of doing so under brutally short two-, four- and eight-year election windows. Also explored are the common stereotypes, contrasted with the common goals and complementary roles of appointees and career personnel. The chapter concludes with suggested strategies to help career staff "get on the team" and provide value, from offering new ideas to relabeling old ones and using technical budget and appropriations knowledge to support new directions.

Special Challenges—and Opportunities

In order to work well with appointees it's important to truly appreciate their role(s) and what motivates them. In the federal environment, loyal political appointees are arguably *more* critical to the success of the enterprise than comparable executives are to the success of almost any commercial enterprise. This is because accountability is more diffuse and performance is more difficult to measure and reward; because interest groups are more powerful; and because Congress and the media are more attentive to and willing to attack performance failures. Appointees are highly attuned to these issues, including to a whole set of time imperatives that are different from career leaders.

The tight timeframes confronting any administration add to the leadership challenge. A new president's proposed budget is due within a few months of inauguration, and midterm elections make it politically critical to "show some progress" in eighteen short months. First-term administrations, meanwhile, need concrete "results" within three years to advocate for reelection. This provides a clear need for career staffs to "get the ball rolling" on projects aligned to a new administration's agenda, sometimes even before appointees have arrived.

For second-term presidents, the four-year imperative is no less imposing, although the need switches to "secure a legacy" and provide "a leg up" for the party's next nominee. Having appointed leadership that the administration can count on to implement the president's agenda quickly and without doubt is essential to meeting its commitment to the people.

Rapid action to get the right team in place is essential, but it can be a fairly brutal process. In early 1977, within a few weeks of President Jimmy Carter's inauguration, newly confirmed HEW secretary Joseph Califano fired all 357 Nixon-Ford presidential and political appointees in all parts of the department—from the Food and Drug Administration to the National Institutes of Health, the Office of Education, and the Centers for Disease Control and Prevention (at the time simply the Center for Disease Control). Califano's newly appointed executive assistant ushered all those appointees into his office through one door and out a second in three-minute intervals. The only distinctions made were whether they were to clear their desks that day, stay for a week to assist the replacement, or accept a one-month consulting retainer for remote transition support.

Those of us in career positions greeted this ritual with gloom-and-doom predictions that it would take years to reestablish the momentum needed to keep the place running. Califano's rationale: with the right team, named quickly, things would be better in a month and fully "humming" within three; he believed he would have the needed urgency, alignment, and action from the right new team. The secretary was right: within three months the department was humming on the new president's agenda.

Unfortunately, today's poisonous political environment makes this speed very difficult to achieve and many highly qualified individuals choose not to accept a nomination because of the lengthy and often torturous confirmation process, sometimes dragging family and personal lives through the proverbial "mud."

This all presents substantial challenges for federal career staffs and leaders. The sheer number of US political appointees is far larger, even proportionally, than in comparable democracies like Britain, France, Germany, and New Zealand. According to Jitinder Kohli, a globally recognized expert on government reform with fifteen years of experience as a senior British government official, this tends to "atomize" management at leadership levels, like an atomizer sprays thousands of droplets in a mist rather than focusing policy like a sharp spray. In such a diffuse environment it can be extremely difficult for career staffs, already held in lower regard than in other governments, to work toward a manageable number of focused goals.[5]

In Singapore—admittedly an extreme example—there is no debate about the importance of strong management or the government's authority to implement needed actions.[6] Civil servants are highly compensated and held in high esteem, and their directives are followed.[7] In Great Britain, working in government is a coveted career.

Adding to this is the totally different timeframes that shape the attitudes of career versus appointed leaders. Career leaders and staffs are "in it for the long run," pursuing careers that can exceed thirty years or more to full retirement. Appointees, on the other hand, need to do something *now* in order to help fulfill the president's commitment to change and improvement. In a perhaps extreme example, Labor Department CFO Sam Mok awoke daily asking himself, "What will I do for [Labor Secretary] Elaine Chao today that will make her look good?"[8]

The rapid movement of political appointees in and out of positions (with average tenures of eighteen to twenty-four months) creates a training burden for career staffs and leaders as well. Robert Knisely, a veteran of Vice President Al Gore's National Performance Review and seven cabinet departments, points to the "extensive amount of time career leaders must spend dealing with people totally inexperienced in your enterprise or in management at all, in which you are constantly 'training-up' new leaders and bosses. . . . No corporation could succeed under that strain."[9]

When government does succeed it's due in no small part to the fact that career and appointed leaders actually *do* have common goals and interests, especially achieving results for the taxpayer. In her book *Unsung Heroes* Norma Riccucci concludes that highly successful senior career executive bureaucrats ("execucrats") understand the political intricacies of their environments, have finely honed political skills, and are good at choosing political allies.[10] As career leaders, our success can be enhanced as well by the mastery of appointee goals, personalities, and needs.

Understanding Appointees' Goals and Challenges

The simple message to appointees arriving in this "foreign" land of unfamiliar operating norms and established culture is that you need the help of the natives in order to survive and thrive, so the smartest thing you can do is befriend the career leaders (see chapter 10). Conversely, career staffs and leaders should use your insights and wisdom to *befriend the political team* to help them find their way and thereby gain their support for your needs as well.

Shared Goals

As a career staffer it can be daunting—and sometimes downright frightening—to witness 8,000 new high-level people landing on your shores, "juiced up and ready to transform!"[11] Both sides too often view the other through a stereotyping lens that frequently lacks subjectivity or accuracy.

Just as in our personal lives, when we react based on these expectations we usually miss the less threatening, more positive reality. In this case, the reality is that appointees bring new and potentially transformative ideas and leadership, based upon their prior experiences, along with political perspectives that reflect voter desires for government improvement. Career staffs offer the institutional knowledge critical to successfully implementing such changes, along with the stability and continuity necessary to keeping the highly complex US government operating from administration to administration. It actually can be a good combination.

The bottom line is that career and appointed managers (and leaders) both benefit from a close working relationship. They actually share many continuity and performance goals and operate under the same constitutional responsibility to "faithfully execute the laws." Political appointees arrive with one additional imperative: to execute rapidly the changes and improvements that were promised by the president and reflected in the vote of the electorate. That's something that must be respected as appointed personnel work to implement an administration's agenda.

Promised Changes

Most of those promises will be a clear part of the public campaign record, so at least when it comes to programs and policies there shouldn't be a whole lot of surprises. This means you need to have been keeping up with the positions and commitments of the incoming administration, or, in the case of more limited changes, the new department or agency head. Confirmation hearings also provide valuable validation of these. Get the ball rolling on the needed analyses and preparations, as suggested earlier in the chapter, so you are a valuable early member of the new team.

Challenging Timeframes

All administrations have important time lines—usually aligned with the two-year, four-year, and eight-year cycle of legislative and executive elections—and a certain degree of impatience for getting things done and making their mark. Hearkening back to the **Four Dimensions of Success**, an excellent strategy for supporting appointees is to help them sort their input, output, and outcome goals along these three timeframes. While doing so you can align longer-term outcomes with your program's mission goals and your personal performance metrics.

The first key milestone for a new administration is the very quick eighteen-months-in midterm elections, and so it's smart to work with appointees on some clear, achievable input and output goals that fit that calendar. For example, shift funding to higher-priority programs or services in high-profile areas like transportation, defense, the environment, or health and human services. Realistically, these short-term markers will likely be inputs such as increasing defense spending or enacting a new program, with the chance of some output impacts if you really move fast.

Likewise, also work on some midrange goals for the end of the administration's first term—the three-and-a-half-year marker—just in time for the reelection campaign. Two full fiscal years will have elapsed, so it is possible to show some *output* achievements (often needed to get reelected), like stronger border security or reduced wait times on tax or social security hot lines. You also can try to attain some high-profile *outcomes*, which every president wants, like stronger economic growth or a nationwide improvement in veterans' health.

Politically attractive goals need not always be *outcomes*, though. In fact, high-visibility *outputs* can do nicely, such as higher national vaccine rates, fewer out-of-wedlock pregnancies, reduced cross-border drug traffic, or renegotiated trade agreements. There might be time enough to report on outcomes, such as improved economic performance or reduced highway morbidity and mortality, but achieving such significant national improvements in just a few years is tough to pull off.

The longer-term eight-year window provides ample opportunity, on the other hand, to highlight progress and success in outcomes. This may include an overall improved economy (the holy grail of every administration); higher real income for Americans; or a more secure, peaceful military position globally. Polling data can be a helpful tool to showcase increased confidence in government or optimism about America's future.

The Right Attitude

To be able to help political appointees achieve these goals, career staffs have to understand the political and management environment in which they live. Appointees will be searching for wins the administration can take credit for once timeframes get compressed and pressures build for results in the highly charged political environment. An attitude of understanding, tolerance, and generosity will serve you well in this situation. Remember the admonition that there's no limit to what can be achieved if people don't worry about who gets the credit. This is especially true in a political environment, so give credit freely and often to your new leaders.

In fact, evincing tolerance and generosity should pay *you* dividends as well. It can help you win added resources, be part of an important initiative, or even be considered for a leadership role. Newcomers need guides. Savvy natives use that to help them navigate the terrain in ways that benefit both.

Political Appointees and "Managing Up"

Nobody wants to be "managed" (or worse, manipulated) by subordinates, least of all presidential appointees looking forward to implementing transformative changes. And yet the concept of "managing up" described in chapter 2 is directly applicable here.[12] To achieve your program and personal goals, understand and play to the appointee's temperament and needs.

Sometimes this can be difficult. After the Nixon-Ford Administration gave way to Jimmy Carter's, the tone at HEW shifted dramatically. Newly named Secretary Califano brought with him a much different style than Cap Weinberger had used, and Califano's subordinates reflected his impatience with the bureaucracy and suspicion of career personnel. I was eager to make a positive impression in my career role as assistant to Carter appointee Henry J. Aaron, the new assistant secretary for planning and evaluation. Califano's new public affairs chief, Eileen Shanahan, a former *Washington Star* editor, came to visit and, failing to find the assistant secretary, she turned to me: "Who released these welfare reform research results to the media?" she barked. Shanahan wasn't keen on what the numbers had to say.

The release had been fully approved, so I had gone ahead and issued it, just as we had done dozens of times under the prior administration. "But why do it in time for the 6:00 p.m. news? Why not tomorrow [Friday] after dinner . . . you idiot," she replied. The conversation ended abruptly with our new media leader pronouncing me the "worst civil servant she had ever met" and assuring me I would "pay the price."

I considered my alternatives: pack up right now, find a lawyer, visit Shanahan with a clever plan to call all seventy-five press outlets and beg them to ignore the release. Henry Aaron sent me to Ben Heineman, Califano's chief of staff, who smiled and said, "Don't worry about it. Nobody listens to Eileen's tirades about incompetent career staff." Then Heineman added two pieces of advice: first, since this administration is super-attuned to the press, be sure my new boss conferred with Shanahan on the timing of every release; and, second, be sure my first interaction with Califano himself was a good one, since "first impressions are key with Joe."

In reality, Heineman was sharing advice on the administration's priorities, on how to successfully "manage up" with both Shanahan and the new secretary, and how to better serve my new assistant secretary as well. He taught me, too, that I missed a transition red flag: Aaron or I should have prepped Shanahan *before* issuing one of the department's first media releases following the transition to the new administration.

Of course, learning at mega decibels is not the preferred way to discover a new administration's culture, although it did get me great exposure to Heineman (and later his help with Califano). You need to tune in to the policies, practices, and culture of new appointees. Some suggestions follow.

Key Takeaways

As long as there are elected presidents there will be appointees with legitimate and important roles to play. The question, of course, is how to help them and yourself as well.

Create Your Offense

1. *"Do Everything You Can to Make Them Successful."* That's the advice of Todd Grams, former SESer at OMB, the Veterans Administration, and IRS. In Grams's view this means "listen first, determine where they're coming from, and what they want to get done." Learn their agenda by reading white papers, research abstracts, media coverage, backgrounds of key incoming appointees, and commitments made to constituencies. In essence, do what it takes to understand what "success" might look like for the new appointees.

2. *Demonstrate Your Value to the New Team.* Use the two key advantages you bring: significant institutional knowledge (including "where the skeletons are buried") and how the policies developed and resources committed by previous

administrations might be reconfigured and/or redeployed in support of the new administration's priority goals.

3. *Have a Strategy for How You Will "Tell the Story" of Your Organization or Program.* A four-inch-thick briefing book is not going to achieve this. How will you *personally* communicate goals, status, strengths, and (yes) weaknesses of the existing program or organization? Where do you see the need (and opportunity) for changes and improvements, particularly where those might align with the new team's priorities? What would you need and want to know, if the roles were reversed? Work to provide these.

4. *Anticipate the New Regime's Expectations.* As Ben Heineman noted, first impressions are important. Be ready to demonstrate that you know your stuff in a nondefensive way. Always start with the presumption that the new team will want and welcome what you have to offer by way of institutional knowledge. If they don't—and sometimes they don't—there will likely be an information gap for the new team and, therefore, subsequent opportunities to use what you know in some strategic way.

5. *Find Allies Among the Appointees.* Sometimes these are people with whom you share common views on policy or management; at other times it's just senior officials who respect your role or value your judgment based on prior interactions or common acquaintances. Effective "execucrats" find alliances with appointees who are positioned to help them with things like funding or administration support at OMB or on the Hill.[13]

6. *Offer Up New Ideas That Might Be Helpful, or Even Exciting, to the New Folks.* Don't offer "exciting" ideas until you have established enough alliances and working relationships to gain some respect; and don't force it. My colleague Jitinder Kohli did time running the United Kingdom's Performance Management Office when Gordon Brown became prime minister (PM). Apparently Brown had a habit of endorsing ideas and approaches before careful consideration, which was creating difficulties for careerists like Kohli in "managing" the PM's commitments and resulting in a "scattershot" program of potentially untargeted and ineffective initiatives.

So Kohli approached Brown's key aide and got this bit of timeless advice: "It's part of your job to give Gordon Brown new and exciting ideas that make *you* a 'thought partner' to the PM. That's what will 'capture' him and create your value." Today, working with US federal government clients, Jitinder has generalized this advice into a concrete strategy: hear what they say and understand what they want to do; become a "thought partner" in bringing stimulating, exciting ideas to the appointees; and then help them make those ideas reality.[14]

Execute Effectively

1. *Do Some Advance Work*. Career SESers are in a good position to begin analyses of what process, resource, or policy changes should be considered to advance the new agenda and to have this information ready for a presidential appointee upon nomination or confirmation. You need to be careful not to go beyond analysis, which could be considered presumptuous and trigger some defensive reactions.

2. *Understand the Appointee's Learning Style*. Different people take in information differently. Ask any teacher. Some of us are visual learners while others absorb more audibly. Few of us learn best by reading hefty primers on "how to" versus learning from examples of what has been effective (and what hasn't).

3. *Pick Up On and Use Nonverbal Cues*. Comptroller General Bowsher repeatedly used "bread-breaking" events to signal his desire to build relationships that transcended political or audit differences. He would frequently invite cabinet members to join him in the comptroller general's dining room to discuss GAO insights into their organizations or address specific problems an organization might be experiencing. (The practice was so effective and well-received that appropriations were specifically earmarked for it, even in the tight budget environment.)

Setting and style are both important. What is your appointee used to for relationship-building: is it having a beer or wine after work, or a quick breakfast before the day starts? As Arthur Andersen's global government services leader I was schooled by our French partners on using food, wine, and setting for political communications purposes. Naturally, all the meetings among our French partners began at noon over fine food and wine, often with spouses present to assure the absence of premature business discussions. The more important the issue, the more important to "take the time to get to know one another" (and perhaps soften everyone up?). Across the English Channel, the British partners began at 7:00 a.m. in a room with a white board, markers, and breakfast tea and crumpets.

Again, there is no right or wrong, but nonverbal cues send very clear signals, so look into the cultural background of your new appointees. Does the person "enjoy the debate" or take offense at socially abrupt disagreements in front of others? Is he or she used to starting late in the morning and working into the evening, like many Hill staff and private attorneys do, or is a 6:30 a.m. to 3:00 p.m. workday the norm, like some GAO staffs preferred?

4. *Control the Briefing Books*. No discussion of career-political interfaces would be complete without acknowledging the existence of "briefing books." Stephen Goldsmith, former Indianapolis mayor and chair of the federal Corporation for

National and Community Service (CNCS), and now director of the Innovations in American Government program at Harvard's Kennedy School of Government, offers the following vignette. Goldsmith notes that some of the senior staff at CNCS, a particularly partisan-sensitive agency when Goldsmith was appointed by George W. Bush to head it,

> retained the view that they were guardians of the institutional history against the heretical attacks of a new administration. Others however saw a more constructive future in adapting the institution to the new themes and interests of the incoming administration. The top holdover leadership prepared very thorough briefing books containing descriptions of each program and possible areas of interest. These books however did little to help the new administration understand how it could legitimately incorporate an existing agency into its agenda.[15]

Instead of relying upon hefty briefing books, Goldsmith used a combination of conversations with senior executives and staff to reposition the mission and show the new administration how CNCS could help meet commitments made by the president during the 2000 campaign.

In today's information-on-demand world, briefing books still retain some usefulness as reference documents, demonstrations of the depth of program issues, and, of course, as doorstops when printed out. If someone in power wants one, surely deliver it. A desktop shortcut icon on a laptop can be a great reference source. Know that some people still prefer to devour decks and binders over the weekend or late at night perhaps. Don't forget to summarize the key points in bullets up front.

As tools for communicating, as Goldsmith says, conversations are really the key to transmitting knowledge accompanied by the needed relationship building. I ran into one former boss, after my successor had walked him through a thick loose-leaf binder, who said he yearned for the "one-pagers" I usually brought to our meetings because those allowed us to spend his limited time discussing the issues and choices rather than poring through mountains of underlying data.

5. *Practice Active Listening.* Based on what you know about the incoming administration's commitments, personality, and aspirations, use open-ended questions to connect with new officials. Ask the appointee to be very clear on what he wants to achieve, says Clay Johnson, and repeat back what you have heard, perhaps with some added discussion about how the goals might be attained. When

designed to collect unvarnished information and stimulate a bond of empathy with the speaker, "simply asking" is valuable in establishing communal goals and personal connections.[16]

6. *Be a Tour Guide*. Steer the newbies through the learning experience as an open-minded and fact-savvy guide. Include field trips to be sure they see how your program really operates at the local level. Find a way during the tour to insert key insights and a few ideas about how your organization could get better. One way to any newcomer's heart is to help her see the value *she* can bring to the organization's operations.

7. *Use the Appropriations Process to Interact with Appointees*. Unless they are veterans of previous regimes, few appointees will enter with an appreciation for the intricacies of managing three appropriations cycles (see chapter 4) or the specifics of your particular program's budget. They will need seasoned careerists to help them understand where the funding needs (or excesses!) are and which stakeholders can help or hurt, and also alert them to when funding decisions are imminent.

8. *Understand the Pace*. Often, especially with new appointees and new administrations, you'll be part of a "hurry-up offense." You get only one chance for a first impression. Get your running shoes on and plan for some extra hours in the shop, at least early on with a new team.

Play a Smart Defense

1. *"Don't Leave Wet Babies on Doorsteps."*[17] This phrase, a Todd Grams favorite, means to bring solutions when there are problems; don't just bring the problem. Make yourself a constructive participant in the problem solving. If you don't, you're less likely to relish the answer the new team comes up with. Worse, in absentia you could be viewed as part of the problem. It's all too easy for the "new" folks to blame the "old" folks when there is nobody present to explain all the dynamics involved or why things are as they are.

2. *Freely Rebrand the Good Stuff*. When an existing program or great idea can be aligned with the goals of the new team, consider renaming it. Administrations love to announce their new programs and seldom enthusiastically embrace ideas or programs championed by the prior team. A renamed program, with a few adjustments, can become theirs.

3. *Always Recall the "Deal."* Realistically, it's not always possible to conciliate, befriend, reconcile, or adjust. Sometimes the elected team wants to make changes with which you may disagree. Remember, your job is to "faithfully ex-

ecute"—within the limits of law and ethics—so you have a duty to perform as a responsible civil servant, accepting the electorate's choice on policy and priorities whether you agree or not. The success of both short-term policy decisions and long-term government management integrity depends on it.

4. *Sometimes It's Good to Move On*. Even the most dedicated and flexible civil servant may find herself unable to gain entry or acceptance into a new administration's team or to implement their desires. As acting associate commissioner of family assistance at the Social Security Administration at the end of Jimmy Carter's administration, normally a political position, I wound up "persona non grata" when the Reagan team arrived. They didn't really care that I was career SES; they saw me as part of the old way of thinking about welfare. After some ignored attempts to build bridges, I concluded it was time to find an assignment elsewhere. When my SSA successor was named, we agreed I would stay the few months needed to solidify my move to GAO. In return I committed to giving her the support she needed with the inherited team and lots of counsel, always privately, on the people and issues she was inheriting.

Ultimately you do need to stay true to yourself. It's fine to be flexible, but there may be some occasion where an administration wants to do something counter to your core beliefs on policy or law, on the stewardship of taxpayers' dollars, or on answering citizen needs. Even then be cautious. It's not unusual for career staffs to incorrectly believe we are compelled by some law or rule when in fact it's only a matter of being "the way we have always done it."

The new administration may have valid reasons for making changes or new interpretations. Don't forget that while they're learning lots from you, you may have something to learn from them, so be open to that. You might even suggest some alternative approaches that you would find more acceptable, but ultimately a change in position could be best if you cannot implement in good faith.

For extreme situations of law or ethics, whistleblower processes offer mechanisms for review, but that has generally been a perilous path best reserved for extremes.[18]

Conclusion

Democratic activist Patricia Harris was secretary of health and human services when Ronald Reagan was elected in November 1980. In the aftermath of the election, the secretary called together the department's leadership—appointed and career—and pronounced what she termed "the call to the battlements." Having fought the good fight, Harris said, we now must fight tooth and nail against the changes the new administration intended to implement.

It struck me as denying the fact that "the people had spoken" and had rejected a second Carter term in favor of Ronald Reagan. I asked her about that, somewhat timidly, under cover of the question, "Madam Secretary, do you have advice for those of us who are career staff and plan to stay on?" (To this day I think she was surprised to learn that career staffs were actually present.) Harris paused, thought, and responded that while appointed staff should "man the bastions" from whatever outside-of-government platform they can, civil servants have a responsibility to stay on and "keep the boats afloat," serving the people with distinction, as is our democratic tradition. Then she paused and smiled, deciding how to finish the thought. "Just remember, though, in four years we will be back. . . ."

Notes

1. "Life and Death in the White House," National Museum of American History website, accessed June 8, 2015, http://americanhistory.si.edu/presidency/3d1d .html.
2. Christopher Hammer, "Booth's Reason for Assassination," TeachingHistory.org, accessed June 8, 2015, http://teachinghistory.org/history-content/ask-a-historian /24242.
3. "Presidential Key Events: Chester A. Arthur," University of Virginia Miller Center website, accessed June 8, 2015, http://millercenter.org/president/arthur/key -events.
4. US Congress, House Committee on Oversight and Government Reform, *Policy and Supporting Positions*, 112th Cong., 2nd sess., 2012, 203, http://www.gpo.gov /fdsys/pkg/GPO-PLUMBOOK-2012/pdf/GPO-PLUMBOOK-2012.pdf.
5. Jitinder Kohli, in discussion with the author, August 2014.
6. "Go East, Young Bureaucrat," *The Economist*, March 17, 2011, http://www .economist.com/node/18359852.
7. Seth Mydans, "Singapore Slashes Officials' Salaries," *New York Times*, January 23, 2012, http://www.nytimes.com/2012/01/24/world/asia/singapore-slashes -officials-salaries.html.
8. Sam Mok, in discussion with the author, June 2015.
9. Robert Knisely, in discussion with the author, July 2014.
10. Norma Riccucci, *Unsung Heroes: Federal Execucrats Making a Difference* (Washington, DC: Georgetown University Press, 1995), 236–40.
11. Mike Causey, "Surviving a Second Term," Federal News Radio, January 23, 2013, http://www.federalnewsradio.com/20/3202391/Surviving-a-second-term.
12. See chapter 2.

13. Ricucci, *Unsung Heroes,* 235–37.
14. Kohli discussion.
15. G. Edward DeSeve, *The Presidential Appointee's Handbook* (Washington, DC: Brookings Institution Press, 2009), 46.
16. Clay Johnson, in discussion with the author, December 2014.
17. Todd Grams, in discussion with the author, November 2014.
18. An Act to Amend Title 5, United States Code, to Strengthen the Protections Available to Federal Employees against Prohibited Personnel Practices, and for Other Purposes, Public Law 101-12, US Statues at Large 103 (1989), 16–35.

CHAPTER 12

Tips for Consultants–and the Feds Who Use Them

Until recently, if you needing parking when visiting the White House, you called ahead for someone to find you a spot and then actually bring a parking pass out to the gate. To get a conference room in the Old Executive Office Building you had to track down the conference room scheduler and try to find an open room. If an authorized staffer wanted to arrange a West Wing tour, he needed to find an open time with White House security.[1]

Management processes comparable to these, like personnel administration and property management, were similarly outdated. To anyone who has scheduled an airline trip or spec'd out a new car using a smart phone, these processes were inefficient and people-intensive—and totally out of step with the Obama Administration's push for e-government.

As a result, in 2012 the White House solicited help in creating digital applications to handle various Executive Office of the President (EOP) support activities in a more efficient, twenty-first-century tech-savvy way. An initial piece of work was awarded to a vendor at a very low price. What happened next is a valuable lesson for both contractor and buyer and highlights an important difference between a "contractor" and a "consultant."

The winning bidder for a second part of the job—who was sensitive about pricing itself out of the high-profile work, given the competitiveness of other qualified vendors—won the new work with a low fixed-price offer, which put them in a tough spot. They *were* capable of doing the work well, but the economics of the deal compelled them to make a significant mistake right off the bat: they approached the job as a contractor rather than as a consultant.

This is a key distinction that many in the world of federal contracting and consulting don't think much about. *Contractors* respond to detailed requests for proposal that largely spell out what product or service is being requested, such as a building, a missile, a correspondence management system, or answering phones at a call center. These do not require much new thinking on the contractor's part; the contractor is expected to follow the specifications to provide the products or do the task. *Consultants*, on the other hand, are tasked with helping customers figure out *how* to do something better or solve a problem, like improving customer service, reducing cyber risk, or finding an innovative solution to a new challenge. It's higher-end and more expensive work.

Under self-inflicted cost pressures, the winning bidder first approached the job as a contractor and relied on available junior personnel to submit some turnkey apps that would modernize the Executive Office's scheduling and administration processes. Therein lay the seeds of a big problem: the West Wingers were counting on the contractor to analyze how, when, and why executives and staffs would use the new mobile apps and then use a rapid-prototyping approach to determine the best ways to streamline tasks like scheduling in an environment where such a system had never been used before. Contrary to the contractor's understanding, the White House was looking for a *consultant* first, to understand all the needs, and a *contractor* second to build the application.

Adding to the difficulties—for both the White House and the consultant—early in the contract the federal government shut down for a month due to a budget stalemate with Congress.[2] Although work was halted during this time, the White House held fast to the agreed-on delivery dates. After all, the White House does not shut down, and EOP, like all smart customers, expects its contractors to understand the working environment. It was a damaging double hit for the contractor-*cum*-consultant: after underbidding the job it was now under severe deadline pressures with an increasingly dissatisfied customer.

A high-visibility job for the highest-visibility institution in the world isn't one you want to fumble. Nobody wants to tell (or at least nobody *should* want to tell) the White House chief of staff or CIO that a deadline is not going to be met. Yet confrontational contract-centered finger-pointing did ensue, and it appeared that a deal between a well-known consulting firm and a high-prestige client was about to end in collapse.

That's when the contractor-consultant did something smart: it threw in all the upgraded resources needed to get the series of apps designed, up, and launched, even working with EOP to train its staff on the new applications prototyping process. It was a clear case of reputation being more important than short-term profitability, although all understood that success would demonstrate app-development prowess to other federal buyers.

The full court press paid off. The White House, pleased with the rapid turnaround, asked the consultant to stay on, awarding another year's work under terms that recognized the need for both consulting *and* contracting skills.[3]

The lessons here cut both ways: in this high-expectations environment, the client might have benefited, in the long run, from using a labor-hour contract rather than a firm fixed price for the early work. More in-depth involvement from client experts may have helped potential users understand the new prototyping process. Distinguishing between contractor and consultant skill sets to get this particular work done, along with an understanding of their differences in cost, might have helped as well.

For the contractor's part, from the start it should have paid closer attention to the client's needs and desires. High-profile clients require more senior attention from the get-go, regardless of pricing, so it was unwise to assign junior talent mismatched culturally to the high-performance, high-speed profile of the client. But the final lesson is probably the most important: reputation is everything. If you commit to a job, whether as a consultant or contractor, do the job right no matter what it takes.

Having spent half my career on each side of the divide between government and consultant-contractor, I am continually surprised at how opaque each side's view can be of the other. This chapter is intended to help both consultants and those federal leaders and managers who hire and work with them to be successful. It is a relationship that is too often fraught with confusion and disappointment when it really can be about partnership and success.

The discussion focuses on the specialized problem-solving role of a consultant and the listening skills and customer-centric attitude essential to doing that role well. I highlight some lessons from my own experiences on both sides of the table, illustrating how important one's contracting approach, the partnership, and having frank communications are to satisfactory outcomes. I conclude by borrowing fourteen pointers from an award-winning expert, and personal mentor, ranging from active listening to adopting client priorities to bringing new ideas and pilot-testing solutions.

Who Do You Really Need?

To paraphrase the Cheshire Cat in *Alice in Wonderland*, if you don't know where you're going, any road will get you there. Similarly, if you don't understand the difference between the benefits of using a contractor versus a consultant, you will inevitably pay too much when you need contractor support and fail to get the help you need when you really need a consultant. Neither skill set is better or worse; each is required for different needs.

Contractors provide personnel who are skilled in performing specific tasks, such as standing up a call center, building a tank, or managing a housing project.

The government uses contractors for defined products or services not core to the government's role where the requirements are clear and specific, especially when the need is episodic or temporary, as in the case of meeting surge needs or building and maintaining facilities. *Consultants,* on the other hand, should be called in when government needs some specialized advice or insights in identifying and implementing the right solution to a problem or finding new pathways to meeting needs.

Janet Foutty, named by GovConExec as a 2015 Wash100 "Most Influential Government Consulting" leader, served commercial clients before moving to federal consulting. Foutty notes that the contractor-consultant distinction is one the private sector understands well but that seems more muddled among the public sector. "In the commercial world, a noticeably different approach and closer trusted relationship exists for consulting than for contracting. Buyer and seller understand that," says Foutty. "Federal buyers, maybe because of the arms-length procurement process, have to work much harder to see the difference and get the value for taxpayers."[4]

Consultants bring problem-solving skills and new ideas that can provide huge value, says Foutty, now CEO of Deloitte Consulting LLP, at a cost that is higher on an hourly basis but actually small compared to a project's full cost, especially when tough problems need to be solved. For example, if the need is a new bridge, consultants might help you figure out how to finance the structure using private rather than public funds. If the goal is a process improvement, a consultant might help you analyze and streamline your processes *before* you buy new software to manage them or even help you find an effective way to handle immigrant registration. In our White House case, *consulting* skills turned out to be necessary to develop smarter, more efficient ways to schedule visits.

Consultants bring to the table content background and problem-solving skills, combined with a dose of knowledge on how such problems have been solved successfully in comparable environments. Good ones work in partnership *with* a client rather than just *for* a client. "If the government buyer is open to the give-and-take, there can be tremendous value to the taxpayer in finding the right solutions," says Foutty. "If they're not, they're wasting the government's money."[5]

Being a Great Federal Consultant

A great consultant must be focused on *the customer's* problem, says Wade Horn, a consultant who once was head of the Administration for Children and Families under President George W. Bush. "You have to accept *their* problem as your own and not try to convince them that a different agenda should be addressed," says Horn.

It's also essential to understand the *unique* constraints within which federal clients operate, says Horn, especially constraints that don't exist for commercial clients. "Their reward structure is different. They can't raise capital. If they need more people, they can't just go out and hire them without a congressional appropriation to do so. And the ROI calculation is entirely different than outside government."

Horn is right about that. You have to understand what the client really wants and needs, and the environment in which that client operates. Indeed, the turnaround in the White House case study was fueled by the consultant's "just in time" recognition of the client's rapid-paced, real-world environment and political constraints.

It's a lesson I learned early in my consulting career. Immediately after I left GAO for private consulting, I inherited work that my new consulting group was already doing for the Nuclear Regulatory Commission's CFO office. Reaching back to a retired GAO leader in nuclear management, I incorporated "Ted" into the team, figuring he'd bring valuable experience to the job. A few months later I got a call from the CFO, politely asking that I "get him out of here."

It turns out that Ted—who had been engaged to help solve a specific budgeting issue—had decided that the client was focusing on the wrong thing and repeatedly hijacked the conversation to focus on what he viewed as bigger problems along with his approach to solving them. At my request, albeit with some "coaching" and "coaxing," Ted went on to other life pursuits after helping us rapidly solve the problem on which we were engaged. So, again, the simple lesson is: listen, listen, listen.

What You Don't Know Can Hurt You—and the Client

This is not to say good consultants take the presented facts and statement of needs at face value. In fact, there is often a difference between the client's stated "wants" and their true "needs." A simple construct I have used in the past emphasizes a deeper, more thorough, and more sophisticated look at all the issues and circumstances surrounding a defined problem—without changing the stated problem as defined by the client.

There may be issues that the client hasn't been willing to discuss for a variety of reasons, whether political (internal and external) or personal. There may be issues that the client hasn't thought of at all, which an outsider is better able to spot and surface. Shorthand for this phenomenon is that there are *stated* needs, *unstated* needs, and *unknown* needs (see chapter 6). You need to understand and recognize all three categories if you're going to be a successful consultant and not waste client time and money, whether because you failed to recognize known problems or got blindsided by others you didn't know were out there.

Again, it's something I learned from personal experience. We had been asked to do an efficiency study for NIH, which had been ordered by Illinois congressman John Porter, whose committee oversaw NIH appropriations. We were told the goal of the study was to find $1 billion in savings out of NIH's $13 billion administrative budget—a daunting challenge for any consultant. That is, it was daunting until I had an illuminating side conversation with the director of NIH, who—about two-thirds of the way through our work—casually mentioned that, in reality, if we found $300 or $400 million in savings that would suffice.[6] The *stated* goal was to find major reductions in expense. The *actual* goal was to identify a modest set of changes—"low-hanging fruit," as we called them—that were just enough to silence critics. That information would have been extremely helpful to know going in.

Similarly, I've been involved in other contracts that were presented as "reorganization." Several of them weren't actually aimed at efficiency or effectiveness gains but rather at removing certain powerful personnel from key positions in order to install a new team.

Whatever the actual differences between *stated*, *unstated*, and *unknown* needs, conversations focused on *getting the underlying needs straight* are key to your effectiveness and that of your client. The question is how to discover "what you don't know."

Stay Humble and Listen

It's tricky. Oftentimes federal officials already are wary when it comes to consultants, perhaps because they have had bad experiences; or they resent paying a "highly paid" outsider to do something they feel the government can handle on its own; or they have been offended by experiences with some private-sector "whizzes" who have no clue of the special federal constraints Wade Horn acknowledges. The key here is to win the confidence of your client by evincing a level of humility that is commensurate with the client-contractor relationship, that is, boss-employee. Establishing yourself as a "trusted business advisor" is the goal here, so it's always wise to keep one other bit of Foutty's advice in mind: "The client knows more than you do, so be humble in your approach."[7]

It's amazing to me how impressed customers are when I just listen. I repeat back occasionally, sometimes summarizing what they've said in ways that allow the customer to see facts combined into a more coherent whole, along with potential insights they may lead to. The general rule is to talk less than 10 percent of the time and use most of your 10 percent talking time to ask questions—an important technique for finding out what the goal of a project *really* is. Had I sat down privately with the director of NIH early on in the overhead-cutting project, we could have saved time, money, and angst. Of course, others can provide needed information as well, points out Horn. Since you don't know what you don't know, don't be shy in corroborating information with other involved players as well.

To be candid, there are good *business* reasons for developing a "trusted business advisor" relationship with your client: it helps grow a business based upon true client value. If clients respect me and believe I provide value, they'll figure out how and where to give me consulting work again, which provides important professional gratification, not to mention remuneration.

Be Honest about What You Can (and Can't) Deliver

It is absolutely crucial that a consultant not break the trusted business advisor relationship by claiming capabilities you don't actually possess or promising solutions you can't deliver. Friends don't "sell" to their friends. In fact, you can use a three-step process for determining if you can help a prospect in a very personal, service-oriented way: first, listen well and truly understand the prospect's needs; second, carefully review your ability to meet that need (including capabilities you can bring from elsewhere, but only if you really can produce them); and, third, if the capabilities can meet the need, discuss with the potential client how you can help—but, again, only if you really can help.

If you cannot really help, a trusting relationship demands that you say, "You know what? Given your issues and your situation, I can't help you." Make a referral if you are confident that that person can meet the need. The prospective client will respect you for that, and you will live to help another day. If you try to do what you (or your firm) cannot do well, you will seldom get a second chance.

Federal alums who "consult back" to their friends and agencies will recognize this trust issue as a major one. When I left GAO, I followed the advice of a former fed and scheduled strictly social lunches with every federal leader I knew to let them know I had gone into consulting and where to find me. Knowing that under federal ethics rules I couldn't discuss business issues for at least a year, my goal was to simply renew acquaintances over lunch. My second goal, of course, was to capture and reinforce the trust that existed when we were federal colleagues. In fact, most of my former federal colleagues, even before the closing coffee, were chatting freely about their job challenges and frustrations. Some even explicitly asked for help; in many cases, after running it by counsel, I was able to refer them to one of my new consulting colleagues. Once my ethics "probation" period was up, I then went on to work with many former colleagues as well.

It can be an uncomfortable dance. Mary Corrado, herself a former CFO at both the National Reconnaissance Office and the Central Intelligence Agency, describes her fear of being viewed as a "sleaze" trying to "sell back to my friends" in the intelligence community when she hung out a shingle as a consultant.[8] But Corrado was able to overcome that squeamishness by viewing her new position as merely a continuation of her lifelong support for the intelligence community mission. The change was just that she was now trying to accomplish it from the outside, which is probably the key to her effectiveness and success as well. "What you have," Corrado notes, "is knowledge of the culture and value system that outsiders don't have. That helps me make sure my team delivers great work. Most of all, I protect the relationships I have with my client agencies by making sure I stay involved in the work. You have to keep 'client first' at the top of your mind."[9]

Winning Trust

Winning trust is harder in the federal realm than in the private sector, according to Gene Procknow, who in 2004 switched from serving commercial clients to serving federal ones and by 2011 was named a top consultant by *Consulting Magazine* for his public sector work. "It's more difficult to be on the same side of the table [as the customer]," says Procknow, "because of procurement rules, or the fear that federal officials sometimes have of getting too close to one consultant." When Procknow consulted to private-sector clients, for example, they often urged him to use their offices for all his business simply so he would be close at hand when they needed him. That arrangement is allowed in the federal government but only for doing the work of that agency.[10]

Understanding a client's motivation is also more difficult at the federal level, says Procknow. "Generally, commercial clients are motivated by fear [of some threat] or greed [the desire to make more money]. Not so in federal. I have to focus on truly understanding what their motivations are in order to serve them well."[11]

On the other hand, Procknow thinks it's worth the added degree of difficulty because the federal work is far more intellectually stimulating and because clients are often free to share their strategies and plans at a level of detail that competitive commercial enterprises are reluctant to disclose.

Collaborating to Get Value

We are in the "collaboration age," and this is as relevant to finding and working with the right consultant as to any other twenty-first-century initiative or enterprise.[12] Consultants like to speak of "goal alignment," meaning if you achieve your goals then I achieve mine. When there is good goal alignment between client and consultant it makes layers of management and expensive processes unnecessary.

Teach and Incentivize

Creating a value-based arrangement with consultants and contractors can go a long way to achieving this alignment. The important contribution from a share-in-savings or value-based arrangement is the clarity it brings to the buyer's real needs (see more in chapter 6). It's far easier, then, to clearly define what you want the consultant to help you achieve.

For example, if you, as a federal official, want help in reducing per-bed costs in federal prisons, incentivizing the consultant to achieve that by tying compensation to documented savings makes sense. If you're looking for ways to make the TSA experience more pleasant for frequent business flyers, incentivize that.

It helps to explicitly address with the consultant how the work contributes to the broader mission(s) of the agency or department. This provides more than just motivational value because good consultants will define and refine their skill needs, activities, and goals if they understand how the work is expected to affect important stakeholders and outcomes. In the EOP apps development project scenario, the client adopted a more collaborative approach once the consultant accepted that its mission was to help the client be successful rather than just meeting contract requirements. The joint adoption of a more collaborative approach, with alignment of goals, was critical to turning the project around.

To take full advantage of your consultants, you need an efficient way to get them up to speed. Good consultants will want to understand the history behind a project, including if and why various strategies have worked or failed in the past. A "best practice" among top consultants is to train and prepare federal employees and leaders to "carry on" once the project is complete and the consultant departs. Do not engage a consultant who doesn't want to help you embed long-term, ongoing improvements institutionally.

Know who you are hiring. If it's not a person you already know and trust, and who you know has the knowledge and skills to take on the challenge you're facing, then get a reference from a trusted colleague—preferably one whose allegiance to you is stronger than to the consultant. Find a way to meet in person so you can see if the consultant is a cultural and temperamental match for your organization, including someone who understands the often tricky internal and external political environments that overlay federal operations.

Once you have found a great consultant, in the words of the song, "never let him go." It sounds self-serving, but a truly great jockey can ride multiple different horses to success.

Another tip for hiring the right person is to hunt for someone with experience in solving commercial problems similar to yours. For example, consultants who have advised commercial supermarkets on logistics and display strategies might be asked to bring similar insights to help military commissaries. Or if you are charged with implementing legislation like the 2010 Dodd-Frank Wall Street Reform and Consumer Protection Act, it makes sense to include someone who has consulted to banks on regulatory matters so you can better understand their internal environments (although from a conflicts viewpoint, not to lead).

Create Key Channels of Communication

Personal relationships and good communication can greatly enhance a working partnership for both the client and the consultant. Matching senior-level staffs who can relate to each other is a great way to do this. On the government side, it should be a senior leader who plans to be on the job for a long time or someone with whom the consultant can share challenges and who can provide high-level help if needed. Matching that person with a senior leader in the consultant organization opens up a strong channel for counsel and advice going in both directions.

Often these relationships can provide great value by pairing functional leaders—such as technology leaders or contracting leaders. A major turnaround strategy for the White House project discussed earlier was to have individual pairs of executives begin to meet, one on one, to find common ground in their respective areas: contracting executives, technology leaders, program executives. Without this collaboration, and the signal it sent that both sides wanted a resolution, I doubt the recovery could have occurred.

Don't be afraid to get close. Neither government leaders nor consultants bite (generally), and rules encourage both sides to know each other better. (See especially OMB's "myth-buster" guidance in chapter 6). Follow all ethics rules, of course, but find space—literally and figuratively—to facilitate informal and frequent interactions. It will pay big dividends.

Procknow's Personal Pointers

Rather than end this chapter with the usual **Key Takeaways**, I'm going to turn to some tips from *Consulting Magazine*'s 2011 Top Public Sector Consultant, Gene Procknow, based on his long experience in consulting to commercial and federal clients. Procknow is preternaturally good at what he does because he clearly understands the positive power of a strong and healthy client-consultant relationship:

1. **Gain insight and trust by active listening.** It's the 10 percent rule outlined earlier in the chapter: you won't be learning anything about your client's needs if you're doing all the talking.

2. **Always make the client's best interests your top priority.** It's astonishing how often consultants make *their* interests the top priority and fall back on what they know versus what the client needs. One size rarely fits all, so don't try to deliver the same product to every client.

3. **Be rapidly responsive.** Clients expect you to be there to serve them. They find it frustrating to have to leave voice-mail messages. Confer with the client about the best way to make contact, and then pay attention to doing it. The more proximate to them you can be, the better.

4. **Be politically aware but not politically driven.** You shouldn't be playing politics, but you should certainly be aware of what's going on politically, both inside your client's world and in the larger political world. Don't give your client advice or counsel that is contrary to political reality at either level.

5. **Bad news gets worse with age.** Too many consultants and clients flout this time-tested adage. If you see a problem—or, better yet, if you see a problem looming—bring it to the surface and do it quickly. "We got

this" doesn't cut it. This is advice that cuts both ways: a client who sees a looming issue should surface it ASAP as well.

6. **Don't blame the client.** You accepted a job, and that job is to help your client accomplish his or her key goals. Blaming the client will only make it harder to do that. If there are issues that need to be worked out, approach them from the perspective that the client is competent and trying to do the best job possible.

7. **What's in the news?** Literally. It makes you look both caring and aware if you bring relevant news items to your client's attention.

8. **It's never really about the cost.** When clients complain about the cost it really means they're not satisfied with the value you're providing. How many times have you heard the phrase "They're expensive, but they got the job done".

9. **Avoid consultant fatigue by finding new needs.** Once you've worked with the same client a few times, they sometimes start taking you—and the presumably good job you've been doing—for granted. Be on the lookout for other issues you might help your client with. It makes you look like you care, that you're thinking ahead, and that you understand the environment in which your client operates.

10. **Keep the dialogue going.** It is important to be hyper-aware of how your client is feeling about progress, so there should be high-level and honest ongoing dialogue between executive levels. This cuts both ways: have a back channel the consultant can use to get to government executives as well.

11. **Build a brand with client executives.** Develop a reputation for being great (or the best) at the things you want to be known for. Is it crisis intervention? Organizational transformation? IT troubleshooting? Don't try to be all things to all clients. When people hear your name, what do they think of?

12. **Informal meetings are best.** Crucial to a successful consultant-client relationship is ongoing conversation. The conversation is more likely to be open and frank if you're sitting over coffee, one on one in your shirtsleeves, rather than in a meeting room with twenty people taking notes.

13. **Pilot-test solutions.** Develop, test, and refine. Develop, test, and refine. Then go live. That allows you to improve your product and processes in a low-key, high-value way, and it will save a whole lot of embarrassment in final rollout.

14. **Career counseling and career help will cement the relationship.** Talk to key staffs in your client agency about their career aspirations. Friendly, informal career advice helps build trust with a client. That person may get promoted to a position where he can turn around and hire you . . . and he will remember that you helped him get the job.

Conclusion: The Trusted Business Advisor

Ultimately, a healthy and productive consultant-client relationship depends on value, trust, and partnership. A successful consultant to the federal government brings a wide range of skills and personal strengths, ranging from the ability to listen and read between the lines to being able to provide personal value in an environment shaped heavily by rules and regulations. As Wade Horn notes, knowledge of the special constraints federal officials operate under is essential to success. A successful client embraces the added value from a trusted business advisor and knows how to use that to improve program and organization.

In the end it's about becoming a trusted business advisor. To be good at this at the federal level, you've got to be "all in" for the client and ready to do whatever it takes to ensure their success.

Notes

1. Bob Capuano, in discussion with the author, March 2015.
2. Sylvia Burwell, "Impacts and Costs of the Government Shutdown," whitehouse .gov, November 07, 2013, https://www.whitehouse.gov/blog/2013/11/07/impacts -and-costs-government-shutdown.
3. Capuano discussion.
4. Janet Foutty, in discussion with the author, December 2014.
5. Ibid.
6. "Arthur Andersen Delivers Mixed Review of NIH Administrative Acumen," *The NIH Catalyst*, January-February 1998, http://nihprod.cit.nih.gov/catalyst/back /98.01/arthur_anderson.html
7. Ibid.
8. Mary Corrado, in discussion with the author, March 2015.
9. Ibid.
10. Gene Procknow, in discussion with the author, March 2015.
11. Ibid.
12. Kimberly McCabe, in discussion with the author, January 2015.

Conclusion: Four Common Threads

I wrote this book in order to offer practical, hands-on insights and advice on how managers, leaders, and students of public management who may aspire to join their ranks can better achieve successful outcomes in the challenging federal political and performance environment. Using lessons from my own experiences, insights from experts and other practitioners, and cases that illustrate positive and negative results, the book highlights concrete actions and strategies federal managers and leaders have adopted to be more effective: from communicating and negotiating with stakeholders to focusing on achievable goals and motivating people to pursue them; from aggressively managing technology and contracts to capitalizing on risk and innovation to dealing constructively with oversight.

This is not easy to do in the polarized, fractured federal sphere. To be effective, the necessary activities and strategies have to be thought through in advance, executed well over multiple timeframes, and defended against ever-present critics. In order to help readers focus separately on the needs and actions important to each stage, I structure them into three essential phases—**Create Your Offense**, **Execute Effectively**, and **Play a Smart Defense**—and discuss **Key Takeaways** at the end of each chapter. They are further summarized in Appendix A, which practitioners and students can use as shorthand "prompts" in specific situations or when creating broader strategies.

Throughout the book I have avoided broad issues of federal transformation, choosing instead to focus on what individual leaders and managers can actually do to be effective at delivering federal services under existing conditions. Clearly, this is much more difficult than simply implementing a set of steps or adopting a particular strategy. Many serious constraints are evident in the federal realm—political, resource availability, interest-group power, or the sheer breadth of sector diversity in our federalist system. They often make it difficult to even agree on a common definition of "success" for a specific program or activity, let alone achieve it. In this environment, being effective requires a healthy dose of both "art" and "science." I believe that attention to four common threads, often

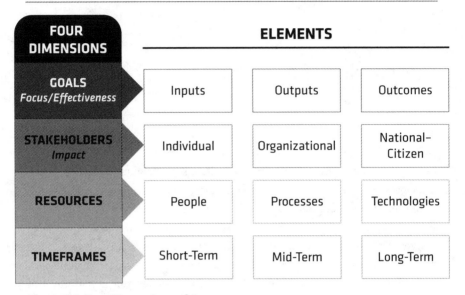

Figure C.1: Four Dimensions of Success

deriving from case studies of success or disappointment, can help us navigate the environment and balance the factors that determine successful outcomes.

One thread is that the **Four Dimensions of Success—goals, stakeholders, resources**, and **timeframes**—are under debate almost continuously and thus potentially changing much of the time. (The Four Dimensions are reproduced here as Figure C.1). It's important to recognize that the four dimensions are totally interdependent in this dynamic environment, and reliant upon one another. They must be managed that way. *Changes in any element of one dimension—whether by choice or by chance—must be accompanied by altering another.* In the federal sphere, with so little unilateral control, recognizing important changes in circumstances or goals and the need to adjust to new information is often the difference between success and failure.

I call this "pivoting," or the ability to change rapidly as goals and conditions change. In one of our case studies, Census pivoted well: it recognized the need to adjust technology and processes and to confront key stakeholders with the risk of failure if they maintained their parochial positions. The Affordable Care Act launch team, lacking the constitutional mandate enjoyed by Census and confronted with shorter timeframes and dramatically higher political discord, did not pivot to a lower-tech launch strategy that might have mitigated at least some of the website launch problems. The literature supports "pivoting," by various names, as an important federal strategy. In *Federal Management Reform in a World of Contradictions*, for example, Beryl Radin emphasizes the wisdom of incremental approaches that are "ever changing and constantly searching for ways to balance conflicting imperatives," including the inevitable federal politics.[1]

A second thread is that *defining and communicating your own goals well* can profoundly affect how your success will be perceived, especially with the cacophony of voices always "spinning" how well or poorly programs are performing in the federal political environment. Negotiating the political and stakeholder agreements and compromises necessary to win over the most powerful allies will be important to your ability to marshal resources to meet those goals. As we saw with the IRS and GAO case studies, how you frame your goals, in particular, can have a significant impact on your ultimate success. In both cases leadership carefully separated output goals along multiple timeframes and created different management, process, and technology plans for each, negotiating resource and output agreements with the most powerful legislative and external stakeholders early and often.

I recognize that "aligning goals and stakeholders" is more easily stated than achieved, especially in our era of divided government and fractious budget and policy discord. There are often multiple and conflicting goals, compounded by unrealistic expectations. Here, as in thread one, we have to accept variability in realistic outcomes. It can be wise, in such an uncertain and risky environment, to stay away from extremes of goal-setting or performance claims, if at all possible, noting the old adage that those furthest out on limbs are usually most vulnerable. A good defensive strategy is to be specific about realistic expectations and potential shortfalls, even if this acknowledgment comes via an off-the-record discussion with your most important leaders and allies.

The third thread is *the role that a clear and present threat—or an outright crisis— can play* in prioritizing a program or policy. Legislators get reelected by increasing services to their own constituents while advocating that everyone else economize. With no firm connection in the federal system between the *commitments* and *available funding*, the former far exceed the latter. Savvy federal leaders use crises (or credible threats of same) to get related program needs moved to the front of the line for resources and leadership attention. In our Y2K case study, for example, some criticized Clinton administration leaders for waiting until 1998 to launch the major federal initiative. But this was principally a nonfederal set of changes to be made and it would have been difficult to justify elevating Y2K to the "threat" and "imminent crisis" level before then. By 1998, with the stated threat "upon us," diverting leadership talent and budget from other priorities became more realistic and achievable.

For programs or initiatives lacking a visible crisis, indeed for the majority of federal commitments, it's important to recognize how much more variable the level of likely attention (and resourcing) will be, and thus how challenging it can be to find agreement on goals and among stakeholders. A number of the case studies illustrate a common pattern of initial stumbles, recovery, enhanced attention, and then success. The sheer overflow of federal challenges makes that pattern predictable, especially with the impact of stakeholders' political power, limitations of talent and funding, power-sharing across sectors, and the ever-changing fluidity of goals. The Medicare prescription drug program stumbled out of the gate, but recovered rapidly and well. IRS's systems modernization succeeded . . . the second time around. Sometimes it takes multiple "stumbles" or learning experiences. Standing as a contrast to this "second-time" pattern is the NASA *Columbia* shuttle accident, which followed an eerily similar accident that destroyed the *Challenger* seventeen years earlier and which has yielded much study about organizational learning and the handling of risk.[2]

There are important implications to this third thread, *principally, that adaptive, motivational, and learning skills are what matter most in federal management*, including awareness of the specific types of issues that are likely to accompany different types of problems. Environmental programs, for example, present different challenges than do education, healthcare administration, or defense readiness. Successful federal leaders recognize that different issues have different profiles and so they identify the needed talent and build coalitions internally and across sectors, *before* the crisis. They anticipate possible crises and learn from them when they occur. Some even use them to gain resources. They anticipate the risks and respond flexibly, rather than defensively, when it comes time to pivot. If the flood is upon you, it's too late to build anew.

Thread four is the overriding importance of having *great people skills and communications capabilities*, something discussed in every chapter. Whether the task is choosing and deploying the right technology, hiring the right contractor, making the right organizational moves, adopting the right risk strategies, or managing your relationships with oversight entities, it's all about investing in people and communications—which, taken together, mean relationships. The limits to a federal manager's ultimate power are manifold, which means that those who know how to communicate, motivate, facilitate, and negotiate will have the most influence—and, therefore, success. This is why the motivation skills discussed in chapter 2 and the communications techniques outlined in chapter 5 stand as threads that run through this book . . . and throughout effective public management.

I do not mean to imply that these four threads—attention to the dynamic relationships among the Four Dimensions of Success and pivoting when things change; defining and communicating goals well; finding or capitalizing on a threat or crisis and using adaptive skills when you can; and recognizing the overriding importance of people skills and communications capabilities—are easy to "pull through" public sector endeavors, or even that they "ensure" success when you do. But it does seem that attention to them gives one a better shot at being effective in the challenging government environment.

Notes

1. Beryl A. Radin, *Federal Management Reform in a World of Contradictions* (Washington, DC: Georgetown University Press, 2012), 173–77.
2. See, in particular, Julianne G. Mahler, *Organizational Learning at NASA: The Challenger and Columbia Accidents* (Washington, DC: Georgetown University Press, 2009).

Appendix: Summary of Key Takeaways

★ Chapter 1: Key Dimensions of Success ★

⌒ Create Your Offense	⌒ Execute Effectively	⌒ Play a Smart Defense
• *Define the goals right.* Make sure you've set the key inputs, outputs, and outcomes that are going to define your mission and align your stakeholders behind you.	• *Pull together the best people.* Your team should include individuals with the requisite technical skills, those with relevant experience along with general problem solvers.	• *Neutralize your opponents.* Identify and be explicit about how to deal with potential opponents, even outright enemies.
• *Focus on your stakeholders.* Assess the relative influence of various stakeholders and then play to them accordingly.	• *Develop the right processes and procedures.* Define which processes and procedures are essential to success.	• *Avoid arguments and appearing defensive.* Appearing defensive compromises your ability to convince key stakeholders that you are the more reasoned, rational voice in any debate or conflict.
• *Set strategic timeframes.* The more ambitious the task, the smarter it is to establish some short-term goals by which you can mark progress or that can provide opportunities to alter strategies (e.g., "pivot").	• *Deploy the right technology.* Identify the simplest, most accessible, and user-friendly technologies.	• *Co-opt the "opposition."* Potential opponents can be pulled into the fold if you evince an appreciation for and understanding of their needs and then make accommodations to gain their cooperation.
	• *Tend to stakeholders (part II).* Listen to and communicate with stakeholders throughout implementation.	• *Build oversight response capacity.* Designate specialized personnel specifically to address—not argue against, but address—oversight reporting and response issues.
• *Balance the four dimensions of success:* Goals, stakeholders, resources, and timeframes are dynamic and interdependent. Attend to keeping them in balance.	• *Use risk-based decision making.* Use RBD to identify risk at every decision point.	• *Use criticism.* Use the momentum of criticism to push forward your own goals.
	• *Deploy force multipliers.* Force multipliers can include specialized personnel, IT, and shared services arrangements.	• *Be ready to pivot.* Build your strategy around short-, mid-, and long-term goals and always be ready to change course.
		• *Negotiate.* The best realistic deal might be a compromise. What's most important to you?
		• *Pick your battles.* In many cases it is smarter (not to mention easier) to sit quietly and take momentary heat.

★ Chapter 2: Empowering Your Most Valuable Asset—Your People ★

↳ Create Your Offense	↳ Execute Effectively	↳ Play a Smart Defense
• *Motivate and manage from mission and vision.* Whether you're managing up, across, or down, clearly articulate what "good performance" is, based on a strong public-service imperative.	• *Help staffs meet their goals.* A key part of your job as a leader/manager is helping them define how they will get the job done.	• *Get ahead of the trends.* Understand and get in front of the trends that have the potential to affect the people in your workforce and how you interact with them.
• *Promote a mentorship-based culture of personal growth.* Help your staff build soft skills, including political insight, negotiating, understanding and balancing risk, persuading, motivating, relationship building, communicating, and compromising. Support the superstars.	• *Take advantage of every tool and technique to communicate and motivate.* You can never "overcommunicate."	• *Address performance disappointments personally.* Be aware of people's "wins" and "losses." Make changes in job match or tenure when needed to address serious shortfalls.
• *Rethink recruitment and retention.* Adopt a social media–savvy approach to finding, recruiting, and motivating talent and stakeholders. Recruit the best.	• *Encourage new approaches to work.* When possible, grant flextime and remote work.	• *Give credit generously.* Buy agreement, if needed, by giving credit to the judgment and skills of others.
• *Listen, listen, listen.* Then listen more.	• *Incentivize and support "best" performance.* Spend more time focused on your top 10 percent than on the bottom 10 percent. Spend the balance of your time improving the performance of the middle 80 percent.	
	• *Manage up, across, and down.* Pay attention to the goals important to your supervisors, your peers, and your employees.	

★ Chapter 3: Managing the Complex New World of Technology ★

⌐ Create Your Offense	⌐ Execute Effectively	⌐ Play a Smart Defense
• *Adopt a helping-first leadership style.* The most effective technology leaders help operating entities achieve their goals. They build and motivate teams to achieve tech goals.	• *Sprint and pivot.* Break tech projects into shorter "sprints" that are punctuated by potential pivot points.	• *Have the people and a plan in place.* Make sure you're equipped with the right talent and decision-making power.
• *Adopt a venture capital approach.* Develop a "portfolio" of prioritized projects, because some will fail.	• *Create a results management office.* An RMO monitors outputs, not principally inputs.	• *Do independent verification and validation.* Either in-house or through a consultant.
• *Pick your IT strategy.* Answer the key questions about the most effective and affordable IT quadrant before you start talking about solutions.	• *Build in resource optimization.* Use analytic tools to define low-cost, high-impact options.	• *Consider "cloud control."* Think "cloud" whenever possible.
• *Choose your "boulder."* There are always a balance and tradeoffs between scope, cost, and schedule. Know which is most important in each program.	• *Embrace crowdsourcing and other social media approaches.* Tap into the broader creativity of both staffs and citizens.	• *Reduce technical debt.* Consider the cost of maintaining subpar software versus the efficiencies to be gained through an upgrade.
• *Think digitally.* Digital applications and solutions provide major efficiency and effectiveness gains.	• *Integrate development and operations.* DevOps can reduce costs and timeframes while reducing risk.	
• *Buy it if possible.* Always question the value of developing your own solution when there may be an existing application already out there.		

★ Chapter 4: Creating and Leading a Well-Designed Organization ★

⌐ Create Your Offense

- **First, define what "success" will look like.** Be clear on the output and outcome goals and measures.
- **Take the time to diagnose.** Is the current business model efficient and effective enough?
- **To reorganize or not to reorganize?** Avoid mega-reorgs; they drain time, energy, and resources.
- **Create a mission excellence vision and a plan to get there.** Create a vision around customer satisfaction.
- **Create a bold shared-services strategy.** Let someone else do your non-core-mission work so you focus better on mission.
- **Find and support innovation.** Innovation is not optional.

⌐ Execute Effectively

- **Use your chief financial officer.** Your CFO will be your top organizational and funding ally and activist.
- **Examine shared-services alternatives.** Use a structured approach. Consider other agencies or an outside provider.
- **Create the incentives that drive successful transformation.** Make the business case and line up your team.
- **Decide where to put the boxes.** It's about efficient and effective workflow.
- **Go flat.** Flatter is usually smarter.
- **Create an innovation incubator.** Think "skunkworks."

⌐ Play a Smart Defense

- **Know the politics.** Understand the players and their constituencies. Groom angels. Having at least one strong supporter, either on the appropriations or authorizing committee, is critical.

★ Chapter 5: Communications—What's the Good Word? ★

⌐ Create Your Offense	⌐ Execute Effectively	⌐ Play a Smart Defense
• *Adopt a communication strategy and style that supports your goals.* Define stakeholders and messaging goals. Understand the different types of communicators in your organization and when and how to use each.	• *Be clear about what you want to communicate.* Don't get behind a podium unfocused.	• *Be forthcoming.* Break bad news yourself.
• *Always listen before talking.* Understand all the key issues before you offer feedback.	• *What do key constituencies think?* Listen 90 percent of the time, talk 10 percent (or less!). Use listening tours and tools. Consider a traceability matrix.	• *Study the history.* What comms strategies worked or didn't work the last time?
• *Align your message.* Pay attention to all three levels of communication: individual, organizational, national/citizen.	• *Pre-plan.* Be ready for bad news . . . and good. Create a comms guide.	• *Put the best communicators on the podium.* Don't hide behind your public information office.
• *Communicate a vision of success and pride.* Effective communicators motivate and inspire.	• *Communicate up, down, and across.* Make sure all key players are in the loop.	• *Never lie.* Your credibility is your most valuable asset. Get the info out fast and include the fix.
• *Use nonverbal signals creatively to support messaging.* Food, drink, events, perks, and celebrations work great.	• *Use behavioral insights.* Market test your message to ensure that it's the right one effective with the right audience.	
• *Get to know media players.* Relationships are key to a media strategy.		

★ Chapter 6: Getting Value from Contracting ★

Create Your Offense

- *Involve all stakeholders.* Pursue a "stakeholder inclusive" strategy when defining the requirements and goals of a procurement.
- *Have a value strategy.* Define value clearly as the driver of your contract strategy.
- *Incentivize your team.* Emphasize that the job is to provide the best value for taxpayers.
- *Cultivate innovative procurement office customer service.* Groom internal staff members who can help your operations improve.

Execute Effectively

- *Use existing contract vehicles when you can.* Preapproval saves time and money.
- *Choose between cost-plus, time-and-materials, or firm-fixed-price* based on the best match to your value goals.
- *Use all your tools.* Federal acquisition regulations offer more flexibility than many in the government realize.
- *Create the right incentive structure.* Outputs and outcomes should shape contract incentives.
- *Consider "risk ratings."* Attach a "risk rating" to each bidder.

Play a Smart Defense

- *Check the rules.* Don't automatically take "can't" for an answer.
- *Consider outside help.* A specialized contractor for technical or performance advice can sometimes bolster performance.
- *Head off problems.* Manage contractor performance attentively.
- *Squeak when you need grease.* If your contractor isn't delivering, make some noise.
- *Use your attorneys.* Lawyer-to-lawyer conversations can sometimes help find solutions.

★ Chapter 7: Risk-Based Decision Making ★

⌐ Create Your Offense	⌐ Execute Effectively	⌐ Play a Smart Defense
• *Create an enterprise-wide risk management program.* Develop in-house expertise in scoping out risk. • *Establish a risk-based decision-making framework.* Adopt guidelines for which steps to take. • *Align rewards.* Good leaders reward intelligent risk-taking.	• *Attend to important stakeholders.* Develop risk profiles and give key stakeholders at least some of what each needs. • *Create a chief risk officer.* Make sure the role is independent and well protected. • *Communicate risks and tradeoffs.* Do this as publicly as possible.	• *Anticipate failure points.* Projects seldom go exactly as planned. Have a pivot ready. • *Listen to tech talk.* Your techies know the consequences of tech risks. • *Don't get complacent.* Success tends to desensitize. • *Accelerate recognition of threats and "surprises."* It's guaranteed that something is out there—you're just not seeing it yet. • *Confront biases.* Overconfidence. Availability. Confirmation. Optimism. Put a "court jester" on your team.

★ Chapter 8: The Wide Wonderful World of Innovation ★

⌒ Create Your Offense	⌒ Execute Effectively	⌒ Play a Smart Defense
• *Identify your best and brightest and give them cover.* Find your innovators, encourage and protect them.	• *Mix mature and young.* Experience and enthusiasm don't always come in the same package.	• *Forget the thousand points of light.* Synergy is a group phenomenon.
• *Create new competencies.* Consider adding "creative," "innovative," and "bold" to some of your talent requirements.	• *Share information.* It makes you more powerful.	• *Avoid the doom loop.* Even the best and brightest get bored or burned out. Move them after a while.
• *Mix it up.* Combine different backgrounds and strengths on one team.	• *Look outside for good ideas.* Innovation isn't exclusive to one level of government or one sector.	• *Don't get too big.* Big breeds bureaucracy. Configure smaller teams that spawn creativity.
• *Mix it up II.* Moving people around in the organization sparks energy and synergy.	• *Create an idea incubator.* "Skunkworks" work.	• *Stay under the radar.* Bureaucracies don't like troublemakers. Give others the credit.
• *Create an innovation calendar.* Set aside time to think about what needs fixing.	• *Use diffusion of innovation.* Connect innovators with early adopters and early majorities.	
• *Create an innovation portfolio.* Find the most vexing problems facing your agency.	• *Find other disruptors.* Form a network.	
• *Channel conflict.* Controlled disagreements often lead to new thinking.		

★ Chapter 9: *Tips* for Living with Oversight Organizations ★

⌐ Create Your Offense	⌐ Execute Effectively	⌐ Play a Smart Defense
• *Play smart.* • *Stay positive.* Consider all criticism constructive. • *Adopt and co-opt the agenda.* Engage oversight agencies early. • *Job swap.* Consider rotating staff on a temporary—or even permanent—basis from your agency to an oversight entity and vice-versa.	• *Play ball.* • *Agree to as much as you can.* Accept whatever findings you can as a matter of general practice. • *Create a unit to handle oversight relationships and communications.* Its job is to establish positive relationships with oversight entities. • *Master the art of testifying.* Know what message you want to deliver. • *Understand the politics.* Politicians are always playing to constituencies; know which they are. Don't take it personally.	• *Play nice.* • *Be a cooperative partner.* Work with—not against—oversight agencies. • *Make constructive changes on the fly.* Fixing problems as they're flagged gets you early credit. • *Use the oversight to request resources.* If fixes require added resources, embrace the recommendations. • *Right problem, right answer?* Scrub recommendations; you may have a better way they'll accept. • *I disagree.* It's expected, if not overdone. Be professional and respectful. • *Develop a thick skin.* You're always going to be on somebody's "radar."

★ Chapter 10: *Tips* for Political Appointees Managing Civil Servants ★

↶ Create Your Offense	↶ Execute Effectively	↶ Play a Smart Defense
• *Embrace career staff.* They hold the keys to your success. You'll gain buy-in. • *Walk them through the administration's objectives, commitments, and agenda.* • *Be explicit about the four success factors:* Vision. Coalition. Timeframes. Agency culture. You'll avoid tissue rejection. • *Befriend the "C-Suite."* Your CFO and the assistant secretary for administration and management are critical to your success.	• *Adopt a visible framework for goals, activities, and results.* Be clear about concrete accomplishments.	• *Showcase and protect career personnel.* It will pay off. • *Beware the praise trap.* Don't let the flattery blind you. • *Use them or move them.* And do it as quickly as possible. • *Challenge precedent.* Don't take "that's the rule" for an answer. • *Manage up.* Stay in touch with higher-ups.

★ Chapter 11: *Tips* for Civil Servants "Managing" Political Appointees ★

↳ Create Your Offense	↳ Execute Effectively	↳ Play a Smart Defense
• *Do everything you can to make them successful.* It will rub off on you. • *Listen early and often.* Understand what appointees are trying to accomplish. • *Demonstrate your value.* Share your knowledge on what's been tried before, what worked, and what didn't. • *Do some advance work.* Begin analyses that can help a new team hit the ground running. • *Tell your story.* Personally communicate goals, status, strengths, and weaknesses of existing programs or the organization as a whole. • *Find allies among appointees.* Make friends in high (appointed) places. • *Offer up new ideas.* Ones that will help move the administration's agenda, and maybe yours alongside it.	• *Figure out appointees' learning styles.* Some are visual learners while others absorb more audibly. • *Pick up on nonverbal cues.* Are they comfortable connecting over lunch or even over a beer? • *Curtail the briefing books.* Keep initial communications short and sweet. • *Engage in active listening.* Use open-ended questions to connect with new officials. • *Be a tour guide.* Give appointees tours of the program and organization at service-delivery level. • *Use the appropriations process to make inroads.* Few appointees will have true appreciation for the intricacies of three budget cycles at a time. • *Tune into the administration's pace.* Welcome opportunities to be part of a hurry-up offense.	• *Do not leave wet babies on doorsteps.* Bring solutions when there are problems. • *Rename it.* Where existing program goals can be aligned with new appointees' goals, give the program a fabulous new name. • *Faithfully execute,* even if you have some qualms on policy and priorities. It's your job and important in our federal system. If you can't, see next bullet. • *There may be times when you've just got to move on.* Ultimately you need to stay true to yourself.

★ Chapter 12: *Tips for Consultants—and the Feds Who Use Them* ★

⌐ Create Your Offense	⌐ Execute Effectively	⌐ Play a Smart Defense
• *Always make the client's best interest your top priority.* Don't fall back on what you know vs. what the client needs. One size rarely fits all, so don't try to deliver the same product to every client.	• *Gain insight and trust by active listening.* You're not learning anything about your client's needs if you're doing all the talking.	• *Be politically aware but not politically driven.* You shouldn't be playing politics, but you should certainly be aware of what's going on politically, both inside your client's world and in the larger political world.
• *What's in the news?* Literally. It makes you look both caring and aware if you bring relevant news items to your client's attention.	• *Be rapidly responsive.* There is nothing more frustrating to a client than leaving messages on your voice mail.	• *Bad news gets worse with age.* If you see a problem—or, better yet, if you see a problem looming—surface it quickly.
• *Avoid consultant fatigue.* Be on the lookout for any issues you might help your client with. It makes you look like you care, that you're thinking ahead, and that you understand the environment in which your client operates.	• *Keep the dialogue going.* Be hyper-aware of how your client is feeling about progress. There should be high-level and honest ongoing dialogue between executive levels.	• *Don't blame the client.* If there are issues that need to be worked out, approach them from the perspective that the client is competent and trying to do the best job possible.
• *Career counseling and career help will cement the relationship.* They build trust, and if the client gets promoted, maybe you helped her get the job.	• *Informal meetings are best.* Conversation is more likely to be open and frank if you're sitting one-on-one over coffee in your shirtsleeves.	• *It's never really about the cost.* When clients complain about the cost it really means they're not satisfied with the value.
• *Build your brand.* Develop a reputation for being great (or the best) at the things you want to be known for.	• *Pilot-test solutions first.* Develop, test, and refine. Develop, test, and refine again. Then go live.	

Index

About the Author

Ira Goldstein has a total of over forty-five years of experience as a federal civil servant, manager, and leader and as a consultant to federal, state, and local governments. He served as policy director and acting associate commissioner of Social Security, responsible for the nation's federal cash welfare program, and was US assistant comptroller general at the Government Accountability Office, Congress's efficiency and effectiveness watchdog. He began his federal career as an entry-level analyst in program planning and evaluation at the Office of the Secretary of Health, Education, and Welfare.

In the private sector Goldstein held positions in government contracting and consulting, starting with a defense contractor during the Vietnam War years. He later became managing partner and worldwide government services director at Arthur Andersen Business Consulting and then a vice president in federal services at Unisys Corporation. Most recently he was instrumental in creating and leading Deloitte's federal consulting business, from which he retired in 2015 as civilian sector leader.

Goldstein is a fellow of the National Academy of Public Administration and a charter member of the federal Senior Executive Service. He is a recipient of the government's Distinguished Executive Award and of a 2010 Fed100 Award for federal technology leadership. He received a bachelor of science degree from the University of Pennsylvania and a master's degree in business administration with distinction from Harvard Business School.